PROFILES OF ANTHROPOLOGICAL PRAXIS

Profiles of Anthropological Praxis

An International Casebook

~:~

Edited by

TERRY M. REDDING
and
CHARLES C. CHENEY

berghahn
NEW YORK · OXFORD
www.berghahnbooks.com

First published in 2022 by
Berghahn Books
www.berghahnbooks.com

Library of Congress Cataloging-in-Publication Data

A C.I.P. cataloging record is available from the Library of Congress
Library of Congress Cataloging in Publication Control Number: 2022008625

British Library Cataloguing in Publication Data

A catalogue record for this book is available from the British Library

ISBN 978-1-80073-466-1 hardback
ISBN 978-1-80539-141-8 paperback
ISBN 978-1-80539-559-1 epub
ISBN 978-1-80073-467-8 web pdf

https://doi.org/10.3167/9781800734661

~: CONTENTS :~

❖ ILLUSTRATIONS ❖

Figures

Table

⌁ FOREWORD ⌁

The Emergence of WAPA and Birth of Praxis

SHIRLEY J. FISKE AND ROBERT M. WULFF

The Washington Association of Professional Anthropologists (WAPA) was organized in 1976 in Washington, DC, and quickly grew into a thriving venue for anthropologists interested in finding and interacting with other anthropologists who were actively applying anthropological precepts and methods to real-world problems. The membership base started locally and regionally, but within a few years had generated national interest, with a robust mix of practitioners, academics, and students.

WAPA became a major player on anthropology's national stage: organizing scholarly conferences and fee-based practitioner workshops, sponsoring events at national anthropological association meetings, and publishing directories and employment manuals.[1]

The Washington, DC, region was (and is) an international hub for social/behavioral research and practice. The region is not solely a "federal town" of government agencies, but it also includes a wide array of private-sector organizations (profit and nonprofit). Anthropologists have been attracted to the region because of the many employment possibilities in both the public and private sectors. For example, by the late 1970s and early 1980s, practicing anthropologists were already well represented throughout the DC employment landscape. These employment opportunities fueled WAPA's growth and visibility.

Still, by working in contexts not directly tied to a university department of academic anthropology, practicing anthropologists often felt marginalized from their anthropologist identity, since achieving career advancement as a program evaluator, policy analyst, or project director almost always required making hard choices within a limited time. Some turned their back on anthropology associations and started attending alternative professional meetings more directly related to their work.

Many practicing anthropologists accepted this path away from anthropology. We did not. As practitioners and active WAPA members, we witnessed daily the powerful problem-solving capabilities of anthropology's knowledge. We were determined to retrieve these lost practitioner colleagues and extract their valuable knowledge and experience to benefit the advancement of anthropological practice. Thus was born the Praxis Award.

Praxis Award Goals and Development

We created the Praxis Award in 1980 to achieve two specific goals:

1. Record and promote the value of anthropology's knowledge for solving problems of interest to government and industry, thereby expanding the discipline's traditional focus beyond teaching and research.
2. Start the long effort necessary to create a professional practice arm as a legitimate career alternative to anthropology's academic arm. The academic arm of anthropology long ago established itself as a legitimate profession: a profession defined by anthropologists' exclusive ability to teach anthropology to students in higher education and to conduct anthropological research for publication in scholarly journals.

Since successful practitioners working outside the academy were not on the publish-or-perish track, there was little incentive for them to take the time to write up a project or result for an anthropological audience. We hoped the Praxis Award, with its cash prize, would offer that incentive. Publishing award-winning entries as case studies in our subsequent *Anthropological Praxis: Translating Knowledge into Action* volume (1987) fulfilled the first goal of recording and promoting the problem-solving value of our knowledge.

How to address the second goal? All successful professions—be they law, medicine, or city planning—share three elements: (1) Clients or sponsors who value or pay for a practitioner's (2) unique skillset capable of solving (3) a set of problems not solvable by an alternative skill set. Wulff argues that anthropological practice is not a profession by these standards. Without the protection of professional status, anthropology practitioners could be limited to a para-professional status that significantly limits their earning and level of industry respect.

To jumpstart the emergence of a professional practice arm, we needed to find anthropological practitioners whose successful careers provided lessons about the specific anthropological methods and theories a practitioner could employ to make a living from nonacademic clients and sponsors.

We operationalized the second goal by creating an award unique in anthropology that valued application and results in a professional context rather than, for example, the more typical lifetime achievement award given to a well-known anthropologist. Only these lessons provided the raw materials to build a professional practice arm. The Praxis Award case studies are designed to provide such a roadmap to professional status.

As initially drafted in 1980, the Praxis Award competition guidelines and entry form required applicants to speak directly to this skill set. These were to be identified as follows:

+ An identifiable, client/sponsor-driven problem.[2]
+ A clear and identifiable role for the anthropologist(s).
+ A demonstrable nexus of knowledge into action documented with identifiable results.
+ Articulation of the "anthropological difference," showing the role that anthropological theory and methods played in solving the client's problem or sponsor's need.

The application criteria were simple. Applicants had to hold a master's degree or PhD in any anthropological subfield. The application had to be based on a specific project or endeavor that occurred roughly within the prior five years. In a multidisciplinary project, at least one team member had to be an anthropologist with the higher degree. Applicants were encouraged to self-nominate, an idea that was ahead of its time.

The initial guidelines and entry form have changed little over the Praxis history, providing an invaluable database to make our argument for professional status. We began to make this argument in 1987 when we edited and published *Anthropological Praxis*—twenty case studies produced from Praxis Award winners and honorable mentions in 1981, 1982, and 1983.

In the forty years since the first Praxis Award, the wide gaps between the worlds of academia and practice have been significantly reduced. The American Anthropological Association (AAA) and the Society for Applied Anthropology (SfAA) have both altered their policies and operations to be more practitioner aware. A significant number of anthropology departments have added a focus on practice and applied anthropology to their programs, including components such as internships, courses dedicated to applied anthropology, and applied masters degrees.

There are many reasons for the decreasing gap—not least the steadfast efforts of many hundreds of individual academics, department chairs, and practitioners to improve communications within their local anthropology institutions and communities. At the national level, the creation of the National Association for the Practice of Anthropology (NAPA) in the early 1980s as a AAA section was an essential step toward improved integration. In addition, the creation of the Consortium of Practicing and Applied Anthropologists (COPAA), an independent, national consortium of university-based applied anthropology programs dedicated to integrating practice in their applied programs, was an important building block. To a lesser extent, perhaps, we believe that the Praxis Award and its casebooks—*Anthropological Praxis* and now *Profiles of Anthropological Practice*—have been, and will be, successful textbooks that continue to stimulate improved relations between academia and practice over the last four decades.[3]

Organizing Principles for *Anthropological Praxis* and *Profiles* Casebooks

We selected the organizing principles underlying the *Anthropological Praxis* volume to highlight the way anthropologists are solving problems in the broad swath of organizations and entities facing "real-world" decisions and actions. We wanted younger anthropologists just starting their careers to see themselves in practice roles and organizations where their work is not only valued and useful but can help make a difference.

We chose categories that reflect problem solving; showing "knowledge in action," such as assessment of results; making policy choices; and defining the problem—the very first thing that needs to be done. We asked each chapter author to write subsections using the general format of the Praxis application: "Problem and Client," "Process and Players," "Results and Evaluation," and the all-important "Anthropological Difference." In our introduction, we state that "our emphasis is on the action—the purposeful use of knowledge—rather than on the disciplinary labeling or typology of roles for an anthropologist" (Wulff and Fiske 1987: 3).[4]

In this contemporary volume, *Profiles of Anthropological Praxis*, the organizing principles are domain areas of anthropology, including cultural preservation, sociocultural change, economic development, the environment, and health promotion and management. *Profiles of Anthropological Praxis* continues the *Praxis* tradition by asking the authors to address similar components in each chapter to allow comparisons and learn from case experiences: project background, project description, implementation and anthropologist's role, outcomes, and the all-important anthropological difference.

Our *Praxis* volume established a high standard for case examples, and *Profiles* continues this standard by bringing the practical action of anthropology into the current millennium, with many of the case examples dealing with equity and social justice issues in the domain areas of anthropology. It is a remarkable achievement to pull these together in one volume and to provide examples of the breadth of anthropological impacts both nationally and internationally. The combination of both books provides a continuous record of action and achievement.

Our book's strong sales and many adoptions as class texts demonstrated that both academics and practitioners were eager for the lessons that these success stories provided. With Redding and Cheney's *Profiles* volume, awardee experiences between 2009 and 2019 are now available to current and future colleagues to experience the breadth of successful work that these stories describe. The publication of *Profiles* makes us hopeful that future Praxis Awards will enable even more anthropologists doing purposeful, results-oriented work in a broad swath of public and private sectors to come forward and report on their work for upcoming generations of anthropologists.

Shirley J. Fiske started her journey in anthropology as an undergraduate at the University of California Davis, with a BA in anthropology, and continuing to Stanford for her PhD. Over the last 40 years she has been a program director in a nonprofit organization, faculty member at the University of Southern California; a policy advisor, research, and program manager in a federal agency (National Oceanic and Atmospheric Administration), and a senior advisor in the US Senate. She is now a research professor of anthropology at the University of Maryland, where she is conducting research on subsistence fishing and ethnographic resources for the National Park Service. Over the years, she has played a leading role in a number of anthropological associations, serving as president or board member of WAPA, the National Association for the Practice of Anthropology, and the Society for Applied Anthropology. She was an original co-director of Praxis, serving with Robert Wulff for the first three Praxis Award competitions in 1981, 1982, and 1983. She also coedited (with Robert Wulff) *Anthropological Praxis: Translating Knowledge into Action*.

Robert M. Wulff was introduced to the concept of professional practice while taking electives in the UCLA school of architecture and urban planning while in their PhD program for urban anthropology, and thus accepted with enthusiasm an offer to join the faculty of the new MA in applied anthropology program at the University of South Florida (USF). While at USF, he helped create *Practicing Anthropology* and served as the publication's founding editor. Raring to walk the talk of practice, he left academia and moved to Washington, DC, with the Carter administration to accept a position in the US Department of Housing and Urban Development's Office of Neighborhood Development. Carter lost, and Wulff left government and took his anthropological and urban development knowledge to the private sector, spending the next thirty years designing and developing residential and mixed-use communities. He retired from practice to direct George Mason University's Center for Real Estate Entrepreneurship. He has served as president of WAPA, where he founded the Praxis Award. He co-directed the award with Shirley Fiske for the first three competitions (1981, 1982, and 1983), which resulted in their coedited case-book *Anthropological Praxis: Translating Knowledge into Action.*

Notes

1. One of WAPA's first publications was *Stalking Employment in the Nation's Capital.* WAPA pioneered the development and implementation of workshops designed specifically by and for anthropologists on finding jobs outside of academia, both regionally and at annual professional meetings: Adam Koons, Beatrice Hackett, and John P. Mason, eds., *Stalking Employment in the Nation's Capital* (Washington, DC: Washington Association of Professional Anthropologists, 1989).
2. Over the years, the Praxis Award "client" has been interpreted broadly by applicants and Praxis jurors. A client can be an organization that employs the practicing anthropologist full-time, a sponsor of the anthropologist's work, a beneficiary of the practitioner's work, or a corporation that hires a consulting anthropologist. Examples of clients from winning entries include government agencies, development foundations, self-help groups, for-profit companies, nonprofits, and small-scale voluntary associations.
3. For over twenty-five years, NAPA graciously hosted the Praxis Award ceremony during its business meeting at the AAA meetings, affording WAPA the opportunity to present the award receptions for a national audience—for which WAPA is extremely grateful. We also acknowledge the role that SfAA began to play as of 2020, as a new home for the Praxis Award presentation on the annual program.
4. Wulff, Robert M. and Shirley J. Fiske. 1987. *Anthropological Praxis: Translating Knowledge Into Action.* Boulder, CO: Westview Press.

~:~

Introduction

TERRY M. REDDING AND CHARLES C. CHENEY

A s practitioner anthropologists, we are asked throughout our careers what exactly it is that we do. If you are a student, questions will revolve around what you hope to do someday with *that* degree. These earnest queries will come from acquaintances and strangers alike. You may even find yourself wondering from time to time about what your far-flung peers are doing. This book is designed to help answer these types of questions.

Profiles of Anthropological Praxis gives readers firsthand descriptions of applied anthropologists at work. What makes this book different from potentially similar publications about applying anthropology is that all cases presented here have been vetted by a Praxis Award Committee and ranked by a jury of expert practitioners as part of the competitive Praxis Award process. These chapters are based on the original award applications of the author(s). For all awards within the discipline, the Praxis Award receives among the highest number of applications; these cases are the exemplars, representing biennially the best in class.

The book serves as a sequel to *Anthropological Praxis: Translating Knowledge into Action* (Wulff and Fiske 1987), described in the foreword. The two volumes differ somewhat in the organization and presentation of their contents, but they share the same applied anthropological orientation and thrust.

This volume draws from successful submissions for Praxis Award competitions between 2009 and 2019; the projects described have occurred in roughly that same timeframe. The volume editors served as competition chairs during all but the last award cycle, and we are pleased to note that all awardees in that span, either Praxis winners or honorable mentions, have contributed chapters to *Profiles*. Their descriptive narratives are about the roles the anthropologist(s) played in projects carried out in a wide variety of settings in the United States, Africa, Asia, and Latin America, with scopes of work ranging in dimension from small community efforts to national and multinational endeavors, and which addressed a broad spectrum of human problems.

The chapters focus on the story of how and why the authors applied anthropological approaches and insights to solve these human problems and the strategies and methods they used and actions they took to ensure their projects were beneficial. The chapters for the most part share the same organizational components:

+ Project background: The problem or issue to be addressed.
+ Project description: The action designed to address the problem.
+ Implementation and anthropologist's role: How the anthropologist(s) set about, either alone or as part of a team, to undertake the project and deal with ongoing situations and circumstances.
+ Outcomes: What happened as the result of the project, and why.
+ The anthropological difference: Why anthropology provided the best tools to apply to the issue or situation.
+ Epilogue: When appropriate and available, many authors have included an update on events and results since the initial project was described in their award applications.

Based on the central concerns of the project chapters, they are grouped into six broad, topical sections that comprise the main body of the book: economic development, communities and the environment, cultural preservation, health promotion and management, sociocultural change and adaptation, and policy change. Not all projects fit neatly into a particular category. This reflects the nature of our holistic, multidisciplinary, broad-ranging work and highlights again why it is sometimes challenging to describe our discipline. Some projects involved millions invested by an international donor, while others came about on a shoestring budget by a lone anthropologist, but they share the common thread of being exemplars for the discipline.

The text and highlights of the chapters also reflect the subjectivity that comes into play in our work. The individual experiences and backgrounds, the different preferences and priorities, all shape the project approaches and outcomes that you will read about here. The projects demonstrate that there is no one "right" way to design and undertake a successful project. The multidisciplinary and holistic anthropological toolkit contains many options to deploy, depending on the unique circumstances presented. This is combined with choices anthropologists must make on the occasions for which there are no clear guidelines.

Back to that question of how to describe our work, this book demonstrates that we really do everything; thus, it can be something of a conundrum to adequately answer what it is we actually do. But whether a project is small or large, several months or several years in duration, involving factors that affect dozens or potentially millions of lives, the primary connection is the achievements made possible through the proper application of anthropology to best address human problems. The "Anthropological Difference" sections of each chapter, which represent the real soul of the book, detail how this application often provides the most insightful and effective solutions to these problems.

You have likely already read the foreword by the creators of the award, Robert M. Wulff and Shirley J. Fiske, which reflects on the award's foundations. Be sure to also read the afterword by Riall W. Nolan, which looks to the future of the discipline. In between, you will find fascinating, insightful, and revealing accounts from anthropologists of how they go about their work. Applied and practicing anthropologists can have a substantial role in making the world a better place for us all. Our authors show you just a few of the possibilities.

Note: For those interested in delving more deeply into the history of the award, or to access the application materials, the Washington Association of Professional Anthropologists website (www.wapadc.org) provides abstracts of all awards to date, descriptions of the award and process, and the application forms.

Terry M. Redding is currently a strategic communications specialist with a maternal and child health project funded by the US Agency for International Development (USAID). He received a Master of Arts in anthropology from the University of South Florida in 1998. In 1999, he contributed to and edited *Applied Anthropology and the Internet*, the first-ever, fully online publication of the American Anthropological Association. He joined LTG Associates, Inc. in 2000 on a USAID-funded population project and was then involved in a variety of research and evaluation projects before working for several years as an independent editorial and evaluation consultant. He has served as president of the Washington Association of Professional Anthropologists, communications chair for the National Association for the Practice of Anthropology, and chair of the Praxis Award competitions of 2013, 2015, and 2017.

Charles C. Cheney completed a dissertation on cultural change among the Huave Indians of southern Mexico and received a PhD in anthropology from the University of California, Berkeley, in 1972. He then began what would become a career in applied medical anthropology by taking the job of "culture broker" between a south Texas pediatric hospital and the predominantly Latino population of the Texas-Mexico borderlands. After that, he served as director of sociocultural research in the departments of community medicine and psychiatry of Baylor College of Medicine, and later was director of program development for the National Association of Community Health Centers. Further, as an independent consultant, he has conducted extensive needs assessment and evaluation research into the provision of healthcare services to US low-income minority and immigrant populations for community health centers, public health departments, and a range of federal health agencies. He has served as president of the Washington Association of Professional Anthropologists, member of the board of directors of the Society for Applied Anthropology, and chair of the Praxis Award competitions of 2009 and 2011.

References

Wulff, R. M., and S. J. Fiske. 1987. *Anthropological Praxis: Translating Knowledge into Action*. Boulder, CO: Westview Press.

PART I

~:~

Economic Development

CHAPTER 1

~:~

Emergency Food Security Recovery
An Afghanistan Case

ADAM KOONS

Project Background

When this project was first conceived in 2008, rural Afghanistan had been experiencing severe food insecurity following years of drought. For three years, the staple crop, wheat, had mostly or totally failed in much of the country. Farm households had depleted their seed stores in failed crops, and in extreme cases farm families consumed their seed. The resulting production scarcity and food insecurity had several consequences, including a dramatic increase in (primarily illegally) imported food from Pakistan. Although a viable agricultural season was being predicted, households no longer had seed stocks and other inputs on hand, and they could not afford new seed, fertilizer, and other items. The local credit-based network of private agricultural suppliers was unable to provide additional support to household farms.

There was also real concern over an alternative and lucrative strategy for farmers: growing poppies for the illegal drug industry, which in turn supplied substantial resources to insurgent forces in Afghanistan. Although risky and dangerous, numerous farmers adopted this tempting option.

In parallel with the US government's military and political stabilization efforts in the country, the US Agency for International Development (USAID) had many large-scale economic development, infrastructural, and humanitarian programs underway, as did the British government and many other donor countries and international agencies.

USAID had several concerns over the increasingly widespread food insecurity. Providing emergency food aid was extremely complicated logistically, enormously expensive, only a short-term option, and unsustainable, and it did nothing to assist in restarting local agricultural self-sufficiency. In addition, neither the Afghan nor US governments wanted farmers to resort to poppy production.

USAID sought therefore to restore local livelihood capacities in an effort not only to enable small farmers to produce sustenance but to actually revitalize Afghanistan's wheat production sector to make it appealing to farmers and support the economy. To achieve this, farmers would need seeds and other inputs such as fertilizer on a massive scale. But there were many financial, logistical, operational, political, cultural, and agricultural complexities.

At the time, I was the global humanitarian director for a US-based international nongovernmental organization (NGO) that already had large-scale, USAID-funded infrastructure programs in Afghanistan. In Kabul, I lunched with a USAID officer with whom I had worked on several successful programs, mostly in Africa. He was serving there as a short-term food security advisor and was looking for ideas to address wheat cultivation.

Admittedly, I did not know Afghanistan or its culture(s) very well then, and I had never worked or researched there. Nonetheless, I pitched an idea based on a strategy I had successfully implemented in Lebanon after the Hezbollah hostilities with Israel in 2006, a very different country and context. The officer was intrigued and asked to see a "concept paper," a two- to five-page summary laying out basic strategies, goals, objectives, and an implementation plan. This would give USAID an idea of whether they would be interested; if so, they would invite us to prepare a full, detailed, and precise technical and budget proposal for possible funding.

My colleagues and I immediately set about preparing the paper. We met with senior members of our NGO's Afghan team, some Afghan field staff, and members of my headquarters humanitarian team to work out elements of the prospective project. We provided the concept paper to USAID in a matter of days. Shortly thereafter, instead of asking for a full proposal, they unexpectedly requested a more detailed and expanded concept paper, along with a reasonably detailed budget. So, instead of a fifty-page proposal, we had to focus in on a fifteen-page paper.

However, in order for us to really know if our ideas were operationally, culturally, socioeconomically, and financially valid, viable, feasible, and appropriate, we needed to quickly conduct careful analyses on a number of topics. We achieved this by calling on numerous local experts. Afghanistan is a very complicated and expensive place in which to operate, particularly in isolated rural areas, and local knowledge was key in understanding what was realistic and achievable.

When we submitted our expanded paper, we were nervous about our estimated $30 million budget, a figure that seemed very large. We received back a totally unexpected and entirely unprecedented response from USAID. They, along with the British government's aid agency at the time, the Department for

International Development (DFID),[1] would fund the project. However, they were so optimistic about our strategy and approach that they asked us to expand the coverage to accommodate a $60 million budget. Although no one in our organization had previously experienced such a request, we excitedly but cautiously agreed. Our participant target would now be 250,000 farms instead of the original 176,000. As far as we could tell, this would now be the largest project of its kind in USAID history and quite an overwhelming undertaking. (We must have done something right because USAID subsequently requested that the project be expanded in a follow-on phase.)

Project Description

Our plan laid out a project goal of providing accessible and affordable agricultural inputs to drought-affected subsistence farmers to promote wheat and other staple production during the fall/winter 2008 and spring 2009 seasons. The two specific objectives were to (1) increase the access to seeds and fertilizer by 250,000 (household) farms to improve wheat yields and food availability in those seasons and (2) to provide vulnerable farmers access to income-generation opportunities.

Our strategy was very innovative and virtually unique at the time. Generally, similar projects designed and implemented by international organizations used a simple, decades-old approach. Ideally, though not always, from an initial field assessment, the organization would decide what supplies and materials were needed for each farm, and how much. The project would then purchase the supplies from a large-scale wholesaler and deliver them directly to villages for farmers to collect. We did not think this strategy was locally appropriate or viable because it would likely create resentment on different fronts, as it did not take any local human, agronomic, or economic considerations into account.

Instead, based on our initial ideas pitched to USAID and subsequent field validation assessments, the farming supplies would be provided through a flexible voucher system. This was based on several realities: (1) although small, the farms were different sizes; (2) some farmers had seeds, and some did not; (3) farmers may not want to grow only a particular crop or crop mix, or a particular amount of certain crops; (4) some farmers may have sold some of their tools; and (5) farmers knew their own needs best, therefore a one-size-fits-all package was not appropriate. Also, men and women typically grow different crops, and there were many woman-headed households. Flexible vouchers sought to address all of these issues.

Selected communities would be informed of the intended project and the voucher approach carefully explained to community leaders and members, both men and women. They could then apply for vouchers, and project staff would work closely with and through preexisting local Community Development Councils to review the applications. Eligible farmers would receive vouchers worth approximately US$145. Recipients could use the vouchers up to their monetary equivalent on any agricultural inputs they felt necessary to restart their wheat cultivation and support household food security. The project arranged for vouchers to be redeemed at the agricultural supply depots where farmers typically got their supplies.

The volume of depot-supplied goods was unprecedented, since in normal times most farmers used their own seed. The project had to ensure that the depots would be adequately supplied with seeds, fertilizer, and other needed inputs. To address this, the project worked directly with large-scale wholesalers that typically supplied the depots to ensure they had the financial and logistical capacity to support an effective supply chain. Additionally, to promote successful germination, seeds purchased by the wholesalers for the depots were required to be certified and tested.

Also, and very importantly, to enhance each voucher recipient's involvement and "ownership," a 15 percent copayment (equal to about twenty dollars) was required from the farmers upon their voucher redemption. The amount was calculated to be within the means of the recipients and was part of the original voucher application criteria that farmers agreed to, with support from the Community Development Councils. These copayments could be reinvested back into the communities for various agriculture activities, thereby further extending the impact of the program.

To further maximize production, agricultural training would be offered at each depot. There was no requirement to accept training, but it was available at any time during the cultivation season. It was promoted as an on-demand way for farmers to learn new techniques for potentially increasing their yields of wheat and other crops such as vegetables, but it did not force the training or promote a fixed curriculum that might not respond to farmer interests. The trainers were government agricultural officers who had been largely inactive because of lack of resources and demand. Their salaries would be partially supported by the project.

As the project was getting underway, the US government held such high hopes for its efficacy and importance that it was specifically singled out and recognized by US special envoy Richard Holbrooke as a key point in nonmilitary assistance to Afghanistan.

Project Design and the Anthropologist's Role and Impact

The project team knew that this novel approach required "buy-in" from a variety of stakeholders at all levels. We were facing the challenge, particularly at the local level, that it was not the "normal" way things worked and that the approach was brought in externally by foreign aid workers. Still, we did not want the effort to appear distasteful or strange.

An important element of my contributions as anthropologist was insisting on, and designing, a very rapid ethnographic research activity to assess the model viability. Our specialized assessment was tailored for the proposed strategy by using an integrated, community-level approach that sought to examine not only the intended, direct beneficiaries but also, in a holistic manner, the relationships and potential consequences of interactions between the different stakeholders. We wanted to measure the potential acceptance but also identify or predict any possible, secondary, or negative consequences. In doing so, we also examined the potential roles of male and female community members, local businesses and the private sector, local traditional leaders, local project staff, local government officials, the national government, ourselves, and the US government. All of this data collection had to be done at lightning speed, somewhat in contradiction to the "normal" duration and depth of ethnographic or applied research. The analysis, also by necessity, had to be largely qualitative and performed in a "quick and dirty" manner. The research used a mixture of local professional expertise, existing sociocultural literature, random but limited field interviews, focus groups, and key informants (including our own local staff). We were able to quickly pilot a small field sample of test questions before implementing the actual research. Because of our own field staff limits in coverage, time, effort, specialized training, logistics, and ongoing insecurity, we contracted with an Afghan-owned social science research organization and worked with them in close consultation and supervision to undertake the actual field research. The analysis was then conducted jointly.

Key learnings included the following: (1) there were no agricultural resources remaining for the coming season; (2) local farmers knew there were alternate, albeit illegal, crops they could cultivate; (3) the selected remote regions were unaccustomed to aid and suspicious of and uncomfortable with dealing with nonlocal persons; (4) the high level of local dignity and pride indicated that farmers would be offended by charity, even agricultural inputs; (5) perceptions existed among the population that the Afghan government takes from its citizens and does not give back; (6) there are strongly established and time-honored relations between local producers and local agricultural supply depots, and these include providing inputs credit and access to harvest sales. These findings, along with many others, supported our belief that the project model was feasible.

However, there were also considerable challenges in undertaking such a large and complicated project in a country as difficult as Afghanistan, particularly under such insecure and politically sensitive conditions and in remote, rural locations. We were also working within an almost impossibly short time frame. Most large projects, even urgent food-security-oriented efforts, take many months to launch and get underway, and these often take years to show measurable results. Once started, we had to show tangible results during the very next growing season. This challenge was particularly stressful when the funder doubled our starting budget and therefore the magnitude of coverage and objective targets. For a few moments, we considered if we could or should ethically and operationally accept the doubled budget on an as-yet untested project. Ultimately we decided that, as the framework had already been designed, scaling up was possible.

Connected to our time constraint was the process of orienting our partners, stakeholders at every level, and the communities to this new and very different approach. We had to gain their trust and get their concurrence and collaboration while also establishing and maintaining a level of operational transparency that was not the norm. This was particularly true for the transparency we insisted on locally regarding developing, communicating, implementing, and monitoring the criteria and process used in selecting the voucher recipients. This transparency was very important to help mitigate jealousy among those who did not receive vouchers and to avoid the implications or accusations of bias.

A particularly thorny challenge was our insistence (and the donors' requirement) to fully include women. In Afghan society, women's roles are very strictly prescribed, and their access to goods, along with their capacity to make decisions, is severely limited. We sought to address this by ensuring the availability of inputs (vegetable seeds, garden implements) that are generally only used by women and by providing training specifically designed for women, their horticultural activities, and increased family food security. In many cases, we organized women's peer-to-peer training. We also spent considerable time with elders and Community Development Councils to ensure they understood the vital importance of women's roles in food security and thus the importance of women's access to portions of the vouchers. We also stressed the importance of recognizing the high number of woman-headed households that might not otherwise receive vouchers. As needed, our staff assisted women who were household heads to ensure they could complete the applications.

An additional concern and challenge that often weighed heavily was that we were undertaking long-term humanitarian activities in a conflict-ridden country and politically contentious environment in which there were multiple, simultaneous interests, objectives, and motivations. We were very much aware that humanitarian principles are sometimes at odds with political ends and that there were any number of potential military and security issues and consequences to activities. These were factors we could not change or even mitigate, and so we had to focus on the humanitarian goals we intended to address.

Because of the position and authority I held at my NGO, I had the rare opportunity to be involved in almost every aspect of the project, including conception of the initial idea, promoting and testing the idea in discussions with the potential financial supporter, designing the strategy and approach for the project, fine-tuning the strategy details, organizing the research to field test the ideas from a social, cultural, economic and logistical perspective, leading the process of developing a budget, and coauthoring the actual funding request document. It is unusual to have that amount of input, even with a typical NGO project, since many jobs and program phases are somewhat compartmentalized.

I was fortunate to have the opportunity to design my role in the NGO in this way. I was involved only indirectly in the actual project management and in its monitoring and evaluation. The responsibilities of the team I led included all aspects of developing and launching programs, but not the ongoing operational management or the evaluation—these would have presented a conflict of interest. Although my level of input may have been unusual in general for an anthropologist in this particular arena, it was not uncommon for me in this organization to have a similar role in numerous other humanitarian and disaster responses.

In this case, I did what applied anthropologists are very good at, as are many other seasoned aid workers across a range of disciplines: innovatively connecting the dots to address new challenges. As noted above, a few years earlier I had helped design what turned out to be a very successful flexible voucher-based humanitarian program in Lebanon. Although Afghanistan was a very different setting, the concept I applied was the same.

Still, it is important to make a clear distinction between a "typical" voucher program, used increasingly in relief and development, and our model for a flexible voucher, since many project elements rest on this distinction. Normal vouchers would enable recipients to redeem a predetermined and fixed amount from a predetermined list of goods—that is, one size fits all: wheat seeds and fertilizer in a set quantity, regardless of what quantities or other supplies were needed. Our design facilitated farmers in choosing, as they best determined, any supplies in any quantities up to a maximum monetary value.

The project was therefore designed with a grounding in economic anthropology, exploring knowledge of local exchange and livelihood systems as cultural traits. In anthropological terms, cultural relativism was used to assess how project components might fit into a beneficiary worldview of individuals, of family members and providers/decision-makers, and of community members. For example, we considered the differences in effect on locally perceived self-esteem and respect if goods were provided entirely free as charity rather than if they were distributed through vouchers.

Additionally, to ensure the effective articulation of the roles of various stakeholders at different levels, from the community leaders to the government officials and donors (USAID and DFID), each set of responsibilities and commitments was designed after careful examination of differential self-interest and motivating factors, and in consultation with these stakeholders.

Implementation and Outcomes

Because of our organization's structure, my team was involved with the elements described above, but a different group took over project implementation and management. This implementation group comprised a headquarters-based project supervisor and a country-based project director (sometimes called "chief of party" in US government jargon) who reported to the country director in Afghanistan and the headquarters manager. The project director was responsible for the recruitment of in-country staff, management of the budget, and local government relations and was also accountable for the efficient implementation, ongoing management, and ultimate results of the project. The design team and I had no further official role. We did spend time and effort trying to ensure that the project implementation group understood our design rationale, intent, and ideas for effective implementation, and we kept the door open for follow-up consultations.

Although we had to move on to other assessments and project designs in a busy office, we sometimes sought informal updates and progress reports from colleagues during the Afghan project implementation; we also had access to formal monitoring and reporting documents.

At the end of the original one-year project, evaluation data from internal monitoring, six separate internal and external studies and surveys, and other sources showed that the distribution of vouchers directly to farmers was a primary reason for the program's success in reaching target beneficiaries. Among other outcomes, the project:

+ provided 297,000 vouchers (at a 99.9 percent redemption rate), aiding 1.7 million family members;
+ reached 3,000 women-headed household farms, benefitting 18,000 family members;
+ reached 341,301 farmers with agricultural training;
+ supported 175 local agricultural depots with additional business;
+ increased wheat yields in planted areas by 55 percent for irrigated farms and 94 percent for rain-fed farms (as compared with nonrecipients);
+ showed that the percentage of farmers selling wheat at local and regional markets increased from 14 percent in 2008 to 59 percent in 2009.

Overall, household food security was reestablished, while self-esteem and self-determination for farmers were maintained by avoiding a charity-oriented donation system. This particularly resulted from the open-ended vouchers and the farmers' copayments.

In a country where a frequent alternative crop to wheat is opium poppies, there was constant concern by the US and Afghan governments that as wheat became more difficult to grow, farmers would turn to poppies as their only option for an accessible livelihood. This program was able to reestablish wheat as a viable and productive crop for household support. According to USAID, in the season following project implementation, wheat harvests were both impressive and sufficient for recovery-level production, a result partially due to the project.

Existing local social, agricultural, and economic systems, protocols, and processes were respected and left intact, such as working through local leadership structures and maintaining close existing and symbiotic relations between producers and depots. This was done without the perception of external imposition, interference, or prescription by working consultatively through the local social and political mechanisms.

The deliberate use of local agricultural depots had several intended positive effects. First, bypassing the local depots by providing the goods directly from a central supplier would have undercut local commerce and created bad feelings and lack of support for the project among local businesses. Also, farmers had long-standing relationships with the depots for supplies, and sometimes they utilized the depots as links to buyers at harvest time. Additionally, the project added considerable new farmer business, which could serve to expand relationships and create enhanced local market system linkages. It could even later lead to potential access to credit or other mutual arrangements.

A critical and rather smart element introduced by the donors (which we appreciated and very much endorsed) was the farmer copayment. This approach is very rarely used in humanitarian programs (or development programs), as beneficiaries are usually considered too poor to participate. However, the cash investment from the farmers turned out to be a further opportunity to instill the sense of program ownership. Since they were personally invested in the supplies, the vouchers were not regarded as charity; rather, the farmers felt like they were in partnership with the donors. We felt that this aspect was a very important factor in enhancing the normalcy of self-determination and the feeling of personal responsibility. Operationally, the project plan was that all of the collected copayments would be pooled at the local level, managed jointly by the project, the Community Development Councils, and the local government, and allocated for reinvestment activities by the communities, who would participate in selecting how the funds would be used, thus serving as a further affirmation of local control.

We noted a somewhat unplanned but very welcome and impressive collaborative multiplier effect. Agricultural depots often carried larger and more expensive farm equipment, such as small motorized two-wheel tractors, which were usually far too expensive for individual farmers. However, we found that in a number of cases a group of farmers would pool their vouchers to purchase a tractor to share. In the same way, other shared tools were purchased jointly to defray costs.

For all of the reasons described, this program's effectiveness led to it becoming a model within Afghanistan as well as for the organization I worked for in our other country programs. The flexible voucher model was replicated in a major expansion (see epilogue below), and other donors have shown significant interest in this approach. The model generated lessons learned about program design and implementation that were used in general program design strategies for both our NGO and USAID.

One disappointment we had, which is almost universally common among humanitarian programs, is that no in-depth ethnographic or sociocultural research was conducted in the post-project period to examine or truly validate longer-term and deeper project efficacy, sustainability, and sociocultural impacts.

The Anthropological Difference

It may be difficult to distinguish the anthropology here from good, sound, appropriate economic development, and humanitarian practice. Much of the anthropological influence is rather subtle. Gratifyingly, anthropological perspectives, data collections approaches, and vocabulary, such as qualitative and participatory assessment, holism, cultural relativism (i.e., cultural sensitivity), and integrated and interrelated community systems, have suffused the thinking in this and other good project design in diverse cultural and economic settings. Though it will never be as rigorous or as in depth as formal ethnography, what was once described as "development anthropology" is now just good development design. Recognizing the differential roles of women and men and how they affect projects, understanding different economic, social, and political statuses and power relations, or ensuring that projects do no harm are ideas grounded in anthropologists' in-depth knowledge but are now common considerations among aid workers. The fact that I, as the design team anthropologist, ensured that such principles and approaches were appropriately used could be considered "action anthropology" (e.g., Tax 1975), or just responsible project design.

The project was complicated, and it involved many delicate and sensitive issues, any of which could have derailed it if things did not go according to plan. It was probably the most complicated humanitarian project I have been involved in—and this in a domain where every single project is complicated. Without the input and design sensitivity described above, the program could have been yet another prescriptive, "foreign," centrally mandated, and externally controlled aid program that would have been perceived as an imposed last resort that farmers had to accept in order to survive, and it might have been unsuccessful.

To summarize, project success was achieved by the following culturally grounded, research-informed, and anthropologically influenced features.

Building Confidence: Being Locally Appropriate

The project required decision-maker and gate-keeper acceptance. These were necessary to receive the support, permission, and validation of the funding agencies, national government authorities, and local authorities and leaders. Our efforts to carefully consider the socioeconomic and cultural aspects and consequences of the project design, and pilot test it, were key to gaining full support from all authorities.

Establishing Trust

In a country with extreme suspicion and distrust of foreigners (associating with Americans can be dangerous or fatal), particularly in the remote rural areas, we arranged for the project to be introduced to communities through local NGOs and then validated by the local Community Development Councils. There was no overt association with foreign agencies or governments. This was a deliberate decision that avoided the often-used emergency project approach of sending centrally based international NGOs or UN agency staff who are unknown locally. To further add local validation and prevent any stigma of foreign involvement, the inputs were transported, and the redemption process undertaken in the presence of known and trusted local government officials. All of this also further supported and reinforced efforts to strengthen a "national solidarity program" publicized by the government in combating the ongoing insurgency.

Another area of concern we identified was our original idea of using cell phone–based data entry for field staff, which we thought could greatly assist in record keeping and monitoring. This technique was coming into vogue globally at the time and was regarded as a significant advancement in saving time, effort, and cost. But we decided against implementing this because it could invoke suspicion, which could place the staff in danger, and also such technical uses would contradict what was supposed to represent a "local," home-grown project.

Sustaining and Protecting Self-Determination

We initially agreed with the donors that wheat seeds and fertilizer provided through transactions of locally redeemable vouchers was culturally appropriate because the alternative of using direct delivery of supplies would seem too similar to charity handouts. The recipients were and are a proud, independent, and self-sufficient people, unaccustomed to "relief." However, we also expanded and modified the approach: we made the vouchers open-ended and redeemable for any agricultural supplies stocked at the farm depots. In the end, almost all farmers chose seeds and fertilizer anyway, and some also got hand tools. Many, particularly women, selected gardening seeds and supplies. The farmers very much appreciated having a choice, recognizing it as an acknowledgment of their expertise and ability to devise their own solutions. The extent of ownership and self-reliance that was instilled (according to farmers' own feedback) created a sense of hope and relief about their future, and the project received considerable respect.

Transparency and Participation

There were elements of the voucher recipient selection, delivery, and redemption process that required procedures that were culturally acceptable locally and ensured effective project operations. As is always the case, there were insufficient resources to allow all households to receive vouchers. However, the communities were not entirely homogeneous economically, and some farmers had less need and were less vulnerable than others. An externally devised selection process might neglect, omit, or misunderstand local characteristics. Therefore, selection criteria were developed in consultation with local community leaders. During implementation, the criteria were applied transparently and uniformly so that no impression of favoritism or bias could emerge.

Using the locally guided recipient selection criteria, farmers had to actually apply for vouchers. Applications were reviewed and chosen by the Community Development Councils, with monitoring and oversight by project staff. To prevent misuse and corruption during redemption, recipients had to "sign" the vouchers. To accommodate the sensitive issue of illiteracy, thumbprints were used. This practice satisfied community members with the strong impression that misuse would be identified.

All these culturally appropriate activities worked to ensure that the project would be accepted and achieve its goals. The holistic and culturally relative approach of anthropology and sensitivities to local needs worked together in a very difficult geographic and geopolitical setting.

Epilogue

Note

This epilogue was written just prior to the US withdrawal from Afghanistan in August 2021.

The US and Afghan governments' satisfaction with the project led to a follow-on, one-year project in 2009 called AVIPA Plus, which covered the same eighteen provinces; however, its funding was increased to $360 million. Added components included temporary employment through cash-for-work community projects, grants-in-kind for local cooperatives and agribusinesses, and an increase of the copayment to 35 percent, all with a focus on rural economic and political stabilization. In the following year, AVIPA Plus was expanded yet again, to cover thirty-one (of the total thirty-four) provinces, including conflict zones. Funding then reached $431 million, while the United Kingdom and Japan undertook projects in the remaining three provinces.

Some cumulative results reported up to March 2011 include:

+ the provision of 1,146,439 agricultural voucher packages worth $164 million;
+ the distribution of $19 million in small grants benefitting almost 60,000 farmers;
+ the provision of agricultural training for 501,000 male and female farmers (275 percent of the target);
+ improvement of 338,040 hectares of arable land;
+ collaborative implementation of 2,235 agricultural project activities between communities and the Afghan government;
+ generation of $17 million by voucher copayments; this was used to support new agricultural support projects, which provided a 34 percent subsidy for farmers to purchase locally appropriate, low-cost, two-wheel tractors.

Finally, whether or not directly consequent of the original project, in the wake of the follow-on projects, USAID supported four 4-year regional agricultural development programs ranging in value from $28 million to $178 million.

Adam Koons currently works for the US Federal Emergency Manager Agency's (FEMA) Office of Disability Integration and Coordination. He holds a PhD in applied anthropology from American University (1987). His career has focused on poverty reduction, food security, disaster management, emergency response, and humanitarian assistance as a full-time practitioner. Until recently, he worked on international programs, and he lived overseas for over twenty years. He has held senior management and executive positions at a range of international NGOs, and he has worked for USAID several times. Koons has served on the Society for Applied Anthropology's Nominations Committee and twice on their annual program committee. Starting as a charter member of WAPA, he has been president twice, chaired the program committee, served on the board of directors for many years, and has been on the Praxis Award committee twice (2017, 2021). He has often written and mentored young anthropologists on practitioner employment.

Note

1. In 2020, the British government merged DFID and another government department to form a new agency, the Foreign, Commonwealth and Development Office (FCDO).

References

Greenfield, Victoria A., Keith Crane, Craig A. Bond, Nathan Chandler, Jill E. Luoto, and Olga Oliker. 2015. "Rural Development Programs in Afghanistan." In *Reducing the Cultivation of Opium Poppies in Southern Afghanistan*. Santa Monica, CA: Rand Corporation, 85–166.

International Relief and Development. 2014. "Empowering Citizens, Engaging Governments, Rebuilding Communities: Afghanistan." Case Studies in Community Stabilization, International Relief and Development in Afghanistan, 2006–2013. https://reliefweb.int/sites/reliefweb.int/files/resources/IRD_Afghan_CaseStudy_29Apr14.pdf.

Tax, Sol. 1975. "Action Anthropology." *Current Anthropology* 16(4): 514–17.

USAID. 2012. *Afghanistan Vouchers for Increased Production in Agriculture (AVIPA) Plus: Final Report*. 1 September 2008–15 November 2011. US Agency for International Development and International Relief and Development.

USAID Afghanistan. 2010a. "AVIPA Pumps Hope into Marja." Fact Sheet. USAID Afghanistan.

USAID Afghanistan. 2010b. "Afghanistan Vouchers for Increased Production in Agriculture (AVIPA Plus)." Fact Sheet. USAID Afghanistan.

CHAPTER 2

~:~

Ecotourism in One Amazon Community

My Role as Anthropologist, Witness, Scribe, and Facilitator

AMANDA STRONZA

Project Background

Southeastern Peru is a region of tropical rainforest with a state named after the River of the Mother of God, Madre de Dios. On a tributary of that river, the Tambopata, 180 families of the Native Community of Infierno share nearly ten thousand hectares of forests, oxbow lakes, and clear-running streams. Their land is in the heart of a biodiversity hotspot, an expanse of forest sustaining more species of plants and animals than does most any other place on earth. Though the forests and traditions of Tambopata are threatened by outside forces—land speculation, commercial agriculture, illegal gold mining, logging, and more—the inhabitants of Infierno are stewards of their natural riches. They use ecotourism as one of their tools for protecting what they value.

Infierno's residents first converged in 1977, coming from Ese'eja Indigenous heritage as well Quechua and mestizo traditions of the Andes and Amazon. The families joined to form a "Native Community" on the banks of the Tambopata River. They had an incentive: the Peruvian government had passed a "Law of Native Communities," which stipulated that Indigenous peoples of the Amazon were entitled to legal recognition of territorial rights if they agreed to settle together. For decades, the families of the different cultural groups in Infierno shared land, waters, and wildlife under a communal governance regime. They shared, too, a subsistence lifestyle. Everyone farmed a little, hunted a little, fished, and gathered fruits, medicines, and fibers from the forests. In one area of the community with the oldest growth forest, they created a two-thousand-hectare reserve, a kind of sacred forest, that they called Nape, after an Ese'eja shaman.

Their lives began to change in the 1990s. The Madre de Dios region had become a boom area for ecotourism, which was being promoted by conservationists, the business sector, and the government as a form of "sustainable development," a way to balance economic needs of local communities with the need to protect rainforests. The Tambopata National Reserve had been created, and plans were underway to create the Bahuaja-Sonene National Park. Infierno was in the buffer zone of both parks as well as at the heart of the ecotourism boom, where increasing numbers of motorized canoes plied the Tambopata, carrying tourists from distant lands to new lodges upriver. The people of Infierno hoped to gain a foothold in the new economy. They had the Indigenous knowledge, cultural resources, biological riches, and a reserve they had established in their territory. All that they lacked was financial capital, business skills, and marketing reach.

In 1996, they started meeting with the owners of an ecotourism company called Rainforest Expeditions. The company, based in Peru's capital, Lima, was founded by two entrepreneurs with a history of research on macaws in Tambopata. The company had often hired locals from Infierno to help with the research, and personal friendships developed along with the idea to partner. Within months of negotiations, the people of Infierno and the owners of Rainforest Expeditions agreed to a contract to create a joint venture partnership to build and operate an ecotourism lodge called Posada Amazonas. They agreed to split profits, with 60 percent to the community and 40 percent to the company, and to share equally in management. A community based "Comite de Control" of ten persons from the community, a mix of men and women, Ese'eja, Andino, and mestizo, would oversee decision-making on all things related to product development, investment, marketing, management, and revenue sharing. They agreed on a twenty-year timeline. In that span, Infierno's residents would gain the skills and knowledge to assume full management of the lodge.

Project Description

I began my PhD research in Infierno the same month that the partners signed the contract. I had lived in Tambopata for several years, first working for Conservation International and then as a master's student at the University of Florida. I had done a study on local grassroots organizations of colonist farmers and Indigenous peoples in Madre de Dios. The ecotourism boom was just beginning, and I wanted to understand how this new market in Tambopata, a new marriage of business and conservation, would affect local communities.

Figure 2.1. The author takes a break near her host community. © Amanda Stronza.

Arriving in Infierno at the start of the ecotourism partnership gave me the opportunity to watch the story unfold. I had been steeped in the ideas and ideals of applied anthropology as a graduate student. I wanted to be sure my research was meaningful and relevant to the residents of Infierno. I also cared very much about producing more than research articles. My aim was to provide support in whatever way I could, to serve as an advocate, and to collaborate with the community and their partner, not just observe. This meant my work would be quite subjective and biased, not able to "predict" what ecotourism could "cause" or enable in other places. But rather, my work would be to document and share the story of how ecotourism was understood, planned, and experienced by people in this one place, among the members of this one community over many years, and then to use that understanding in ethical and supportive ways—ways that led to project awards, grants, and recognition.

After gaining permission from the community assembly to conduct research with them, learning with them as they began their venture into ecotourism, I set up my first home in a tent near the clinic in the center of the community. This was near the soccer field and the communal house, two meaningful hubs for all kinds of formal and informal meetings and conversations. In subsequent years, I had other homes—a thatched hut overlooking the Tambopata River, and a storeroom inside the craft shop where artisans were carving figurines for tourists. I spent my days over three periods of field research—totaling fourteen months between 1996 and 1999—walking from home to home, traversing forest trails and often paddling a dugout canoe up and down the Tambopata, talking with residents, conducting semistructured interviews, taking photos and notes, and participating in daily life. Life included cooking rice over fires and minding children, washing clothes in the Tambopata River, feeding chickens, carrying sacks of papayas, oranges, and avocados to transport canoes heading to the market, and shelling Brazil nuts, among countless other household routines. With time, I came to know all of the families very well, and as our friendships developed, the trust expanded too, and people shared more and more of their lives and thoughts with me. They allowed me to participate in and document all formal meetings, and in many instances, people sought me out to share what they wanted me to document (rather than the other way around: me asking for interviews) or to ask for help in matters of the joint partnership or in reaching out to authorities. The trust people gave me also allowed me to conduct detailed, lengthy, and repeated interviews over the three years of the dissertation work (as well as many years after that), discussions focused on household economic measures, livelihood activities (including farming, hunting, fishing, and gathering), and attitudes and perceptions about a wide range of topics, from ecotourism to conservation to Indigenous identity, and what it means to be Ese'eja or mestizo in Infierno.

In addition to the conventional ethnographic methods of participant observation, field notes, and interviews, I conducted a series of participatory methods such as group discussions and interviews, meant to include local stakeholders in the research process, where they could formulate questions with me and analyze what we learned together. This included focus group meetings to hear opinions and concerns about the ecotourism lodge. I facilitated a whole series of meetings over many months with the Comite de Control, which were focused on building their mission and sense of purpose as well as their organizational skills so they could hold their own in meetings with Rainforest Expeditions. I also led a social network analysis using pile sorts of cards with people's names and then visually representing the consensus data on hand-drawn maps that showed clusters of knowledge, resources, and information sharing between households in Infierno. This was meant to help locals see how their physical location within the community and in relation to the ecotourism lodge was tied to their social organization and where and how they could turn to each other for support. My participatory approach to gathering data also included "social photography"—or gathering visual data as seen through the eyes of community members. I distributed cameras to a cross-section of families, taught them some basic skills in photography, and asked them over the course of several months to capture images falling into one of four categories: (1) things that make them proud, (2) things they might like to share with tourists, (3) things they perceived as challenges or problems in the community, and (4) things they want to be sure to keep private, away from the gaze of tourists. I printed two copies of all the photos and left them with the families and also used them as talking points for subsequent interviews.

All of the information I gathered throughout the field research I wrote up in regular reports, in Spanish, to deliver to the community and to the tourism company as well as to the Indigenous federation in the region, among other stakeholders, including the Peru Program for Conservation International. This was my effort to serve as witness and scribe, documenting the changes as they were happening and facilitating a process of ensuring that local concerns and priorities in Infierno were understood and addressed along the way rather than after problems had taken root.

As an applied anthropologist, I made an effort to be a part of the story too, to support the people of Infierno as they represented themselves as ably as they could (and they did) in the partnership, the first of its kind anywhere in the world. My goal then and for the decades following—I've returned to Infierno after my PhD nearly every year up to 2020—was to write ethnographic, longitudinal, and holistic accounts of the initiation and development of the lodge and its associated activities. The opportunity to live with and learn from the people of Infierno for many months and then over repeated visits between 1996 and 2020 helped me to understand how ecotourism can support local governance of forests, waters, and wildlife and how it can change social relations and feelings of cultural identity. Over the years, my role shifted from cultural broker between the company and the community to other positions, including facilitator of participatory research, ally for monitoring ecotourism impacts, fundraiser and supporter (bringing grants and new resources to the community), and lifetime friend who stays in touch with multiple generations of families I love as my own.

In the sections that follow, I share the results of what I learned—what I learned in collaboration with the members of Infierno—and how ecotourism has shaped life in the community. I begin with a description of the lodge and how people participated in building the lodge and making it a part of everyday life the community. I describe my role as an ally-anthropologist—or what I prefer to call a "cultural broker."

Posada Amazonas

The complex of thatched buildings known as Posada Amazonas is nestled beneath forest cover on the Tambopata River. The Tambopata is a lifeline of biodiversity that flows from the Andean slopes of Peru through the low foothills of the Amazon. Along its way, the Tambopata passes some of the most species-rich communities reported on earth for birds, butterflies, and dragonflies. The lodge is rustic and beautifully appointed with locally designed furniture and art. It includes five main cabins, each with six guest rooms that can accommodate sixty guests.

Shortly after signing the contract with Rainforest Expeditions in 1996, the people of Infierno built the lodge themselves, using locally harvested wood, palm fronds, and wild cane. They depended as well on significant support in architectural design and capital financing from their partners at Rainforest Expeditions. They completed construction of the lodge in two years and opened their doors (and canoes and trails and canopy tower) to tourists in 1998.

Nonetheless, for many in Infierno, the idea of participation was confusing. Before Posada Amazonas had done so, they had never been invited to engage so actively in a project of such magnitude. Historically, the role of decision-making had been left to outsiders. Locals had little experience in being architects of their own change, and they had even less experience building from the ground up a luxury ecotourism lodge with thousands of dollars of capital investment. People felt limited in their abilities, and compounding the lack of experience was a general uncertainty about social roles. Many felt uncertain about how to treat the company as a partner rather than as an employer. In fact, this new kind of interaction was a leap for both sides. In the initial months of the joint venture, the owners of Rainforest Expeditions were accustomed to talking to their community partners rather than with them, delivering tasks rather than converging on plans. The intention of acting as equal partners was there, but neither side was prepared, either practically or psychologically, to deal with the other on such progressive new terms. It would take time, and yet the company needed the community to get involved. It was not just a noble social experiment, it was a new kind of business model, partnering with an Indigenous community on equal terms.

As everyone grappled with the issue of how to build participation, we discovered a point of disconnect on the question of who should participate and how they should do so. I found that we needed to pay attention to the heterogeneity of priorities as well as to different kinds of participation. Not everyone in a community would participate equally. Some may join directly, interacting with tourists on a regular basis as guides or performers, while others may work only behind the scenes as support staff or as wholesalers. Community members differed also in terms of how much time and energy they could invest. Some would work as full-time staff, while others would contract their labor occasionally or earn cash only through the sale of goods. Others would choose not to participate at all.

The expectation for Posada Amazonas, especially from the perspective of outsiders, was that participation would broadly lead to economic benefits and could be summed up as cash earned or employment gained. As an anthropologist, I perceived participation and its impacts more holistically. Participation in this community-owned lodge became more than just income and jobs. There were and are many ways to participate in Posada Amazonas, including joining the Ecotourism Committee. With attention to such differences, I discovered that gender was key in determining who participated in what. Virtually no women were represented in high levels of decision-making, at least not at the beginning. This was not surprising given gender roles around childcare. It was difficult for women to work at the lodge, which is far upriver from the center of Infierno where most people live. Through participant observation, I learned that although most women had no plans to get involved, the situations in their households were changing. Women were not the ones clearing trails, debating the bylaws of the partnership, or learning to guide, but they were affected by the project, often through the participation of their spouses. If their husbands or older sons were involved, that meant there would be new constraints on men's time for farming and other household work. Changes for the men implied subsequent and tremendous shifts in women's responsibilities too.

When I began the fieldwork in 1996, the idea of a private company partnering with an Indigenous community to run a tourism operation was quite controversial. Some feared the company would "rob the natives blind." A history of violence, exploitation, and boom-bust cycles in the Amazon certainly fueled the controversy. A joint-venture partnership was a pioneering idea, but not one that everyone supported. In fact, most people were not supportive, including the local Indigenous federation and many anthropologists internationally who advocated on behalf on Amazonian Indigenous peoples.

As an applied anthropologist starting my PhD dissertation research in the middle of the controversy, I was often challenged about my role, my ethics, and my objectives. Some wondered if I were a plant, a spy for Rainforest Expeditions. They said I was biased and would surely favor the company against the community. I had read from the anthropologist Dennison Nash that indeed many anthropologists had turned down consulting possibilities with tourism companies for these very reasons, the assumptions of bias and of "selling out." I had not been hired by either Rainforest Expeditions or the people of Infierno, but I did plan to share what I was learning with both partners. That heightened worries about me on all sides. Was I sharing sensitive information? How could I protect people from risk?

Despite the concerns, my collaboration with both partners offered opportunities. My role as insider on both sides made me privy to the company's records, as well as to many candid conversations. Had I been more of an outsider, especially one opposed to the project, it is likely that this would have been impossible. It is also likely that my findings about Posada Amazonas might have been slanted toward the hearsay and rumors that surrounded the project. I tried to build my interpretations on all aspects of the project: not only the published success stories produced for the brochures but also the private discussions about the dilemmas and problems the project was experiencing.

These challenges included, for example, jealousies within the community about who was involved or not and the tendency of the company in the early days to dominate partnership meetings.

Implementation and Anthropologist's Role

As an insider, I was able to gain access to the lodge and its clientele on a daily basis. I observed the operations not only from the perspective of a visitor but also from the viewpoint of the owners, administrators, and staff. I spent downtime with locals in their homes and farms in Infierno, and I joined them at the lodge, watching and talking with them as they interacted with tourists, noting how they balanced dual roles. In other moments, I accompanied tourists, surveying them about their impressions of what they were seeing.

There was some uncertainty about my role as an anthropologist and what I could achieve. At times, the company representatives thought it useful to use me as a barometer of general sentiment in the community. They would ask, "How are things going?" or "What does the community think and feel?" After all, I was living there, sharing meals with locals; should I not have my finger on the pulse? Of course, I knew I could never capture the full range of perspectives. People were always changing their minds, and different sectors within the community generally perceived and engaged in the project in fundamentally different ways.

I had learned this in the first year, when I conducted a stakeholder analysis and tried to understand how ethnicity, gender, age, and livelihood correlated with varying opinions about ecotourism and varying levels of involvement with the project. I interviewed the residents of Infierno as well as representatives of outside organizations about their hopes and concerns. In focus groups, I used hand-drawn posters to characterize the tourism project and to serve as launching points for discussion. I discovered that conflicts outside the community, usually on the part of those who wanted to help Infierno, often intensified conflicts within the community. For example, tour companies that were vying for the same socially responsible market had the members of Infierno asking, "Who should we deal with?" Nongovernmental organizations (NGOs) were competing, too, over the role of who should advise the community in dealings with Rainforest Expeditions. The people of Infierno seemed generally open to working with any group willing to offer support. However, once they became enmeshed in the political relations outside the community, they were resigned to taking sides. The result was that outside relations were replayed and then intensified inside the community.

In many ways, my role as an anthropologist working with both sides of the partnership became one of serving as a kind of cultural broker, a translator of insights and understandings. I often encountered points of disconnect. A first point was on the issue of participation. In my first year, I coordinated a process of participatory planning. The company wanted to ensure that Infierno's residents fully understood the project. The first thing I learned was that the community's vote to sign the contract had been called "unanimous," but in fact many persons were either ill-informed or, as in the case of most women, completely uninformed. The company also wanted to give community members the chance to decide whether or not and how they would like to participate in the project. The company saw me as a resource for persuasion. In my mind, it was more important for residents to weigh for themselves the costs and benefits of getting involved. I was focused on facilitating local decision-making, empowering people to feel in control of this big new project.

Another point of disconnect between the partners was how to define participation. We all had an interest in the concept. For Rainforest Expeditions, participation meant filling labor positions. When they were building the lodge, they had an immediate need for people to haul equipment, lumber, and appliances up steep and muddy riverbanks, nail down thousands of floorboards, forge new trails through the forest, and collect enough palm fronds to weave together nearly twenty thousand panels of thatch. The details were endless, down to the last handmade towel rack. Coordinating the effort required both leadership and a significant investment of time, often away from people's families. Spending time working away from home was in some ways quite new and challenging for subsistence farmers. When the lodge opened, so too did many new opportunities for getting involved, for "participation." Everyone talked about it. Who was and who was not participating? Did some have an unfair advantage over others? Were some earning more or less than others? Who decided who participated and in what ways? In my mind, the importance of participation was as much conceptual as practical. I was less worried about getting hammers into people's hands and more about encouraging them to think critically about how tourism on their land might change their lives and how they could ensure real ownership over the lodge.

As more and more residents got more and more involved, concerns began to emerge about limitations. Were people in Infierno truly prepared to run the lodge? Would they be ready to do so on their own in twenty years? They were concerned as well about new conflicts in the community and how tourism might favor some over others. The general question was not "What can we achieve?" but rather "How are we getting along?" I encouraged stakeholders to take things slowly, pursue small but concrete and locally initiated goals, such as pooling resources to purchase a two-way radio. This approach was based on a philosophy of self-determination and the need to build organizational capacity within the community so that individuals could advocate for themselves and plan their own futures. This entailed learning to gather ideas and concerns from their neighbors and families, transforming these ideas into grant proposals for support, however small, and then learning to deal confidently with politicians and NGOs to negotiate for their needs.

While the company supported small-scale ideas, they also encouraged larger projects, including a US$50,000 World Bank initiative to promote handicraft production. Our different definitions of success emanated from our broader visions. I was thinking about the need for autonomy and social sustainability; the company was thinking about getting things done, preparing their community partners to become better businesspeople (taking risks, cost-benefit planning for the future, etc.), and ultimately ensuring a good return on their investments. As a profit-making enterprise, they could ill afford to think like an NGO and give priority to notions of self-determination over practical needs for efficiency.

Aside from the meaning of "participation" discussed earlier, the company and I disagreed substantively on the role of culture in Posada Amazonas. The company was eager to promote culture as an added attraction. They hoped to have an anthropologist who could help push this through. As anthropologists are known to deal in culture, some in the company thought that my presence would be helpful in identifying and "rescuing" an Ese'eja identity. Rather than helping objectify or showcase certain features of Indigenous culture in Infierno to tourists, I focused instead on asking participants to consider what culture meant for them and why. Do some have "more culture" than others? What does it mean to be Ese'eja or mestizo or Andean, and why are some of these characteristics perhaps more interesting to tourists than others? These types of discussions were rich and animated, and, with time, they led to more conscious planning and self-management of cultural resources.

Outcomes

In its first ten years, Posada Amazonas generated over $2 million in local income. The returns created several direct financial incentives for conservation. One of the first conservation decisions the community made in 1996 was to build the lodge in their two-thousand-hectare reserve where they prohibited hunting, timber harvesting, and farming. Soon after they started building the ecotourism lodge, the community agreed to expand the reserve to three thousand hectares. Thus, the very first action associated with ecotourism was the expansion of the protected commons. This was a decision made autonomously by the community.

Posada Amazonas has also prompted discussion and collective planning of how wildlife, habitats, and even cultural traditions should be used, showcased (or not), and protected. Community members have discussed who should have access to the resources, under what conditions, and how they should be managed in new or old ways in the context of ecotourism. For example, some species gained new value in ecotourism, while others lost value. With changing valuations, decisions about management entered community discussions.

Two examples are harpy eagles and giant otters, species of particular interest to ecotourists, though of relatively little direct value to hunters, either for game meat or skins or feathers. When a community member locates an active harpy nest on his or her parcel of land (held under use rights, as all land is community owned), the individual earns a standard fee for every tourist given the opportunity to see it. The fees are charged until the eagle chick fledges, a period that lasts up to nine months. This nest watching program has become an incentive for individual management of harpy eagles, though the rules were determined collectively by the members of Infierno in the interest of supporting the ecotourism project. Similarly, giant otters in the community's oxbow lakes are managed collectively. Before ecotourism, otters were sometimes hunted for their pelts or because fishers treated them as competitors. Once the lodge was built, the community established clearer regulations on when the lake could be fished, what kinds of equipment could be used, and who would have access.

Posada Amazonas has attracted 6,000–7,000 tourists annually, paying $100 per night in the early years and $600 per night in 2020. The lodge generates yearly profits of over $225,000. A typical tourist itinerary includes rainforest hikes, ethnobotanical walks, night walks and information sessions, and visits to Infierno to learn about local farming practices. A 35-meter tower provides canopy access and a view of the Tambopata from a macaw's-eye view. A highlight for many tourists is a sunrise float on a large catamaran on one of the community's oxbow lakes, Tres Chimbadas. There, visitors can search for a family of highly endangered giant otters and other lake species, including caiman, piranha, and ancient hoatzin birds.

As an experimental model for ecotourism, Posada Amazonas was created to provide revenue, employment, and other benefits to Infierno while also protecting the rainforests of Tambopata. Financing for the project included US$500,000 that came partly from a loan from a Peru-Canada bilateral aid program as well as a capacity-building grant from the Sustainable Development Program at the MacArthur Foundation. The dual emphasis on benefit sharing and joint decision-making has made Posada Amazonas a standout among ecotourism operations around the world. The successful partnership has come only as a result of strategic and conscious efforts on both sides to work collaboratively and to make knowledge sharing and capacity building a priority. Infierno's residents assumed work not only as laborers—boat drivers, cooks, guides, and housekeepers—but also as directors, owners, and decision-makers in the company. For its innovation as a partnership, its profits and financial successes, and its meaningful approach to community participation and leadership, Posada Amazonas has received considerable media attention and won numerous awards from conservation and development organizations, including the United Nations' prestigious Equator Initiative. The project has also been the focus of prominent international media and has been featured in articles in *The Economist, National Geographic,* and the *New York Times.*

In many ways, the members of Infierno have gained new management capacity through their involvement in ecotourism. In recent years, they have devoted considerable time to discussing and enforcing rules for how resources can be used in relation to ecotourism. When some were caught hunting in the reserve in 2006, community members gathered to determine appropriate sanctions and decided to withhold the hunters' tourism profits for that year. More than determining how individuals should be sanctioned when rules are violated, those in Infierno have also gained the capacity to organize themselves, combine resources, and work collectively to protect what they share.

For example, in 2003, before the Peruvian government announced new plans for the completion of the Interoceanic Highway, members of the community applied for a concession to manage lands surrounding an oxbow lake, in part to protect the giant otters. Soon after awarding the concession to the community, the government granted access as well to another private petitioner who had sought permission to fish the lake. Leaders of Infierno joined with their business partners to challenge the concession. The request required political negotiation, money, and the support of other tour operators and organizations, including the Peruvian Society for Environmental Law. After several months of petitioning and payments of several thousand dollars, which the community had set aside from ecotourism profits, the government revoked the fishing concession and granted the community and its partners an area of two thousand hectares to function as an ecotourism concession.

Residents of Infierno had some experience in collective action prior to ecotourism—such as in communal *faenas* (group labors) to plant crops and build communal structures. But they had little reason to work collectively to protect their communal resources before the advent of tourism. It is precisely through their engagement with the community-based enterprise that they were able to gain the skills, practices, and relationships they needed to strengthen their organization for activities like expanding their communal reserve, securing rights to an ecotourism concession, or guarding and monitoring their oxbow lake. Much of this increased capacity is related to a wider social network into which the community has entered since the lodge opened. Especially since 1998, the community has received support from a number of national and international organizations. Aid agencies and NGOs have focused their attention on Infierno as a target for investment and training in such things as conservation, leadership, microenterprise development, and handicraft development. With my help as an ally-anthropologist, the community has earned grants and awards from the World Bank, the Inter-American Foundation, and the MacArthur Foundation, among others. I wrote the grants, first while I was a postdoc and then later as a professor, to bring resources to the partnership while also continuing my research. My journal articles and public presentations also helped put a spotlight on the partnership, with data and analysis showing how ecotourism had led to meaningful changes for local governance of forests and wildlife and community empowerment for long-term goals. For example, the United Nations' Equator Initiative Award was granted using my longitudinal data to show how ecotourism had supported balancing conservation and development goals in the community.

In summary, few community-based ecotourism projects have been so carefully documented—largely through my sustained research over more than twenty-five years, with twenty-eight peer-reviewed articles, monographs, and chapters I've published, tracking changes over time—or described as "successful" by various measures and evaluators as Posada Amazonas. The successes include substantial economic returns, a variety of social benefits, cultural revalorization, effective resource management and conservation, and strengthened local self-determination.

The Anthropological Difference

For environmental anthropologists, ecotourism is an especially timely and practical topic. Increasingly, anthropologists are talking with conservationists, development specialists, tour operators, policymakers, and local leaders about ecotourism and its impacts on local communities and ecosystems. This is good, as anthropologists are especially well suited to focus ethnographic attention on the general but critical question of what happens when those in destinations near and in protected areas become involved in ecotourism. Do local residents become better stewards of wildlife, forests, and other ecosystems when ecotourism is introduced? If so, what is the process by which that happens, and what are the challenges? The difference in having an anthropologist involved was twofold: counting on an intermediary, or cultural broker, between the two partners and sharing lessons learned with other communities and companies in other parts of the world.

Anthropologists are perhaps best prepared of all disciplines for this kind of work. It is our attention to culturally meaningful insights—the emic, insiders' perspective—on how phenomena are lived, experienced, understood, and perceived. Other social science data, for example from economics or survey work, is essential, too, for understanding patterns and making predictions, for gathering objective measures of change. However, it is really only with ethnographic and participatory measures of change that we may gain insights about what the patterns and changes signify for people.

Cultural Brokering

My work as cultural broker between Infierno and Rainforest Expeditions was meaningful in two ways. For one, learning and telling both sides of the story enabled us to learn the whole story of Posada Amazonas, beyond just the economic costs and benefits of ecotourism. This meant unraveling why some were choosing to participate in ecotourism and others were not, and how decisions were often related to social and cultural roles and perceptions within the community as opposed to a mere lack of understanding. An ethnographic approach made it possible for me to include analyses of process, in addition to impacts; that is, how and why locals experienced gains and losses from ecotourism, in addition to what the changes were.

The ethnographic analysis also helped to clarify the concepts of "participation" and "community" from locally meaningful perspectives, highlighting the ways in which diverse actors perceived, reacted to, and defined their engagement with ecotourism differently. The holistic assessment also extended beyond calculating economic impacts of ecotourism and focused attention on quality of life, social cohesion, and concerns about the commodification of culture (i.e., how or if "native culture" should be presented and represented to tourists).

Finally, my role as a mediator between the community and the company helped to create a level of transparency and openness in the working dialogue between the partners. As I pointed out differences in their perspectives and expectations, each side gradually learned more about the other, and the partnership seemed to gain strength. When I pointed out disconnects between what was being said, done, and felt, the company was able to gain greater insight into its own actions and into those of the community, while the members of Infierno also began to affirm that their partnership in Posada Amazonas represented a new kind of development, one in which they stood on equal ground with their partners, despite many economic and social differences with Rainforest Expeditions.

Sharing Lessons Learned

When I began my research and collaboration with the partnership, the members of Infierno had just forged their partnership with the company to build and comanage an ecotourism lodge. In subsequent years, I studied the challenges and opportunities that came with reconciling local subsistence needs with those of international tourists, mixing ecotourism development with conservation, the results of community management of ecotourism, and changing notions of cultural identity. These various facets of the applied research have resulted in multiple peer-reviewed articles and book chapters about this project alone. Publications have appeared in a diverse set of academic journals in anthropology, environmental studies, and tourism studies.

I also shared results of the work with practitioners through reports, workshops, websites, and videos. In 2002, I directed a series of exchanges between local leaders from Posada Amazonas and other Indigenous leaders in Ecuador and Bolivia. The goal was to compare experiences, ideas, and concerns about ecotourism as a catalyst for change in their communities. Members of the Ese'eja, Quechua-Tacana, and Achuar communities, in Peru, Bolivia, and Ecuador, respectively, were involved in every phase of the analysis. They collaborated with me to propose the idea of conducting a comparative study to donors at the Critical Ecosystem Partnership Fund, and then all worked together to gather and assess ethnographic data, cofacilitate workshops in the three countries, and present the results to press conferences in Quito, La Paz, and Lima. In 2005, I produced a professional, hour-long documentary, *Amazon Exchange: Effects of Ecotourism on Indigenous Culture*, in collaboration with the communities in Peru and Bolivia.

Epilogue

Two decades into the partnership, some of the results for conservation and community development are emerging. In the Nape communal reserve where the lodge is located, the forest has remained healthy and intact, with no clearance for logging or agriculture. Wildlife populations are thriving, too, and in some cases making a return, thanks in part to a cessation of hunting in the reserve. Community guides report the return of several rarer species, including macaws, white-lipped peccaries, tapirs, jaguars, and harpy eagles. Aside from local monitoring of the community reserve, the success for conservation has come from collective action in Infierno. Comanaging Posada Amazonas has expanded organizational skills within the community, helping individuals to learn to effectively work together to manage and govern their own resources. For example, ten years after the partnership, residents came together on their own, without outside pressure, and agreed to tie yearly shares of their ecotourism profits to whether or not people adhered to rules of the reserve. If anyone breaks the rule of no hunting, for example, they lose their share of profits. This is a clear and communally led connection between ecotourism and wildlife conservation. In another example, the community established bylaws to regulate fishing rights in the oxbow lake that is critical habitat for the endangered giant otters. The people of Infierno decided very consciously and strategically to monitor and protect the habitat for the otters, knowing the animals are a key attraction for their tourists.

Posada Amazonas has been successful for economic development as well. It is just one lodge in what has been a booming market for ecotourism in Madre de Dios Department, and it accounts for 20 percent of the entire market. The financial success has signaled many changes within Infierno, both in terms of employment opportunities, revenues, and opportunities to gain new professional skills. A percentage of the lodge revenues has been invested in community projects, including a secondary school, a computer facility, a potable water well and tank system, an emergency health fund, and loans and scholarships for students. The remaining profits have been split among the families, who are essentially shareholders in the partnership.

In addition to the conservation and community development outcomes, many in Infierno report feeling great pride and accomplishment for what they have done and how they have effectively run a large enterprise, establishing meaningful roles in ownership and management. In some ways, these feelings outshine the material benefits of income, employment, and healthy forests and wildlife populations. The feelings of autonomy and self-determination have given rise to other community-led initiatives and a sense of capacity and competence.

When the partners signed the agreement in 1996, they concurred that, as long as they remained partners, the members of Infierno would be obligated to maintain an exclusive contract with Rainforest Expeditions. They agreed that no one from the community could strike a deal with a competing company to build a second lodge, nor could any individual independently create an additional ecotourism project within communal territory. Also, outside visitors must seek permission from the association before using ecotourism infrastructure in the community, including the lodge itself, trails through the forest, the catamaran in the oxbow lake, and the canopy tower.

This changed with time. It became clear that the ecotourism market in Tambopata was rich and varied enough to allow for more than one lodge in Infierno. More locals wanted to start their own companies outside of any agreement with their Lima partners. Many community members noted that Rainforest Expeditions had maintained the right to expand, build other lodges, and widen their operations, and they expressed that they should, too. In subsequent years, three families in Infierno established their own private homestays and touristic venues for guests. In some ways, Infierno is now a hub for various tourism options managed by a variety of locally owned companies and associations.

When the original twenty-year contract ended in 2016, the company and the community returned to the negotiation table. They agreed the partnership had been fruitful, enriching, edifying, and productive for both. They had each contributed their skills, knowledge, and resources, and they had each benefitted. They had also created something organically new: a hybrid business model, connecting an Indigenous community with a private company and establishing a for-profit enterprise that delivered net returns to conservation and development. Their joint-venture partnership was not an NGO, a community, or a company but rather a combination of all of them. The partners decided to keep working together. They agreed to change the terms of the contract slightly, now with Infierno gaining a greater share of the profits. The spirit of the partnership remains strong, and the forests, waters, and wildlife of the Tambopata are stable and thriving, at least in that part of the river, thanks to this pioneering experiment that will live on as a legacy for future generations.

Amanda Stronza is an environmental anthropologist with thirty years of experience in the Amazon, the Okavango Delta, and other parts of the tropics. She earned her PhD in anthropology with a concentration in tropical conservation and development at the University of Florida in 2000 and was a postdoctoral fellow in Anthropological Sciences at Stanford. She is currently a professor in Ecology and Conservation Biology, with a joint appointment in Rangeland, Wildlife, and Fisheries Management, at Texas A&M University, as well as codirector of the Applied Biodiversity Science Program. Her research and advocacy focus on people-centered approaches to conservation. In 2013, she cofounded Ecoexist, an NGO in Botswana aimed at fostering coexistence between people and elephants. Since 1993, her work in the Amazon has documented and supported Indigenous stewardship of wildlife, particularly through community-based ecotourism. Her recent work includes a film about gold mining in the Peruvian Amazon and applied research on human-lion conflict in the Kalahari.

References

Stronza, A. 1999. "Learning Both Ways: Lessons from a Corporate and Community Ecotourism Collaboration." *Cultural Survival Quarterly* 23(2): 36–39.

———. 2007. "The Economic Promise of Ecotourism for Conservation." *Journal of Ecotourism* 6(3): 170–90.

———. 2008. "Through a New Mirror: Reflections on Tourism and Identity in the Amazon." *Human Organization* 67(3): 244–57.

———. 2010. "Commons Management and Ecotourism: Ethnographic Evidence from the Amazon." *International Journal of the Commons* 4(1): 56–77.

Stronza, A., and J. Gordillo. 2008. "Community Views of Ecotourism: Redefining Benefits." *Annals of Tourism Research* 35(2): 444–68.

Stronza, A., and F. Pegas. 2008. "Ecotourism and Conservation: Two Cases from Peru and Brazil." *Human Dimensions of Wildlife* 13: 263–79.

CHAPTER 3

❧ ❧ ❧

Ethnic Minority Women-Led Routine Road Maintenance in Vietnam

MARI CLARKE

Project Background

In the past, many rural Vietnamese communities were isolated due to missing road links, particularly in the mountainous areas where most ethnic minorities reside. There are over fifty ethnic groups recognized by the Vietnam government, including the Tay, Tai, Mường, Hmong, and Khmer groups. Many had poor access to education, healthcare, and employment opportunities generated by the country's recent remarkable economic successes. Vietnam's poverty rate fell from 58 percent in the early 1990s to 14.5 percent by 2008 and was estimated to be well below 10 percent by 2010. Primary and secondary school enrollments increased, health status improved, and morbidity and mortality declined. Overall, Vietnam achieved and surpassed many of the United Nations' Millennium Development Goals (MDGs). Still, many ethnic minorities remained among the poorest of the poor.

A number of factors contributed to the missing rural road links. The cost of road maintenance was very high due to erosion, flooding, and landslides on steep terrain; these continue to be exacerbated by increasingly unpredictable and extreme rainfall conditions due to climate change. Leaders and the general public did not understand that failing to carry out road maintenance caused roads to deteriorate more rapidly and become impassible, necessitating expensive road rehabilitation. Some local farmers damaged the roads by cutting irrigation ditches across them and dumping trash in the drainage channels.

The extensive rural road network in Vietnam was and continues to be managed mostly by districts and communes, for which they receive a very small allocation from the provincial budget. This funding is inadequate to cover the upkeep of the road networks. The poor, ethnic minority residents of the mountainous areas lacked resources to cover the high costs of local road maintenance because there were few options for earning income, particularly for women. Even when adequate resources were available for maintenance, contractors were sometimes unwilling to work in mountainous areas due to fears of landslides during the rainy season. To bridge the gap between funding and road maintenance needs, commune people's committees (CPCs) arranged "voluntary labor days" for community participation in road maintenance. While this helped to ensure that local roads were at least marginally open to traffic, the participants had little or no training in road maintenance and sometimes actually damaged the roads in their attempts to fix them.

To respond to these economic and road maintenance challenges, the World Bank Hanoi Third Rural Transport Project Team obtained a small grant from the Gender Unit of the World Bank to launch a small pilot project in one district in Lao Cai Province in northern Vietnam. The Provincial Department of Transport trained the Women's Union members to maintain local roads and supervised them and paid them for their work.

The Lao Cai Women-Led Routine Road Maintenance pilot had been completed by the fall of 2010 when I arrived in Vietnam to conduct workshops on gender and transport funded by the World Bank's East Asia and Pacific Region gender advisor. This training grew out of my work on the design of a baseline survey for the Mekong Delta Transport Infrastructure Project, a road and inland waterways project. The team leader for the Third Rural Transport Project recognized the value of the gender workshop and mobilized provincial transport staff to attend workshops in Hanoi and Ho Chi Minh City. I designed the workshop and prepared PowerPoint presentations, including one describing the pilot on ethnic minority women's maintenance of rural roads, which the project team leader presented. Thus, I became acquainted with the World Bank transport team in Hanoi. The Third Rural Transport Project was about to be extended, and the task team leader asked me to help refine, justify, and design the scale-up of the Lao Cai Women-Led pilot approach. I agreed and joined the transport task team.

Project Description

The World Bank has provided financing and technical advice for expansion of rural road access in Vietnam since 1996. The first two rural road projects supported rehabilitation of roads, strengthening of planning capacity, and implementation of road improvements at the national level. The project aimed to reduce travel costs and improve access to markets, off-farm economic opportunities, and social services for poor, rural communities in thirty-three participating provinces in northern and central Vietnam. The Third Rural Transport Project responded to the Government of Vietnam's desire to increase the upgrading of the primary road network with more decentralized management. The original financing for the project was completed in 2012. Additional financing was approved in 2011 through the end of June 2014.

It is important to keep in mind that the World Bank does not implement projects. Instead, it provides low-interest loans, zero- to low-interest credits, and grants, as well as policy advice, research and analysis, and technical assistance to client countries that implement projects. The World Bank project task teams also conduct supervisory visits to observe road project sites, to meet with local transport and government officials to monitor and discuss progress toward project objectives, and to address any problems. The World Bank also conducts an evaluation and prepares an implementation completion report at the end of each project.

The implementation of the Third Rural Transport Project was carried out by the Vietnam Ministry of Transport (MOT), which oversees many offices and departments from the national to the provincial levels, including transport infrastructure, safety, legislation, and science and technology, as well as three transport colleges and three vocational colleges.

The expansion of the Lao Cai pilot model was implemented by provincial and lower-level Vietnam Women's Union branches in Lao Cai, Quang Binh, and Thanh Hoa Provinces. The Vietnam Women's Union is a political and social organization representing and advising the Communist Party and government on the rights of women in Vietnam, women's advancement, and gender equality. The Women's Union has a wide network across the country at the national, provincial, district, and commune levels, encompassing more than 50 percent of Vietnamese women. In 2012, total membership was more than fifteen million. The provincial Women's Unions implement a broad range of development projects using government, donor, and other sources of funding.

The objectives of the expanded pilot of the Lao Cai Women-Led Routine Road Maintenance model were to: (1) raise the awareness among women and their families on the importance of rural road maintenance; (2) train the local population in road maintenance to sustain infrastructure investments in project communes; (3) strengthen the role of the Women's Union in organizing awareness-raising training for both men and women; (4) effectively maintain roads to increase their longevity; (5) develop an effective mechanism in rural road maintenance for women; and (6) strengthen the capacity of women's unions at all levels in coordinating social and technical activities as well as the technical support capacity of the provincial Women's Union. They achieved these objectives by training trainers who coached local people, mobilizing local groups, raising awareness about the importance of protecting local roads through maintenance, and organizing and supervising routine road mainte-

Figure 3.1. A local work team discusses the impact of their road maintenance work in Lao Cai Province. © Mari Clarke.

nance teams composed of women and men to ensure that the work was done according to specified quality criteria. The provincial Departments of Transport provided technical oversight and quality control on the maintenance work. The Women's Union also worked closely with the people's committees at each level due to their lead role in the overall administrative and development activities within the provinces, districts, and communes.

It is important to note that, even though the road maintenance was managed by women, women did not bear all of the responsibility or do all of the work. Men in the local communities carried out the heavier tasks, such as accessing suitable materials for filling potholes, removing large stones from roadside drainage ditches and culverts, and taking away dead trees. Although women worked more hours on road maintenance than men did, their tasks were lighter and needed to be done more frequently, including clearing rubbish and vegetation from roadside drainage ditches and cutting grass and small bushes.

Implementation and Anthropologist's Role

Successful implementation of a community-based, women-led, routine road maintenance project entails much more than handing out shovels and scheduling activities. It requires thorough planning, clear definitions of roles and responsibilities, mechanisms for coordination throughout the project, training of maintenance workers (including standards of performance for specific maintenance tasks), and community mobilization and awareness raising, as well as supervision, monitoring, and evaluation.

As a consultant supporting the World Bank transport task team, my influence on the pilot project was focused on the pilot's design, technical support to the Ministry of Transport on developing the training materials, project supervision and associated technical support, design and analysis for monitoring and evaluating the pilot project, and institutional strengthening of the Ministry of Transport through workshops.

I assisted the World Bank Hanoi transport team in drafting the Project Appraisal Document for Additional Financing for the Third Rural Transport Project, particularly the description of the expanded pilot for Women-Led Routine Maintenance in three provinces. After approval of the project extension, I helped draft the terms of reference to guide the provincial Women's Unions in their preparation of proposals for organizing and implementing women-led routine maintenance in their provinces. Recognizing the ethnic, social, cultural, economic, and environmental diversity and the need for local ownership of the project, we gave the Women's Union leaders great flexibility in their approach so they could tailor activities to best suit the local situations. To address the negative impact of climate change on rural roads, we encouraged the provincial Women's Unions to include bioengineering (planting vegetation on slopes and along roads and adjacent streams to reduce landslides and road erosion) as a part of their routine road maintenance plans.

The provincial Women's Unions collaborated with the local people's committees (PCs) and provincial Departments of Transport to select the participating districts in each province as well as the roads to be maintained. After consultation with the provisional departments and people's committees, each provincial women's union submitted a proposal with proposed districts, roads to be maintained, and a plan for raising awareness about road maintenance, mobilizing women and other workers for road maintenance, skills training, and managing the road work. I joined the World Bank Vietnamese transport team on supervisory visits to discuss these plans and view roads proposed for routine maintenance.

Assessing the scale-up of the pilot in holistic terms, taking into account the different cultures and administrative levels involved, I stressed in my feedback on draft proposals from the Provincial Women's Unions the importance of clearly detailing roles, responsibilities, and lines of communication among the provincial and district transport officials, the people's committees, and Women's Union branches at all levels to ensure effective coordination. To better understand all the stakeholders involved at different levels and their relationships, I drafted a chart with guidance from the task team leader.

To facilitate coordination and promote quality, transport officials at provincial and district levels drafted memorandums of understanding with the women's union branches and local people's committees that clearly describe roles and responsibilities of all parties as well as quality criteria for the road maintenance. Provincial and district transport officials' responsibility was to provide technical oversight and approve completed work based on standards of performance. The provincial, district, and commune Women's Unions' tasks were to raise awareness, mobilize and train routine maintenance workers, organize and supervise their work, report on activities and completed work, and issue payment for work approved by the provincial Departments of Transport. The people's committees were expected to assist in mobilization and supervision.

Before the road maintenance began, training was conducted to ensure that the workers had the necessary skills to carry out quality maintenance that met MOT standards. Awareness raising was conducted on an ongoing basis throughout the project to increase local understanding and support for routine maintenance to preserve the accessibility of local roads.

The Transport and Communication University drafted a handbook for routine road maintenance of local roads to ensure that all of the training events presented the correct methods and the same messages. The initial draft of the handbook included many technical drawings, technical terms, and too much text. My review comments stressed the importance of simplifying the messages and images, taking into account the limited education of ethnic minority women as well as the different languages that they spoke. I urged the trainers to use more pictures (both drawings and photos), remove technical terms, and focus on a few clear, simple messages.

The provincial Women's Unions and provincial Departments of Transport master trainers launched provincial training of trainers workshops for nearly 4,000 participants, including district-level Women's Unions, economic and Departments of Infrastructure , and commune leaders. Those trained in these leadership workshops organized 136 workshops for over 7,000 participants at the district and commune level, using lectures as the primary training technique, combined with visual aids, some demonstrations, and practice on local roads. Awareness campaigns launched by trainees reached 765,000 people in 1,948 villages using a variety of media—songs, traditional dance, quiz games, posters, banners, and signs, as well as radio and loudspeaker broadcasts with content based on the *Routine Road Maintenance Handbook* that was distributed to all participating Women's Union branches.

During supervisory visits to Women's Union training and public awareness-raising events, I noted that lectures and speeches were the predominant modes of sharing information within both the transport and the Women's Union structures. I encouraged my transport team colleagues to stress the importance of using more participatory approaches that actively engaged participants in solving problems, expressing their views, and sharing knowledge as well as demonstrating and practicing road maintenance skills. Our team praised the use of participatory approaches and used them as examples for the groups who were still relying on lecture and rote learning. We reminded trainers that using demonstrations enabled provincial trainers in the initial pilot to cross linguistic barriers with the ethnic minority women.

The World Bank required the provincial Women's Unions to keep records of hours worked, payments, and kilometers of road maintained for those working on road maintenance. I joined the team for some of the supervisory visits to the field to monitor overall project progress, including the women-led maintenance pilots. The provincial, district, and commune Women's Unions mobilized 9,256 women and men in 1,487 women-managed groups. Poor and minority women had priority, resulting in 86 percent women, roughly 45 percent poor, and nearly 45 percent minorities in the women-led groups. Road sections were assigned to each group. These core groups mobilized other community members to participate. The village and commune Women's Unions led the work teams with technical support from the provincial and district Women's Union leaders as well as from district Economic and Infrastructure Department or Municipal Development staff and provincial Department of Transport staff.

Given the aim of raising awareness, building a sense of local ownership, fostering local stewardship of local roads, and changing behavior to protect rather than damage roads, the Women's Union branches mobilized large numbers of people for road maintenance work to promote a sense of local ownership and responsibility for the maintenance of local roads. At least one member of most households contributed to routine road maintenance in the participating communes and villages. A total of 83,545 persons provided 80,938 days of routine management on 3,149 kilometers of commune and village roads between 2012 and 2014. The provincial Women's Unions also managed 2,293 individuals in planting 39,235 trees along 87.4 kilometers of roads maintained by women-led groups.

In addition to project supervision, the transport team also conducted workshops for MOT staff during and at the end of the women-led maintenance pilot projects. I helped the team design the workshops and prepared presentations to make the case for further scaling-up of the Lao Cai Women-Led Rural Road Maintenance model. Participants discussed constraints on routine road management at the local level, investment in road maintenance, and the effectiveness of the women-led model.

The MOT requested technical support for the update of their Gender Action Plan for 2016–20, which describes activities to be carried out to support the goals of the National Strategy for Gender Equality. To better inform the Gender Action Plan update, I conducted a scoping study (similar to a literature review combined with interviews) of opportunities to mainstream gender in

MOT operations and policies, which was not addressed in the previous plan. My report, which was translated and shared with the MOT, offered suggestions for potential actions to strengthen attention to gender in their transport project planning, management, and evaluation.

My role in project evaluation included inputs into the design of the project evaluation, including qualitative ethnographic techniques combined along with quantitative surveys. This approach enabled the Third Rural Transport project team to assess outcomes for their larger project and the Women-Led Routine Road Maintenance pilot in the broader sociocultural context.

I encouraged them to incorporate informant interviews, focus group discussions, and observations along with their quantitative surveys. For the survey design, I advised them to differentiate women's and men's uses of different types of transport, travel time, and uses of transport, along with other data, to get a fuller understanding of any differences in how women and men use transportation. I assisted the team in analyzing the qualitative data and drafting the final report.

I also guided the transport team in conducting a rapid assessment of the Women-Led Routine Road Maintenance pilot. I drafted focus group and interview questions for different categories of stakeholders and accompanied the team as they conducted interviews and focus group discussions with project participants at the commune level to gain more fine-tuned information on the social and economic outcomes in all three provinces. I encouraged evaluators to interview women and men in separate groups to ensure that women had an opportunity to express their views. We spent the most time in Lao Cai Province because the program had been implemented there the longest. I drafted the final report of the assessment, which was translated and sent to the MOT.

One major challenge, by no means unique to Vietnam, was the reluctance of Ministry of Transport officials to consider "soft" investments, such as gender and other social research and social impact evaluations, as opposed to "hard" investments in roads and bridges. Fortunately, some of the bilateral donors, such as the United Kingdom's Department for International Development (DFID; now known as the Foreign, Commonwealth & Development Office) and Australian Aid, offered trust funds for "soft" gender-focused research and evaluations, and so I drafted proposals to access these funds to supplement the work subsidized through the MOT loan. In the longer term, it will be important to convince the ministry of the value of empirical social research and evaluation data to assess and inform their programs.

On another level, language was a great challenge, as I did not speak Vietnamese—a rather complex tonal language in which a compliment can turn into an insult with the wrong inflection. I relied on my English-speaking World Bank colleagues to translate for me in meetings with Ministry of Transport and Women's Union officials as well as with community members. I took detailed notes on their translations and asked follow-up questions for clarification. I also relied heavily on observations, particularly in the communities. Workshops were conducted in both English and Vietnamese, with simultaneous translation so expatriate World Bank officials could participate. Most documents from the Ministry of Transport were available only in Vietnamese. When I could get an electronic version of a document, I was able to get an amazingly reasonable English translation from Google Translate.

Another challenge was working remotely most of the time. I traveled to Vietnam once or twice a year for supervisory field trips and workshops, as did most Washington-based World Bank staff. I was still able to provide a great deal of input by attending videoconference meetings, communicating via email, reviewing and drafting reports, developing evaluation designs and questions, etc. Maintaining ongoing communication and providing useful inputs in a timely manner was essential. Given the thirteen-hour time difference, I sometimes found myself on Vietnam time, working very late and sleeping quite late. When there was a tight deadline, it was possible to work double days, operating on both Washington and Vietnam work hours.

A more specific challenge came in addressing the recommendations from a sustainability review of the Third Rural Transport Project prepared for the UK's DFID by a consultant who focused narrowly on cost-effectiveness and individual road workers without taking into account the sociocultural context. I suggested including questions about those recommendations in interviews with local leaders, women's union leaders, and people's committee leaders during the qualitative assessment of the program. Their answers confirmed that the sustainability reviewer's preconceptions about the efficacy of involving women in routine road maintenance by establishing microenterprises rather than working with existing organizations, along with generalizations based on limited data, and the failure to recognize the importance of the sociocultural context, led to a misinterpretation of the Women's Union program and roles and an underestimation of the importance of the awareness-raising campaign.

Collecting this feedback from those involved in the project was very important to ensure that the follow-on project would be guided by findings and recommendations that reflected the views of the project participants, would take into account the sociocultural context, and would build on the positive outcomes of the Women-Led Routine Road Maintenance pilot.

Outcomes

The women-led pilots contributed to improved road access, which increased access to markets, healthcare, and education. It also increased community cooperation, improved women's status and voice in household and community decision-making, and created a "culture" of community road stewardship.

The pilot project contributed to improved road access through routine road maintenance. Women-led groups in three provinces maintained 3,191 kilometers (1,628 kilometers of commune roads; 1,131 kilometers of intervillage roads; 390 kilometers of roads to fields). A total of 83,545 persons participated in routine road maintenance in the three provinces, 82 percent of whom were women. Sixty percent of participants were poor, and 63 percent belonged to ethnic minorities.

At the local level, women and men viewed well-maintained commune and intercommune roads as means to facilitate easier access to healthcare, particularly when urgent care was needed, and cleaner, safer means for children to travel to school, particularly during the rainy season.

Local citizens as well as officials and Women's Union branches at all levels realized that the economic gain from maintaining the road to ensure road access was much more significant than the money earned doing road maintenance. While the income earned in road maintenance was valuable for the poor, especially ethnic minorities, the economic gains from having a well-maintained road were much greater. These gains included increased opportunities for the development of small businesses, greater access to markets and market information leading to expanded crop production, and increased income. At the same time, travel time, accidents, and costs for fuel, maintenance, farm inputs, and consumer goods decreased.

Working together in groups on routine road maintenance also improved communication, cooperation, and social cohesion between husbands and wives and among neighbors. As one participant explained, "We enjoy the program and feel more cheerful because it is collectively done by more women. . . . It is interesting to get together and talk about agricultural production, prices, how to make use of products, how to care for children and elders. We are becoming closer to each other." Women and men shared information about many topics, ranging from crop prices, pig raising, and fertilizer suppliers to avoiding a drunk husband and raising children. One participant noted that, in the past, "men rarely worked together with women. Now they can work together, and they can talk together very openly."

Women's leadership roles in the management of routine maintenance enhanced their status and self-esteem. Husbands were more respectful and willing to help with childcare and housework. Women also began to offer their opinions in community meetings for the first time. The leader of a provincial Women's Union said that women-managed projects provided "opportunities for women to act as pioneers in the protection of rural roads, environment, and other movements." A commune vice chair observed that "these [routine road maintenance] activities have been very positive in the way they have improved the status of women. Before, women were second class, doing housework only. Now they participate in public and community activities." A senior Ministry of Transport expert noted that, in her view, "the Third Rural Transport project is the only [Vietnam transport] project that treated women as actors, not just as recipients."

The provincial Women's Union's awareness-raising campaign reached 765,000 persons and engaged 83,545 community members in basic road maintenance, fostering a "culture" of road maintenance at the local and provincial levels. The sense of ownership of and responsibility for the protection of local roads, fostered by the awareness-raising campaign, resulted in behavior changes that decreased damage to roads. Those who participated in the awareness-raising and road maintenance activities convinced others to stop damaging roads. Local residents also became more willing to donate land for village roads. In Lao Cai Province, where the women-led road maintenance was first introduced, the positive outcomes of the Women's Union pilot convinced the provincial people's committee to allocate funds for routine road maintenance by the Women's Union and other local groups and contractors.

Presentations to the MOT about the positive outcomes of the Women-Led Routine Road Maintenance pilot at national roundtables and workshops on the successful outcomes of the Women-Led Routine Road Maintenance program encouraged greater MOT investment in local road maintenance and further scale-up of the women-led maintenance model. A roundtable for MOT staff explored the women-led maintenance model as a key component of a potential road map for sustainable rural road maintenance. The vice minister of transport noted that the rural transport support provided by the World Bank and DFID has "changed the landscape of the countryside, contributed to poverty reduction, and provided the impetus for a national rural development program." Noting that insufficient funding and lack of awareness by leaders and residents had resulted in road degradation, he suggested that "the women-managed model of Lao Cai, if properly implemented and rolled out in other provinces, would raise awareness and engagement in maintenance of local roads and thus support government policy on sustainable transport at all levels."

The Third Rural Transport project wrap-up workshop reported on the outcomes of the Women-Led Routine Road Maintenance program, broader gender and transport issues, and suggestions for increasing attention to gender in MOT programs. These discussions increased high-level attention to addressing road maintenance mechanisms below the provincial level as well as the need for institutional changes, the value of fostering a "culture" of local stewardship of commune roads, and more extensive replication of the women-led road maintenance model.

The positive outcomes of the Women-Led Routine Road Maintenance pilot also provided the institutional impetus for the Ministry of Transport to integrate gender into transport planning. MOT attention to increasing employment and leadership opportunities and benefits for women staff has been impressive. However, the MOT had not, by the end of my involvement, addressed the integration of gender equality in transport sector policy, program design (for services and infrastructure), budgeting, or monitoring and evaluation, except where required by donors. The different travel patterns, needs, and constraints of women and men users of rural and urban transport were not being routinely assessed or addressed in project planning. Also, monitoring socioeconomic impacts on beneficiaries of transport projects was not sex-disaggregated. Gender equality training reportedly targeted management-level staff but not transport-implementation staff. Recognizing the need for institutional strengthening on gender, the deputy minister of transport indicated in a meeting with World Bank staff that he had increased the resources for transport staff to work on gender equality issues. He noted that the MOT planned to distribute documents for mainstreaming gender issues into projects. Given the time necessary to change attitudes, behavior, and policies, these were very significant outcomes.

A senior transport reviewer of the final assessment of the Women-Led Routine Road Maintenance pilots noted that "this work is really groundbreaking and puts Vietnam in a small group of countries that I know of where there has been such impact from the empowerment of women in road works and road maintenance." He strongly encouraged the transport team to incorporate the positive lessons learned in the Third Rural Transport project into the follow-on project. DFID's Project Completion Review of the Third Rural Transport project rated the Women-Led Routine Road Maintenance component as "substantially exceeding expectation," which is their highest rating.

Finally, the Vietnam Women-Led Routine Road Maintenance pilot was nominated as a best practice by the World Bank Social Development Network and Operations Policy Country Service's Results Unit, naming it an exemplary project that made a real impact on transport in developing countries and that is innovative, sustainable, and representative of good practices in the field. The women-led pilot also received a Second Prize for Innovation from the International Finance Corporation, and the International Road Federation gave an honorable mention in the 2012 Innovation Award Competition for Transport in Developing Countries.

The Anthropological Difference

Overall, the holistic analytical framework used to look at the interaction of people, sociocultural contexts, organizational cultures, knowledge, and the physical environment, combined with ethnographic methods in monitoring and evaluation, was essential to understanding the dynamics of the various participating organizations and ethnic groups. The holistic framework also helped to better document the broader impacts of the Women's Union program in a way that could influence Ministry of Transport decision-makers. Rather than an economist's narrow focus on individuals earning income for road work performed, the analytical framework employed through the anthropological lens was one involving interactions of people, sociocultural contexts, organizational cultures, knowledge, and the physical environment.

Anthropological concepts and methods contributed significantly to strengthening coordination between various stakeholders in the project and in raising awareness and routine road maintenance skill training appropriate for the ethnic minority women and men. The design of the monitoring and evaluation effort helped to guide the program scale-up and to inform the wider scale-up in the future. It provided the framework for analysis of the development of the "culture" of rural road maintenance and stewardship from the "bottom up" (commune level) and from the "top down" (Ministry of Transport).

An anthropological lens made it clear that the longer-term results went beyond ensuring that women as well as men were actively engaged in the project and benefited from it. The long-term goal was leveraging the project outcomes to facilitate culture change. At the grassroots level, the aim was to facilitate change in community perceptions of women's roles and status. At the national level, the goal was to influence the Ministry of Transport's organizational culture to recognize the importance of addressing gender gaps and to incorporate gender analysis monitoring and evaluation into the way that it does business. Anthropological research also informs the recognition that such culture change is a complex and often very slow process, particularly when many levels of bureaucracy and multiple ethnic groups are involved.

Epilogue

Since this project, I have continued to work with the World Bank Vietnam transport team; I helped draft the project appraisal document for the follow-on Local Asset Management Project and joined the task team. The follow-on included rolling out the Women-Led Routine Maintenance model further, incorporating other social organizations (Farmer's Union, Youth Union, Veteran's Union), and refining the routine maintenance training materials.

I helped the transport team successfully apply for trust funds for an impact assessment of the Third Rural Transport Project and participated in the evaluation design and review of the qualitative data analysis. I also assisted the team in securing trust funds to conduct a gender-inclusive pilot of performance-based contracting for local road maintenance. I coauthored a technical note on the implications of those pilot results. I also drafted a paper on gender and transport for a National Assembly forum on revisions of the road traffic laws. Gender was a topic among the expert reports that the organizers requested from the World Bank. I also drafted a note on gender and transport in Vietnam, which was incorporated in a multidonor Country Gender Equality Profile for Vietnam and incorporated gender into a note on performance-based contracting for road maintenance. I continue to forge ahead toward facilitating culture change in and through transport.

Mari Clarke, World Bank senior gender consultant, has provided technical support to rural transport projects in Vietnam since 2010. She also advised the World Bank Water Practice, and she has supported Cooperation on International Waters in Africa (CIWA) on mainstreaming gender, the Papua New Guinea (PNG) National Electricity Rollout Plan (NEROP), and the PNG Road Maintenance and Rehabilitation Project II. Earlier, she helped design a web-based knowledge base on gender and transport; developed tools for gender and transport, water, and information, communications, and technology (ICT); and led portfolio reviews on gender and infrastructure. She also helped design and guide studies of gender, poverty, and the environment in Africa and gender and climate change in Bangladesh. Previously, she consulted for the Asian Development Bank, USAID, Catholic Relief Services, and other NGOs. She holds a PhD (1988) in economic anthropology from the University of North Carolina at Chapel Hill; an MEd in instructional design, UNC, Chapel Hill; an MA in economic anthropology from the University of Pennsylvania; and a BA in anthropology from Michigan State University.

References

Asian Development Bank. 2015. "Paving the Road to Better Income Options: Case Study on Promoting Women's Livelihood and Employment Opportunities in Vietnam."

Clarke, M. H. 2009. "Thematic Note on Rural Roads." In *Gender and Agriculture Sourcebook*, 372–82. Washington, DC: World Bank, Food and Agriculture Organization, and International Fund for Agricultural Development.

———. 2010. *Making Transport Work for Women and Men: Tools for Task Teams*. Washington, DC: World Bank Social Development.

———. 2013. "International Development." In *A Handbook of Practicing Anthropology*, edited by Riall Nolan, 222–36. Chichester: Wiley-Blackwell. https://doi.org/10.1002/9781118486597.ch20

———. 2020. "Transport and Change through an Anthropological Lens." *Business Anthropology* (30 November). https://doi.org/10.22439/jba.v9i2.6122.

Dalakoglou, D., and P. Harvey. 2012. "Roads and Anthropology: Ethnographic Reflections on Space, Time, and (Im)Mobility." *Mobilities* 7(4): 459–65.

Harvey, P., and H. Knox. 2016. *Roads: An Anthropology of Infrastructure and Expertise*. Ithaca, NY: Cornell University Press. https://doi.org/10.7591/9780801456466.

Lewis, D. 2005. "Anthropology and Development: The Uneasy Relationship." In *A Handbook of Economic Anthropology*, edited by James G. Carrier, 472–86. Cheltenham: Edward Elgar. http://eprints.lse.ac.uk/253/.

Mannava, A., and E. Perova. 2019. *Who Benefits from Roads and Why? Mixed Methods Analysis of the Gender Disaggregated Impact of a Rural Roads Project in Vietnam*. Washington, DC: World Bank East Asia and Pacific Gender Innovation Lab. https://doi.org/10.1596/1813–9450–9216.

Tran, P. T. M. 2011. *Pathways to Development: Empowering Local Women to Build a More Equitable Future in Vietnam; International Finance Corporation Smart Lessons, October 2011*. Washington, DC: International Finance Corporation, World Bank Group.

World Bank. 2006. *Project Appraisal Document for a Third Rural Transport Project, Vietnam*. Washington, DC: World Bank, Transport Sector Unit, East Asia and Pacific Region.

———. 2014. *Empowering Women to Build a More Equitable Future in Vietnam: Assessment of the Provincial Women's Union Woman-Managed Routine Rural Road Maintenance Program*. Washington, DC: World Bank, Transport Sector, East Asia and Pacific Region.

PART II

~:~

Communities and
the Environment

CHAPTER 4

~:~

Co-management of Natural Resources in Puerto Rico

Applied Anthropology, Public Access,
and Environmental Public Policy

FEDERICO CINTRÓN-MOSCOSO

Project Background

Connecting the public with natural resource management is critical in promoting pro-environmental values and practices, such as those related to environmental justice, nature stewardship, and ecological and socioeconomic
sustainability. The US Forest Service, part of the US Department of Agriculture, acknowledged in a 2010 blog posting that it is critical to proactively engage
diverse views, cultures, and sources of knowledge in resource management, and
that local, national, and long-term needs should be considered to reinforce the
linkages between people and the environment.

In 2012, the Forest Service approved a new planning rule that stressed the
need to actively engage the public in the process of revising and developing
forest plans. Prior to this, the Forest Service noted that the rules were obsolete,
complex, costly, lengthy, and cumbersome. The new rule presented an added
emphasis on climate resilience, social and economic sustainability, and collaborative planning—especially the engagement of youth and minorities—and
made clear the agency's desire to rebuild trust among the public by encouraging
feedback and to support more inclusive and transparent processes.

When the new planning rule was adopted in 2012, eight out of 150 Park
Service "units" selected to first implement the regulation. For these "early
adopters," it was a rare and exciting opportunity to influence planning at the
national level. Each forest plan is revised at least every fifteen years to accom-

modate new scientific knowledge and any changes in ecological, social, and economic conditions within and around the forest. The new regulation mandated that the revision should last approximately three years.

The selection of El Yunque National Forest in Puerto Rico as one of the eight units should not have been a surprise, given the forest's ecological, administrative, and cultural significance. El Yunque has six discrete ecosystems, some of which are endemic, that provide habitats for a great diversity of species, including 150 ferns, 79 orchids, 107 birds, 19 reptiles, 16 mammals, 15 amphibians, 7 freshwater fish, 10 crustaceans, and 225 native trees—greater than that found in all other national forests combined. Administratively, El Yunque is the only tropical forest in the Forest Service system, is located on an island, and is a member of the UNESCO Biosphere Reserve network. Additionally, El Yunque is in a Spanish-speaking territory.

It should also be noted that El Yunque is an important cultural landmark for Puerto Ricans. The park's current name was devised in an effort to connect the park with local lore. Historic research suggests that "El Yunque" comes from a corrupted derivation of a Taino word, *Yuké*, in reference to the white clouds covering its peaks. It is also the name of one of the highest peaks in the forest. According to the archaeological record, Indigenous practices within the forest seem to have been numerous, covering multiple aspects of Taino economic, cultural, religious, and political life. The Forest Service has officially identified at least 140 historic sites and 10 Indigenous sites within forest boundaries, and it is commonly known that many more prehistoric sites are scattered throughout.

Although the policy changes were welcomed by most stakeholders, the historical, political, economic, and cultural context of Puerto Rico, a colonial territory of the United States since 1898, still presented a barrier to incorporating the public into federal planning.

It was therefore unsurprising that the colonial experiences of historically top-down decision-making and public mistrust in federal administrators had become intertwined with other issues specific to the management plan revision. These included limited knowledge about local residents' uses of the forest, lack of interest from some public sectors—e.g., municipal administrators, religious communities, professional associations—forest administrators' preconceptions about the public's capacity to participate, and a shared conception of the forest as an isolated space divorced from outside dynamics, values, and meanings (see Soto et al. 2017; Maldonado, Valdez-Pizzini, and Latoni 1999). In addition, the Forest Service had in prior years fostered scientifically based arguments that were prioritized over other needs—economic development, tourism, cultural practices, co-management—during the planning process.

Project Description

To address the planning and management issues noted above, the administrators of El Yunque entered into an agreement with an environmental nongovernmental organization, Centro Para la Conservación del Paisaje (CCP), to design, coordinate, and evaluate a process of public participation to be incorporated into the otherwise traditional approach of technical forest planning. I led the CCP effort with the assistance of an interdisciplinary team that included another anthropologist, an environmental sociologist, a forester, and nine college students who participated in different project stages. The CCP also hired communication specialists to develop educational and promotional materials for outreach and dissemination of information throughout the project.

Our initial, informal interviews and meetings with staff, as well as archival analysis, demonstrated that indeed the public was not typically consulted on decisions about how to manage El Yunque. For the most part, Forest Service technicians in Puerto Rico and their supervisors in the Atlanta regional office had designed plans based on US national agendas in internal agency discussions. The previous management strategies and visions resulted in conservationist approaches toward the resource, prompting a more contemplative and restrictive use of the forest and limiting public access and the possibility of other management philosophies and practices.

These and other historic, cultural, and economic factors confirmed that the project would have challenges. While the forest receives an estimated 1.2 million annual visitors, spending approximately US$3 million in related recreational activities, more than 40 percent of area families still live under the poverty line. The sentiment of abandonment and discouragement is quite entrenched among the population surrounding the forest reserve, making some persons furious with the Forest Service and others very suspicious of the collaboration process. We constantly heard expressions such as "The forest belongs to the federales, as does the responsibility to take care and maintain it," and "I don't go there. I am not interested [in El Yunque] because it is for tourists." Metaphorically, many residents live with their backs toward the reserve, which is significant, given the importance of El Yunque to Puerto Rican identity.

The forest's contentious history frames the scope of the public participation project and commands a deeper understanding of the social, cultural, economic, and historical context surrounding the reserve. For instance, we had to tackle local residents' feelings of abandonment and mistrust of government agencies at the municipal, state, and federal levels, especially those in gateway communities who often complain about not receiving any social or economic benefits from tourism activities. Most of the money generated by these activities is spent outside the local area; this is a significant fact, considering that the eight municipalities adjacent to the reserve are among the poorest in the entire archipelago of Puerto Rico.

In addressing the planning and management of El Yunque, we tried to target the specific challenges of incorporating public participation into public policy implementation and developing a collaborative model for planning and managing natural resources in a colonial context. For the latter in particular, policy needs to be translated both linguistically and culturally, as feelings of mistrust and resentment mediate the relationship between locals and administrators. A participatory approach for the forest's management had never been tried before.

Once we understood the complexities of the project setting, we were able to focus on developing a strategy that included five major areas of work:

1) A public discussion campaign that brought the planning process to communities and stakeholders outside of the forest. This campaign included scientific fora, environmental events, and meetings with Forest Service employees, community members, government agencies, municipal planners, protected natural areas managers, and other special groups.

2) A Consultation Committee for Public Participation formed by representatives of various sectors—community organizations, small business owners, environmentalists, and academics. Initially, the group came together to provide guidance and recommendations on how to get more residents involved in the project and to make sure that our engagement strategies, materials, and messages were culturally relevant and inclusive. However, the group evolved, promoting sustainable development efforts, building alliances and networks with other groups and individuals, and elaborating their own vision for collaborative governance in the region.

3) Scientific collaboration with the interdisciplinary team, the Forest Service technicians responsible for the analysis and writeup of the new plan. Our team formed part of this group and collaborated in areas such as cultural resources, environmental education, and forestry, and more generally in conceptual discussions. We also established a peer network of scientists and technical experts outside the Forest Service that could provide additional information on the forest or add different perspectives on relevant issues.

4) Media campaign and environmental education. The media campaign was designed primarily for outreach to inform the public about the revision process and disseminate information concerning the new plan. We created a dedicated Facebook page, and we utilized El Yunque and CCP websites as well as local radio shows and newspapers. Given the limited amount of information that existed in Puerto Rican schools about the forest, we designed a workshop for teachers and environmental educa-

tors. We also connected the revision process to various youth initiatives in the area, including CCP's own Community Environmental Leadership Project and the University of Puerto Rico's Extension Services 4-H Clubs.

5) Rapid Ethnographic Assessment (REA) and Environmental Literacy Survey. We conducted two supplementary research actions to learn more about local visitors and youth. The rapid assessment looked at visitors' perceptions about the forest and the planning process, while the survey established an environmental literacy baseline for middle-school children in the region.

Five general objectives guided these initiatives: (1) to establish a better plan by integrating the public's knowledge, values, and perspectives about the forest, and to develop and strengthen a network of agencies, organizations, and individuals committed to conservation, sustainable development, and co-management; (2) to increase access to the revision process for interested and potentially affected parties; (3) to create open and safe spaces that promote problem solving, creative solutions, and constructive dialogue and deliberation regarding all aspects of the revision process; (4) to gather information on forest visitors and surrounding communities through social science research; and (5) to promote a two-way learning process, in which administrators learn new skills and approaches on how to incorporate the public into management thinking and practices, while local residents increase their knowledge about forest planning and management.

Concordantly, several anthropological principles and methodologies were instrumental to the project: (1) the interconnection of human and environmental interactions and the analytical relevance of social and ecological systems, which could help explain the current conditions of the forest, people's discourses about and behaviors in the environment, and conflicting visions for the future of the forest; (2) a holistic perspective that recognized the complexity of social, cultural, historical, and economic elements, as well as the multiple perspectives of diverse audiences; (3) an ethnographic approach that explored and highlighted local points of view and experiences and contrasted them with official discourses and regulations; (4) utilization of participatory, iterative methodologies to facilitate participation and increase engagement among both Forest Service employees and stakeholders; (5) triangulation of qualitative and quantitative data for decision-making analysis and recommendations; and (6) effective communication and ethical responsibility in managing multiple roles and settings as well as in translating information both linguistically and culturally among clients, stakeholders, the project team, the scientific community, and the media.

Implementation and Anthropologist's Role

Our first major step was to get to know El Yunque's visitors and gain our client's trust. Although this was a major project for the Forest Service, locally and nationally, the public was not aware of it. Additionally, there were many misconceptions about the public circulating among local staff (e.g., that the public did not have an interest in participating or the capacity to do so) that needed to be investigated before moving forward. Our rapid ethnographic assessment helped to gather information on local visitors that we could use to operationalize future activities.

For instance, it was not clear how much knowledge the public had regarding local ecological systems and planning, which are deemed critical to responsibly engage in conceptualizing and writing the new plan. Similarly, little was known about the local public's capacity and disposition to fully participate in the collaboration process or if they preferred to be reached by phone or email. Obviously, the more we can learn about the public, the better the strategies we can design and implement. A semistructured survey, accompanied by field observations, was used as the main instrument of data collection. We interviewed 169 individuals during weekends through July and August (2013), since these are known high-traffic months for locals visiting the park.

The rapid ethnographic assessment provided us with rich information on local visitors. For instance, the majority of respondents had not heard about the project or the existence of a forest plan. Yet, the majority was interested in getting involved, although they did not know how they could do so. Moreover, most interviewees stated that the federal government was the sole entity responsible for managing the forest; only a few mentioned that it was the responsibility of both the government and the people. We were able to confirm how close the individuals felt to El Yunque, and also the mistrust that many harbored toward the agency.

We also learned that, to increase participation, dissemination of information needed to be in Spanish and to incorporate a variety of outlets, including traditional postal mail, regional and national news outlets, and public fora and events; there was no centralized source of information for these types of projects. Above all, utilizing research to learn about local visitors allowed us to speak to our clients in a language they understood and to gather valuable research data.

The second step was building structured opportunities for dialogue and planning. As we designed and conducted the REA, the team recruited a group of twenty-five stakeholders to form a Consultation Committee for Public Participation (CCPP), discussed briefly above. This group represented community leaders, environmental educators, planners, ecotourism providers, academics, and members of environmental organizations and government agencies. Initially, the group came together to help us achieve the goals described above, providing guidance and recommendations on how to get more persons involved and making sure that our engagement strategies, materials, and messages were culturally relevant and inclusive.

After little more than two years of monthly meetings though, the group evolved into a stronger entity. They became an intricate part of the project and the new plan by promoting sustainable development efforts, building alliances and networks with other groups and individuals, and assisting our team and El Yunque staff in elaborating a vision and an agenda for establishing new pathways toward collaborative governance in the region. For instance, the new plan's vision statement resulted from language negotiated between the committee and our interdisciplinary team.

The committee worked on a memorandum of understanding with the El Yunque Forest Service staff to allow them to partake in identifying and selecting the forest's management priorities for the coming years, participate more closely in the implementation and monitoring of the new plan, and serve as liaisons to groups in developing collaborative projects in and around the reserve. All of these efforts, which were new to the agency, reflected a change in policy implementation and management, and they represent one of the most important achievements of the project. The integration of a stakeholders committee facilitated the attainment of co-management and community participation. I believe the CCPP has the potential to become a leading environmental and economic development organization in the eastern region of Puerto Rico.

Throughout the process, and in collaboration with the CCPP, our team organized various cycles of community meetings in the municipalities around the forest with the purpose of addressing knowledge gaps, reestablishing relationships between the agency and the people, collecting public input on plan components, and validating the entire process. These meetings were conceived as a space for planners to present to and work with the public on different aspects of the analysis and development of the new plan. Contrary to historical processes, we wanted planners to leave their offices in the forest and meet with the individuals in their communities. We also wanted them to go through the process of explaining their vision for the future of the forest and listening to what people thought of those visions. Each meeting cycle was different depending on the topics discussed and the specific audience.

Finally, the third step was developing baseline information for monitoring and for environmental literacy. The process identified two potential areas for development that had been deprioritized by the administration because of a funding shortage: better communication with the public and environmental education. We designed a media campaign that produced materials adapted for various audiences, from youth to community residents to technical experts. These materials also translated technical and scientific language in English into lay terms in Spanish. Similar to the public discussion campaign, we prioritized regional media outlets closer to where the community meetings took place. Four radio stations and three newspapers in the region covered the process repeatedly, collaborating with us in disseminating information and reaching out to the public. Other electronic outlets dedicated to environmental and social justice issues as well as national media also reported on the project to a broader audience.

For environmental education, we understood the importance of increasing environmental literacy as a way of enabling the public to better engage in environmental planning and resource management. These are topics that most visitors did not know about, and we believe this lack of knowledge hindered their ability to actively participate. Schultz and Ludholm (2013) have found that by combining environmental education and adaptive co-management, administrators are able to foster mutual and collective learning, develop and renew knowledge (both scientific and experiential) through research and monitoring, produce information and educational initiatives for a variety of audiences, and most importantly, connect stakeholders to policymakers, natural resource managers, and other interested parties.

Although it was unrealistic to make such a significant transformation within the project timeframe, we thought we could focus on laying the groundwork for the agency to continue with this effort. It is important to understand that El Yunque used to have a very active education and interpretation program, which was dismantled around the turn of the millennium. The program included a guidebook with materials for public school teachers, and rangers trained to receive and guide groups into the forest. With past funding cuts, the program had been almost entirely eliminated. Interpretation and education staff were assigned to other tasks, and the strong relationships with the surrounding schools were lost. During the project, we had a chance to interview the person who led those efforts and meet with teachers who nostalgically remembered participating in the program.

Bringing back the program would have been impossible and out of the scope of the new plan and revisions; however, we thought we could collect information, while supporting minimal efforts in the meantime, that would help the agency in reestablishing the program whenever funding allowed. Through the rapid ethnographic assessment discussed above, we gathered information on topics related to planning and management and got a sense of how much people knew about the forest. We also organized, with the assistance of the island's Department of Natural and Environmental Resources and the Department of Education, the first Project Learning Tree workshop taught in Puerto Rico for teachers and environmental educators in the region. Project Learning Tree is an activity guidebook specializing in the study of forests and was indeed the model utilized years ago to develop El Yunque's own guidebook. We provided both guidebooks to participants and a certificate of "contact hours" toward the educators' professional development.

Additionally, we conducted an environmental literacy survey in the region's middle schools to establish baseline information of students' environmental knowledge, attitudes, and pro-environmental behavior and decision-making. We used the Middle School Environmental Literacy Survey, created by the Center for Instruction, Staff Development, and Evaluation, which has been administered nationally in the United States. This instrument had been adapted and validated for use in Puerto Rico, but before this project it had never been widely implemented. The study surveyed close to five hundred middle school students in the eight municipalities around the forest. The results show that students in the region tended to outscore US sixth-grade and eighth-grade students on verbal commitment, environmental sensitivity, general environmental feelings, action planning, and actual commitment toward the environment. These findings could be used in future studies to compare environmental literacy levels and determine if there has been progress, taking into consideration the environmental issues, controversies, and circumstances of the region and the educational activities that El Yunque might provide.

Outcomes

A major benefit was achieved by conducting community meetings, which allowed us to meet with persons from all walks of life and age groups. We estimated that more than eight hundred people were directly affected through the community meetings, scientific fora, environmental festivals and events, and meetings with Forest Service employees and special groups.

Through the other initiatives, such as the two research projects and media coverage, the team has reached thousands of citizens, which significantly contrasts with previous efforts that only included three or four public notices in the newspaper.

After analyzing the information gathered in the meetings, the team discovered that the most recurrent issue had to do with access to the forest. Access was defined broadly and had many nuances, such as physical access to recreational areas, access to information about and interpretation of the forest, access to forest products and cultural resources, access to decision-making and planning, and access to the economic benefits resulting from tourism activities related to the forest. In other words, stakeholders wanted to know how the new forest plan would create a more accessible forest for all and what conditions would be needed to provide such access while conserving and protecting the resource. This vision of the forest differed significantly from those articulated in previous plans, in which the forest had been managed in isolation from surrounding communities and with restricted opportunities for visitors, especially locals.

The most relevant and noteworthy achievement of the community meetings and the interdisciplinary team analysis was the creation of a new management area for the forest that could address the public's concern about access and opportunity. The new management area, tentatively named the Community Interface Resource Management Area, would serve as a designated space around the lower elevations of the forest, in which individuals, groups, and agencies could develop a multiplicity of collaborative and sustainable projects, including agroforestry demonstrations, environmental education, ecotourism, and the production of forest products for local economic development. The management area would not only help to better connect the forest with the community by providing greater access to it, it would also improve the conservation of the forest by spreading out activities and lessening the highly concentrated human impact in the current area; existing recreational areas overlap with recently discovered ecosystems that are endemic to this forest.

Complementary materials produced for the project included dedicated sections on the El Yunque and CCP websites with links to documents and a comments section, as well as a dedicated Facebook page with more than fifteen hundred members. A short, ethnographic video introduced viewers to the planning process and presented the vision of co-management through the voices of both the agency and community members.[1]

As the project advanced, many other collaborators, including those from local universities, the community, environmental and educational organizations, businesses, state agencies, and tourism providers, as well as interested individuals, became involved, all of whom were committed to the principles of nature conservation, co-management, and regional development. The project moved from being a static endeavor in satisfying yet another policy requirement to a dynamic effort of participatory planning. After more than two years of extensive praxis, this project represented a historic collaborative effort in resource management in Puerto Rico between multiple stakeholders from the public, private, and NGO sectors.

This project had numerous successful efforts through the years, but the most significant are summarized as:

1) The development and implementation of a new model of participatory management for the Forest Service that included: (1) a stakeholders' planning committee; (2) a public discussion campaign; (3) an environmental literacy campaign; (4) anthropological research; and (5) technical assistance to Forest Service personnel.
2) The formation and facilitation of a stakeholders committee, which aided in the attainment of co-management practices and community participation.

3) The introduction and support of alternative theoretical and methodological approaches that impacted the way Forest Service conducts business internally and with stakeholders.

4) Participatory policy development—this included the coproduction of the new plan's vision and content, which reflects a shared understanding between the agency, the consultants, and stakeholders—especially in the areas of environmental education, cultural resource management, forest products, and recreation.

5) The gathering of baseline data for long-term monitoring of environmental literacy among middle school students in the region, which was also valuable for sustainability.

6) The conception and development of a new management area for the forest, which was a result of the project.

The Anthropological Difference

When talking about plan development, participants on both sides—the forest administrators and the public—tended to take each other's underlying visions and expectations about the forest for granted, keeping them unshared, unexplored, and unchallenged. A major part of the project required us to look for understanding among discourses and practices that seemed in disarray on the surface. We spent a significant amount of effort and time trying to identify hidden expectations and making them explicit to all. In that way, staff and stakeholders could meaningfully construct a more complementary vision together.

Along with these insights, anthropologists bring analytical and methodological tools for the integration of human values, behaviors, and organizations, as well as other social considerations and meanings. Analytical tools provide administrators with useful criteria for making more relevant and socially acceptable decisions. This means being able to provide policy recommendations as needs arise and to develop precise and focused instruments and methods that can produce timely, relevant, and useful information. This is all part of our praxis. Analytical tools are valuable as well when building consensus and helping translate information among groups and settings. Methodological tools include group facilitation skills, teamwork, qualitative and quantitative data analysis, social network analysis, facilitation of interdisciplinary dialogues, budget analysis, and communication and organizational skills. For the first time in the revision of the forest plan, we conducted interviews with visitors and observations to understand people's behaviors and understanding of the forest. We also conducted community meetings in the eight municipalities surrounding the forest and held separate meetings with tourist providers, environmentalist groups, business owners, and other professionals whose jobs in different ways would be affected by the planning process.

Finally, as applied anthropologists, we have the knowledge and experience to develop meaningful structural opportunities for public participation, reflection, and planning. The public's lack of access to decision-making and planning constitutes a major barrier toward involvement and policy implementation. In this project, developing multiple sites and opportunities for residents to learn about, comment on, and actively engage in the process certainly provided for a broader participatory planning approach while continuing to repair the historically contentious relationship between the federal agency and the local population.

Federico Cintrón-Moscoso is a Puerto Rican anthropologist, educator, and climate justice activist. He holds a PhD in applied anthropology from the University of South Florida and an MA in archaeology from the University of Southampton (UK). He is currently the program director at El Puente— Latino Action Climate Network, a program that brings together environmental justice and community leaders to mobilize and educate around issues of climate change mitigation, adaptation, and resiliency. For the past eighteen years he has been involved in youth development and applied research projects that combine arts, science, and culture in the United States, Latin America, and the Caribbean. He teaches graduate and undergraduate courses at the University of Puerto Rico in the School of Education and the School of Social Work, as well as in the Women and Gender Studies Program. He also serves as an independent consultant on various topics such as climate education and participatory resource management.

Notes

The author would like to acknowledge the work of all CCP team members and their contributions to the success of the project: Alejandro Torres-Abréu, sociologist; Edgardo González, forester; Vivianna de Jesús, anthropologist; Marysol Molina, research assistant; Angélica Reyes, research assistant; María Serrano-Abréu, educator; Natalia Olivero-Huffman, communication specialist; and Mayda Grano de Oro, graphic designer.

1. This was a tremendous voluntarily effort, and we are incredibly thankful to our collaborators for their time and support.

References

Center for Landscape Conservation. 2014. *Final Report: Rapid Ethnographic Assessment at El Yunque National Forest; Assessing Visitors' Capacity and Disposition Toward Participatory Planning.* Submitted to the US Forest Service, 28 March 2014.

Cintrón-Moscoso, F. 2015 *Final Report: Public Participation in the Revision of El Yunque National Forest Management Plan.* Submitted to the US Forest Service, 30 July 2015.

Maldonado, M. M., M. Valdez-Pizzini, and A. R. Latoni. 1999. "Owning and Contesting El Yunque: Forest Resources, Politics, and Culture in Puerto Rico." *Berkeley Journal of Sociology* 44: 82–100.

Schultz, L., and C. Ludholm. 2013. "Learning for Resilience? Exploring Learning Opportunities in Biosphere Reserves." *Environmental Education Research* 16(5–6): 645–63.

Soto, S., S. Munguia, N. Y. B. Britwum, L. Gonzalez, C. Gray, B. Moakley, and C. Pedrozo. 2017. "Ecology, Policy, and Puerto Rico: El Yunque National Forest." *Bulletin of the Ecological Society of America* 98(4): 341–44.

US Forest Service. 2014. "Forest Plan Assessment: El Yunque National Forest." US Department of Agriculture, http://www.fs.usda.gov/detail/elyunque/landmanagement/planning/?cid=stelprdb5411336.

CHAPTER 5

~:~

Deal Island Peninsula Partnership

Applying Environmental Anthropology, Ethnography, and Collaborative Learning

MICHAEL PAOLISSO, ELIZABETH VAN DOLAH,
KATHERINE J. JOHNSON, AND
CHRISTINE D. MILLER HESED

Project Background

Climate change affects coastal communities through sea level rise, flooding, erosion, intensifying storms, and changes in marine and estuarine dynamics. These impacts threaten ecosystem services as well as critical social, economic, and cultural assets and well-being. Rural coastal communities in the United States are especially vulnerable because they lack sufficient financial resources and access to governance systems and associated supports to resiliently adapt to climate challenges. These vulnerabilities have largely emerged from changes in broader social, economic, and political dynamics that undermine historically successful adaptation strategies.

The Chesapeake Bay region along the central east coast of the United States is already facing the impacts of climate change on rural coastal ecosystems and communities. This region is one of the most vulnerable in the United States to sea level rise. The peninsula bordering the bay on the east is especially vulnerable due to its low elevation, which leaves much of the landscape exposed to storms, flooding, marsh encroachment, and erosion. These vulnerabilities are exacerbated by the limited adaptive capacities of county governments and local communities, the latter of which are constrained by declining socioeconomic health as a result of regional economic shifts and limited access to government resources.

Project Description

Located on the lower eastern shore of the Chesapeake Bay, and one of many appendix-like protrusions jutting into the bay, the Deal Island Peninsula is twenty-six square miles of low-lying coastline that is home to approximately one thousand residents. Communities on the peninsula were established by farmers as early as the seventeenth century and later developed into thriving commercial fishing centers. Commercial fishers, known as watermen, remain the staple of the local economy. Methodism and Christian faith are important to local residents. Today, peninsula residents see themselves as belonging to one of two broad categories: "born-heres" or "come-heres." The former are descendants of families who have lived in the area for generations and are rooted in local heritage. Come-heres are a mix of retirees and weekend or summer residents who have purchased property—often along the shoreline—to enjoy the beautiful natural scenery and the maritime character of the area.

The Deal Island Peninsula—much of which sits at just three feet above sea level—is prone to coastal storms, tidal inundation, roadway flooding, and shoreline erosion. These environmental impacts are already affecting property values, access to homes and schools, and the health of local marshes, which buffer the communities from storms. Computer modeling of sea level rise predicts worsening of these effects, with large portions of the peninsula inundated by 2050. These small, rural, and unincorporated communities had few options for support to address these challenges until the initiation of the Deal Island Peninsula Partnership (DIPP) in 2012, which, at the time this chapter was written, represents over nine years of continuing collaboration with rural communities on the Chesapeake Bay.

The four authors of this chapter are applied anthropologists who believe that environmental anthropology can make unique contributions to multidisciplinary and multistakeholder efforts to address the impacts of climate change on communities and environments. To design and implement DIPP, we drew from tenets of environmental anthropology and our shared commitment to applying anthropology to solve human and environmental problems.

Through collaboration and learning, the network of diverse DIPP stakeholders seeks to initiate activities that will increase the resilience of the peninsula's communities and environment to cultural, socioeconomic, political, and ecological change. Historically, closely related families, community civic organizations, churches, and a rich fishery of crabs and oysters have helped local communities be resilient to seasonal harvest declines, unfavorable markets, family health and livelihood challenges, or infrastructure damage from storms and floods. While residents today still rely on community-based resources, local social networks are less robust, communities are smaller, families are not as close-knit, regulations and varying stocks of crabs and oysters are making commercial fishing less viable, and flooding is increasing. Many families now have at least one adult member in salaried employment off the peninsula, and much of everyday life is affected by broader regional and state socioeconomic, environmental, and governmental dynamics.

At the core of DIPP's work is the goal of building a diverse network of stakeholders from the local communities, country and state governments, universities, and nongovernmental (NGO) civic and environmental organizations. In building this network, we want to shift the common understanding of "stakeholder" away from the perspective that this includes only local residents while the rest of us are "outside" experts who bring "objective" knowledge. Instead, the foundation of DIPP's network is the belief that we are all peninsula stakeholders. Some of us live and work on the peninsula; others are responsible for providing public services to community residents, including the maintenance of infrastructure and the development of plans to address future human and environmental challenges (e.g., flood management). Others manage and restore state-owned wildlife management areas or research reserves on the peninsula. Still others are invested in the study of the social or ecological impacts being experienced on the peninsula, bringing a multidisciplinary approach and providing field sites for the training of students. And finally, some seek to integrate the collaborative work of DIPP into larger environmental, climate change, or cultural heritage work around the Chesapeake Bay.

We believe that this more inclusive view of who is a stakeholder is essential in order to accomplish the goal of increasing both community and environmental resilience. The drivers of the peninsula's socioecological challenges are as much regional, national, and even global in nature as they are local. Consequently, expertise and solutions need to come from individuals working at different scales with varied organizational missions. DIPP seeks to focus these different skills and goals on a geographically bound area that is facing significant socioecological change. By doing so, each participant can better understand why and how they have a stake in what happens on this patch of coastal shoreline and how their community or organizational needs and interests are similar or different to those of other stakeholders. Ultimately, our goal is to promote collaborative learning among stakeholders so they can find ways to work together, even if they have different goals and perspectives.

The size and composition of our stakeholder network has varied over the course of this long-term partnership, with some remaining actively engaged while others come and go based on their interests for particular activities. We see this flexibility as key to DIPP's capacity to further adaptability and sustainability, which allows busy stakeholders to decide how to allocate their time and expertise. We use an online newsletter to keep all stakeholders updated on DIPP activities, and we use personal contacts, interviews, community conversations, and collaborative research to reach out and more actively engage stakeholders for specific activities. We are fortunate that our network is large and diverse and includes around one hundred peninsula residents; thirty natural, physical, and social scientists from the University of Maryland—College Park and the University of Maryland Center for Environmental Science; and thirty resource managers and planners from Maryland's Department of Natural Resources, Department of the Environment, and Department of Planning, and from the Somerset County departments of Planning and Zoning, Emergency Services, and Public Works. Finally, there are about twenty-five individuals representing environmental, civic, and heritage NGOs involved in DIPP, including the Nature Conservancy, the Union of Concerned Scientists, the Wicomico Interfaith Partners for Creation Stewardship, the Deal Island–Chance Lions Clubs, and Skipjack Heritage, Inc. We have also expanded the DIPP network to include two additional rural areas beyond the peninsula by connecting with rural churches. A total of twelve churches (five of which are African American) are also connected to the DIPP network.

Implementation and Anthropologists' Roles

DIPP is an example of the ways in which the perspectives and approaches of environmental anthropologists can address the community and environmental challenges of climate change. We rely heavily on the approach of collaborative learning as a conceptual framework to tackle climate change, which can be contentious and create conflict.

"Collaborative learning is a framework and set of techniques intended for multiparty decision situations. It is a means of designing and implementing a series of events (meetings, field trips, etc.) to promote creative thought, constructive debate, and the effective implementation of proposals that the stakeholders generate" (Daniels and Walker 2001).

We integrate ethnographic methods of participant observation, interviewing, meetings, and qualitative and quantitative data collection to assist and strengthen collaborative learning practices and to create and sustain relationships among stakeholders who have little history of collaborating. There can be real disagreement and conflicts among stakeholders, much of it stemming from incomplete and inaccurate perceptions of each other's views and practices. Yet all share a desire to address community and environmental issues on the peninsula and beyond.

Three key initiatives between 2012 and 2019 represent the phases of DIPP and the process by which DIPP's collaborative network emerged.

National Estuarine Research Reserve Science Collaboration (2012–15)

The DIPP stakeholder network was formed as part of a National Oceanic and Atmospheric Administration (NOAA) National Estuarine Research Reserve System's Science Collaborative Grant in partnership with the Monie Bay National Estuarine Research Reserve (NERR) on the Deal Island Peninsula. This initiative employed interdisciplinary science and collaborative learning approaches to create open and inclusive space for diverse stakeholders to engage in discussions about the socioecological challenges of climate change, integrate local experiential knowledge with scientific research to enhance understandings of socioecological change, and develop stakeholder relationships built on trust and mutual respect to facilitate a sustained network to support local climate adaptation. Collaborative learning activities were carried out through collaborative research projects focused on the topics of marsh restoration, heritage, and flooding and shoreline erosion, all core issues affecting local resilience. Collaborative research project activities included group field trips, community conversations, and workshops, and these were used to improve understanding of each topic and identify future adaptation needs to address associated risks and vulnerabilities. This phase of DIPP was about bridging the natural and social science divide, as well as learning from and creating a cross-sector stakeholder network to address local vulnerabilities (see Paolisso et al. 2019).

The Integrated Coastal Resiliency Assessment (2016–18)

The Integrated Coastal Resiliency Assessment (ICRA), supported by the NOAA-funded Maryland Sea Grant, built upon outcomes of the NERRS Science Collaborative initiative to address the need for a more structured process to identify, prioritize, and develop adaptation projects to tackle local socioecological vulnerabilities. The ICRA employed collaborative learning to integrate scientific and local knowledge in assessing vulnerabilities and to guide stakeholder prioritizations of adaptation projects to address vulnerabilities. The ICRA was carried out through a series of community conversations to allow stakeholders to select areas of focus for assessment activities. Collaborative field assessments were used to better understand local experiences of vulnerability in each focus area. In the assessments, we conducted stakeholder interviews, surveys, group field trips, and focus area workshops. DIPP stakeholders then identified and prioritized adaptation projects to address priority concerns. These projects included an engineering study of tidal ditch drainage in flood-prone areas and improved ditch maintenance as well as a state-funded living shoreline project to address a highly erosive shoreline that threatens local communities (see Johnson, Feurt, and Paolisso 2017).

Engaging Faith Communities for Coastal Resilience (2017–19)

The Engaging Faith Communities for Coastal Resilience (EFCCR) initiative expanded DIPP's collaborative networks to include other nearby rural coastal communities and regional governments. Drawing upon the ICRA and NERRS Science Collaborative initiatives, the EFCCR aimed to explore how the development of collaborative networks to support climate change resilience in rural areas could be facilitated through local churches as trusted social institutions in rural communities. The objective was to build collaborative networks with rural churches, governments, and researchers living and working on the peninsula and in rural communities in two neighboring counties. We implemented the initiative by using semistructured interviews with stakeholders and text analysis to identify themes on which to organize a series of collaborative workshops (see Miller Hesed, Van Dolah, and Paolisso 2020).

Outcomes

DIPP has resulted in specific interventions that directly increase the socio-ecological resilience of the peninsula's communities and environment. For example, the ICRA identified areas where shore erosion was significantly threatening community and habitat. One particularly problematic area is a section of highly erosive natural shoreline on Deal Island. Large dunes that once dominated the shoreline in the 1990s have eroded away to a thin strip of sand that provides insufficient protection for nearby neighborhoods—including vulnerable households—and the main roadway for accessing the lower half of the peninsula. During storms, water frequently overtops the beach, flooding an adjacent marsh complex and nearby communities. During the ICRA initiative, DIPP stakeholders identified dune reconstruction on this shoreline as a priority adaptation project. Due to the engagement of county and state government staff in these discussions (who saw an opportunity to protect marshes and people and who had access to key decision-makers), the shoreline was selected as one of five demonstration projects across Maryland for a newly formed, state-funded resilience grant program. The Maryland Department of Natural Resources (DNR) funded the construction of a roughly $1 million living shoreline in this location to rebuild the dunes. Design and permitting were completed, and construction began in early 2021.

Road and nuisance flooding is another major environmental challenge confronting the communities on the Deal Island Peninsula. A network of roadside and on-property tidal and nontidal ditches are in place to help storm water move off roads and property and into creeks or marshes. Unfortunately, this system of ditches has not been maintained. Today, a number of local roads experience intermittent flooding, which, if severe, makes roads impassable and dangerous. DIPP initiatives have all included collaborative learning activities focused on flood mitigation. In particular, the ICRA initiative identified and mapped specific road and community segments where ditch flooding was a significant problem. These community maps were used by county government stakeholders to secure a $75,000 state grant to digitally measure and map the ditches using drones in the community-identified flood-prone areas. As this chapter went to press, this study was completed, and the results were being used by the county to plan ditch maintenance that targets the most vulnerable areas. In addition, this study reinforced the need for better flood documentation tools and provided additional leverage for the DNR to develop a Maryland-specific MyCoast platform, a website and mobile application to enable residents to qualitatively and quantitatively document flood impacts and hotspots to inform flood mitigation planning. MyCoast: Maryland was launched in October 2020 and is being piloted on the peninsula to help improve the tool's usability and applicability for stakeholders affected by coastal flooding.

DIPP has also increased the resilience of rural communities beyond the peninsula by establishing connections between rural churches, government agencies, and NGOs. For example, participating church members learned about different resources offered by government agencies such as planning tools, interactive maps, and grant programs. Importantly, because of the collaborative learning approach, we also saw that government employees learned a great deal about the resources, concerns, and needs of the rural communities. For example, a Maryland DNR representative said that this project had increased her understanding of the complex challenges facing underserved rural communities. This, in turn, led her to recommend at a department meeting that funders consider low-income, tax-based limitations and other factors that hamper rural communities' and governments' ability to compete for adaptation support in allocating adaptation funds. We also saw evidence that awareness of social injustices increased among NGO representatives through, for instance, increased sensitivity to and concern for racial disparities that make it especially challenging for rural African American communities to access adaptation support that meets local needs.

We are proud of what DIPP has accomplished and of our contributions as applied environmental anthropologists. That DIPP is still active and making progress is the biggest testimony to its effectiveness and provides evidence of the usefulness of this approach in addressing climate change. The value of this network to the resilience of this socioecological system is also evidenced by the DNR's commitment to assist in funding the network. The establishment of this network successfully met DIPP's primary goal to improve collaborations among residents, governments, and NGOs in order to enhance the resilience of the Deal Island Peninsula and other nearby rural communities. Leadership provided by anthropologists, as well as applied methods, were crucial in bringing to light the cultural frameworks that shaped stakeholders' perspectives and priorities for adaptation. Stakeholders were better able to understand each other, and that created more successful engagement and a willingness to work toward mutually beneficial solutions.

Ongoing Challenges

Leading and implementing DIPP has not been without its challenges. While our training in the principles of anthropology and tools of ethnography have allowed us to successfully build a diverse network and earn the respect and trust of stakeholders, our principal challenge is how to sustain the network and identify nonresearch funding to support the partnership, develop new initiatives, and communicate our process and outcomes (e.g., the newsletter). Our state partners, principally the Maryland DNR, have been increasing their financial support to the network collaborations, since the department manages large swaths of public salt marsh and a research reserve on the peninsula. The DNR's support has been invaluable, but it has been made available through short-term contracts with no guarantees for long-term support. The lack of dedicated, long-term funding remains a challenge for sustaining the work of the partnership.

DIPP has received significant media attention since 2012, which has been challenging due to media coverage inaccurately representing DIPP and supporting divisive climate change discourses that conflict with DIPP's message of bridging stakeholder divides. These challenges have raised difficult questions about what role we play as anthropologists in facilitating media contact and access to DIPP stakeholders. We are still working to develop best practices for media engagement.

We have also struggled to increase engagement with African Americans on the Deal Island Peninsula. Ethnographically, we attribute this to the limited capacities of these households to engage in the midst of increasing day-to-day challenges as well as to a certain level of distrust of government and outsiders borne from long-standing experiences of racialized injustice. We have, however, been successful in engaging Black communities off the Deal Island Peninsula through the EFCCR initiative noted above.

Our successes in facilitating the development of a shoreline restoration project and improved flood management have exposed DIPP to the complex and bureaucratic world of environmental regulations, mainly through the permitting process. We have had to reorient our research to understand this process and work with stakeholders to try to move permit applications toward implementation. It has been sobering to learn that, even with diverse stakeholder support and funding for interventions that increase socioecological resilience, multiple layers of regulations and permitting, at times in conflict, can stall important components of our work for extended periods of time. We have been considering conducting an applied ethnography of environmental regulations and permitting, perhaps as part of graduate student thesis work.

Finally, we have also struggled to balance the resilience needs of today with inevitable future needs (e.g., relocation considerations) as the impacts of climate change worsen. These challenges are largely due to mismatched priorities between locals who want DIPP to focus on immediate challenges and more regional government preferences to invest limited government resources in long-term adaptation responses. To date, our discussions and actions have mostly targeted ongoing needs, but we are exploring opportunities to integrate more future considerations.

The Anthropological Difference

We have a saying when confronting difficulties in our collaborative work: "agreement is overrated." The goal of DIPP is to help stakeholders learn enough about each other's cultural, socioeconomic, and political backgrounds to understand why they think and behave in the ways they do. DIPP strives for consensus on how to move forward, not on reaching monolithic thinking on all causes and consequences of socioecological change. Throughout, we have used our training in anthropology to build rapport and trust and to ensure stakeholders feel that their contributions are important.

Lessons learned from anthropology's historical reliance upon long-term fieldwork were particularly important to DIPP. Engagement with our partners was more significant than "showing up for a meeting." DIPP activities would not have garnered the presence and level of participation that we achieved without this sustained ethnographic foundation. The idea of cultural relativism also served DIPP well, to help us earn trust from stakeholders, but also to create space in which perspectives, views, and beliefs from across all stakeholder types could coexist. We have been able to talk about contentious issues related to climate change and make space for scientific and religious perspectives side by side. A visible example of our practices to promote cultural relativism across the project was our request for each gathering to be opened with a prayer by a local resident—as they would have if holding a local event without outsider presence.

DIPP is the result of taking what anthropology offers out of academia and into the public domain. Although they may not be able to articulate it in technical terms, DIPP stakeholders recognize that our accomplishments are built upon the perspectives and practices of applied and environmental anthropology. Coastal residents, researchers, resource managers and planners, environmentalists, church leaders, and civic and heritage activists have a better understanding of what anthropology is and how it can help solve real-world problems.

Very few disciplines are positioned to enable tough conversations, collect information, and facilitate meetings among stakeholders with a history of mistrust and misunderstanding on a contentious topic such as changing climate. Working as anthropologists and employing ethnographic and collaborative learning approaches, we are able to advance the sharing of viewpoints and experiences in a nonjudgmental environment so that all can collaboratively learn about each other. In learning about each other, in finding respect and trust, DIPP's diverse stakeholders work together, even if they do not always agree with each other.

Finally, developing, implementing, and evaluating DIPP has significantly expanded our understanding and application of anthropology. The lessons learned from DIPP's evolution from an academic project to an ongoing multistakeholder collaboration helps inform the training of future applied anthropologists through teaching, internships, and thesis/dissertation research. In addition, the dissemination of results through many media formats, including conferences and workshops, project websites, and newsletters and publications, contributes to an awareness of these efforts to larger audiences. All of this will broaden the field of applied anthropology and instill in it valuable insights on anthropology as praxis.

Michael Paolisso is a professor of anthropology at the University of Maryland, College Park. He currently is serving as the SfAA president. He is an environmental anthropologist with decades of research and practice in the Chesapeake Bay region of the United States, focusing on coastal communities and climate change, collaborative learning, fisheries and agriculture management, water pollution, environmental restoration, social justice, and socioecological resilience. He cofounded the collaborative coastal adaptation effort that has become the Deal Island Peninsula Partnership (DIPP). He has taught courses on applied anthropology, environmental anthropology, cognitive anthropology, sociocultural theory, and research methods. He has also conducted research in Venezuela, Honduras, Ecuador, Kenya, and Nepal. He completed his PhD in anthropology at UCLA in 1985.

Elizabeth Van Dolah is a coastal resilience project manager for the Nature Conservancy's Maryland/DC chapter and was the coordinator of the Deal Island Peninsula Partnership from 2018-21, a multistakeholder collaborative that seeks to enhance coastal resilience to climate change on the Deal Island Peninsula, Maryland. She received a PhD in anthropology in 2018 after a master's in applied anthropology in 2012, both from the University of Maryland College Park. Her dissertation research examined the value of a cultural heritage framework for developing more inclusive stakeholder processes in climate change adaptation planning. As an applied environmental anthropologist, she seeks to integrate human dimension considerations into coastal resilience initiatives and to foster more equitable decision-making through multilevel stakeholder collaborations that support a range of coastal resilience goals. Much of her research has focused on climate-driven socioenvironmental concerns on Maryland's Eastern Shore of the Chesapeake Bay, including erosion, tidal flooding, marsh migration, and harmful algal blooms.

Katherine J. Johnson works as a social scientist for the National Institute of Standards and Technology on topics of natural hazards risk reduction. Her PhD in anthropology (2016) from the University of Maryland College Park, with a focus on applied anthropology, has positioned her well to collaborate effectively at a federal agency. She currently works on social science aspects of strengthening components of the built environment to better withstand earthquakes. In addition, she is leading an effort to investigate emergency communications in Puerto Rico during Hurricane Maria in 2017. Prior to this work, she conducted community-based collaborative research to support social-ecological adaptation to climate change in a rural coastal community on the Chesapeake Bay. In all of her work, she endeavors to share the insights and benefits of anthropology with others.

Christine D. Miller Hesed is currently a postdoctoral research associate leading a grasslands synthesis project at the North Central Climate Adaptation Science Center. She received an MS in sustainable development and conservation biology in 2010 and a PhD in anthropology in 2016—both at the University of Maryland. Her dissertation research focused on environmental justice as it relates to coastal resilience to climate change among rural African American communities on the Chesapeake Bay. From 2017 to 2019, she directed a project that examined the use of collaborative learning to bring together local and regional government agencies with rural church communities to build resilience to climate change. She has mentored graduated students in the use of ethnographic and cognitive methods in environmental science research, served as a reviewer for the AAA Task Force on Global Climate Change Report, and volunteered at the "Maryland Day" environmental anthropology display from 2010 to 2015.

References

Daniels, S., and G. Walker. 2001. *Working through Environmental Conflict: The Collaborative Learning Approach*. Westport, CT: Praeger.

Johnson, K., C. Feurt, and M. Paolisso. 2017. "Collaborative Science and Learning as Tools for Climate Change Adaptation Planning." *International Journal of Climate Change: Impacts and Responses* 10(1): 59–75. doi:10.18848/1835–7156/CGP/v10i01/59–75.

Miller Hesed, C. D., E. Van Dolah, and M. Paolisso. 2020. "Engaging Faith-Based Communities for Rural Coastal Resilience: Lessons from Collaborative Learning on the Chesapeake Bay." *Climatic Change* 159(1): 37–75. https://doi.org/10.1007/s10584-019-02638-9.

Paolisso, M., C. Prell, K. Johnson, B. Needelman, I. M. P. Khan, and K. Hubacek. 2019. "Enhancing Socio-ecological Resilience in Coastal Regions through Collaborative Science, Knowledge Exchange and Social Networks: A Case Study from the Deal Island Peninsula, USA." *Socio-ecological Practice Research* 1(2): 109–23.

CHAPTER 6

~:~

Marcellus Shale
Public Health Study

THURKA SANGARAMOORTHY

Project Background

"Fracking" is a colloquial term for unconventional natural gas development and production: the horizontal drilling of a rock layer and the subsequent injection of pressurized mixture of water, sand, and other chemicals to release gas and oil. Fracking is a relatively new technique used to extract previously inaccessible natural gas and oil reserves found deep underground in shale formations. It has been hailed by some as bringing about American energy independence, recharging the economy, and providing relief to millions by way of plummeting prices at the gas pump. Oil and natural gas development rapidly expanded throughout North America, Europe, Asia, and Australia because of fracking, and as a result, the United States was, in the mid-2010s, predicted to become a key exporter of natural gas.

Western Maryland, along with Pennsylvania, Ohio, and West Virginia, sits atop one of the largest shale formations in the United States—the Marcellus Shale—which is abundant in gas resources. Fracking had been only recently implemented in the northern Appalachian region, in states like West Virginia and Pennsylvania; it has had a longer history of development in the western United States in states like Colorado and Texas. At the time of this project, in the early 2010s, the areas where most fracking activities occurred included the Great Plains region, which extends from Canada to Texas, and the Marcellus Shale, which spans from New York and Ohio to Western Maryland and Virginia. Marcellus Shale was the largest producing shale gas basin in the United States, accounting for almost 40 percent of US shale gas production.

The process of fracking remains highly controversial due to its relative novelty and because environmental and health impacts have not been thoroughly researched. For instance, the process of extracting gas from shale formations is complex and often includes several interrelated phases. Critical aspects of fracking include the negotiation of mineral rights with owners of land; tree removal and clearing land for well pads; the construction of roads and other infrastructure, including pipelines and compressor stations; the shipment and management of extracted gas as well as water and wastewater; and the movement of transient workers and populations into established communities. These stages of development have the potential for significant economic, environmental, health, and social impacts on communities where fracking is implemented.

Furthermore, although communities welcome potential economic growth brought about by fracking, uncertainties about environmental and health risks have contributed to tension, anxiety, and stress among many who face the rapid growth of energy development. Rural communities experience both opportunities and challenges as a result of fracking. For instance, fracking can result in varied economic impacts, with some, like landowners who sign leases with energy companies, benefitting more than others. Social impacts, such as fluctuating patterns of community interaction, diminishing social cohesion, increases in crime, and escalation of indirect and direct health impacts, such as increased psychosocial stress, mental health problems, and substance abuse, have also been observed.

Despite these uncertainties and controversies, the State of Maryland, like many places around the world, was grappling with the prospect of large-scale fracking. In 2011, then-governor Martin O'Malley issued an executive order establishing the Marcellus Shale Safe Drilling Initiative to assist state policymakers and regulators in determining whether and how gas production from the Marcellus Shale formations in Maryland could be accomplished without unacceptable risks to the environment and the populace. This initiative required research to assess the impacts associated with drilling in the Marcellus Shale in Maryland on the environment and natural resources, the economy, and public safety and health. In October 2013, a statewide public health impact assessment of fracking, the first of its kind, was commissioned by the State of Maryland. The Maryland Department of Health and Mental Hygiene signed a memorandum of understanding with the Maryland Institute for Applied Environmental Health (MIAEH) at the School of Public Health, University of Maryland College Park, to conduct an assessment of the potential public health impacts associated with drilling in the Marcellus Shale in Maryland (e.g., specifically Allegheny and Garrett Counties in Western Maryland, where drilling was being proposed) and to provide a Marcellus Shale Public Health Report with input from residents and a variety of other stakeholders.

Project Description

The then-director of the MIAEH assembled a team of interdisciplinary re-searchers, composed of environmental and occupational health, environmental justice, and social science experts to carry out this assessment. I was asked to participate as one of four coinvestigators in this assessment; my appointment was based on several areas of expertise, including my background as a public health researcher with methodological experience in conducting health impact assessments and as an anthropologist with extensive knowledge of risk envi-ronments and familiarity with community-based participatory research. I am a cultural and medical anthropologist and an epidemiologist by training, based in the Department of Anthropology at the University of Maryland. I am also an affiliate faculty member with the MIAEH, and I was the only social scientist on the team.

The memorandum of understanding signed between the Maryland De-partment of Health and Mental Hygiene and the MIAEH specified that the project was not designed to make recommendations about whether or when to allow fracking to occur in Maryland. Rather, this study was specifically com-missioned, and subsequently designed, to inform decisions by clearly describ-ing the risks and potential public health responses. Furthermore, we were to focus specifically on public health impacts that would be concentrated in and unique to the Garrett and Allegany County populations living and working near the sites of shale gas development.

Our public health study drew upon several methods of a rapid health impact assessment (HIA). An HIA is a process that utilizes a variety of data and ana-lytic methods to determine a broad range of potential health impacts, including those that may result from social, economic, and environmental changes of a proposed project, plan, or policy before it is implemented. Our HIA included a comprehensive description, derived by using an extensive scoping process, of risks and potential public health responses to fracking, a baseline assessment of current regional population health, an assessment of potential public health impacts, and possible adaptive and public health mitigation strategies. The final HIA report and supporting documents were available on the project website.

To summarize, the study, as outlined in the memorandum of understanding, included the following specific steps:

+ *Detailed scoping* (gathering, compiling, and reviewing any relevant infor-mation, feedback, details, and data), including a timetable for remaining deliverables, methods, and public input to determine study objectives.
+ *Baseline assessment* of current regional population health, including de-mographics, causes of morbidity and mortality, local health priorities, vulnerable populations, local healthcare, and social service infrastructure.

+ *Impact assessment* of the potential exposures, including hazards and known health impacts both directly and indirectly associated with hydraulic fracturing, assessment of current exposures, and data gaps prior to onset of hydraulic fracturing.
+ *Final report*, which included the study findings, monitoring and assessment recommendations, and a public health response and mitigation strategies.

Our scoping process sought input from a variety of stakeholders, including community residents through two public meetings, a review of over one hundred public comments submitted to the state in 2013, two focus groups held in West Virginia where fracking had already been developed, and observational data of fracking operations in West Virginia. These data, along with our own review of the scientific literature and careful consideration of the state mandate, were used to make modifications to the study's scope and were reflected in our final report.

The baseline health assessment examined demographics, potential vulnerable populations, a wide range of health indicators, social determinants of health, and healthcare infrastructure in Garrett and Allegany Counties. Baseline health data, or a profile of existing health conditions, are necessary components in an HIA in order to trace the current health status of a population and to understand any potential needs that may arise with a project, policy, or plan. The impact assessment was based on available data from other states with ongoing fracking, regarding exposure and health outcomes, and also on epidemiologic and toxicologic data from other contexts that are relevant to potential fracking-related exposures.

Our assessments of potential health impacts were not predictions that these effects would necessarily occur in Maryland, where regulation is likely to be stricter than in states where fracking was already underway. Rather, we provided assessments of the impacts that could occur and that needed to be addressed by preventive public health measures if and when drilling was allowed. Thus, the focus of our recommendations was on answering this question: Given the baseline population health, vulnerabilities, and potential impacts of fracking, how can Maryland best protect public health if and when fracking goes forward?

An HIA is not a quantitative risk assessment. Rather, it provides information that is qualitative in nature that can be used to assess whether and how community well-being may be affected, both directly and indirectly. Thus, anthropological methods were seen as integral to the success of the HIA by my colleagues. Drawing from my expertise in conducting community-based participatory studies and ethnographic research, I anticipated that sociocultural factors such as place attachment, place meaning, and place identity—people's relationships to their physical, social, and economic environment—would be significant to communities affected by potential fracking activities. I co-led the design for the scoping and baseline assessments, using participant observation, public meetings, and focus groups with residents in Western Maryland and neighboring West Virginia (where fracking had already been underway) to solicit community perspectives on fracking, especially perceptions of environmental and health risks associated with fracking.

For the impact assessment, I referred to ethnographic and other qualitative studies alongside public health and environmental health science literature in order to make assessments of potential impacts related to fracking, including investigating disturbances to residents' sense of place and community and its influence on negative psychosocial impacts. Throughout the project, I used anthropological approaches to underscore the importance of community input in determining public health impacts of fracking, utilizing their comments and concerns to determine the overall aims and objectives of the HIA, which hazards and impacts to evaluate, and the types of research strategies and methods to use. Anthropology helped us systematically evaluate a full range of potential public health risks and benefits of fracking because we focused on community concerns rather than on issues solely predetermined by our (i.e., investigators') research interests or regulatory obligations.

Implementation and Anthropologist's Role

Our scoping process collected a variety of stakeholder input, including responses from community residents at public meetings and over one hundred public comments submitted to the state. Using this information, along with the results of our review of the scientific literature and careful consideration of the state mandate, we finalized a list of specific study topics. Our draft scoping report was released for public comment, and we received forty-six comments from concerned residents, environmental advocacy organizations, and the oil and gas industry as well as reviews from external experts recruited by the Maryland Department of Health and Mental Hygiene.

After carefully considering all of the input, we made changes to our project's timeline and to the baseline health and health impact assessments. First, we incorporated the baseline health assessment, impact assessment, and recommendations into a single final report rather than issuing a separate baseline health assessment earlier in the process. This provided additional time to develop the baseline health assessment. Second, we presented a progress report with a summary of our findings and recommendations at a community meeting in Western Maryland in June 2014. Third, we released the final report a month later to allow for a public comment period. All comments on the final report went directly to the Marcellus Shale Safe Drilling Advisory Commission for consideration, along with comments from external reviewers arranged by the Maryland Department of Health and Mental Hygiene.

During the scoping phase of the HIA, I worked alongside our project manager to determine the wide range of stakeholders with whom we would need to engage, and I planned an intensive recruitment strategy for two public stakeholder meetings, which were critical to our study. I then facilitated public stakeholder meetings in Western Maryland and sought input from the public on their perceptions and needs regarding the scope of our study. I led our research assistants in analyzing transcripts and public comments in order to frame the scope of our study. I also conducted observations of fracking sites and moderated focus groups with community members affected by fracking in neighboring West Virginia, analyzed health data, wrote reports and recommendations, and published findings.

An unanticipated challenge during the scoping phase included community concerns that reflected a strong desire for us to examine climate change issues and their relationships to fracking. Such community concerns were made clear during the public stakeholder meetings, in which residents expressed concern about the interrelated effects of climate change, natural disasters, seasonal weather changes, and community public health. For instance, a resident asked, "Will you be taking into consideration the effects of climate change in the coming decades on Western Maryland? It may affect some of the health effects." In our reports, we acknowledged that fugitive methane emissions, which can occur throughout the fracking production and distribution process, can contribute considerably to climate change and threaten public health.

However, we chose not to examine this issue for a variety of reasons. Adequately assessing these impacts would have required specific types of scientific evidence to support eventual conclusions (where few exist), climate simulation computations, and major assumptions about what policy alternatives are politically realistic. We determined that exploring this issue fell outside not only our expertise and available resources but also the scope of our state charge, which was to focus on health impacts primarily restricted to the local areas where fracking was set to take place. Aside from climate change, all other community concerns were examined in the study, including air and water quality, noise pollution, earthquakes, social determinants of health, healthcare infrastructure, cumulative exposures and risk, and occupational impacts.

In the next phase of our study, we conducted a two-step process that first described the baseline health status of the affected population and then assessed potential impacts in order to evaluate the progress and effects of potential fracking operations. A robust understanding of the health trends and issues currently affecting a community is an important step in the HIA process. Stakeholders during the scoping phase urged us to collect primary, representative, individual health, and exposure data, but a lack of time and resources did not allow for this. Instead, we created the baseline health assessment using a variety of existing data from national, state, and local public health sources. In order to assess the baseline health of Allegany and Garrett County residents, we considered demographics, potential vulnerable populations, a wide range of health indicators, environmental health, social determinants of health, and healthcare infrastructure, based on county-level and census tract–level statistics.

In addition, during the scoping phase, community members wanted us to compare county-level data for Western Maryland to that of neighboring counties in Pennsylvania and West Virginia rather than to the rest of Maryland for an overall health profile because they felt that their health profile (as well as their social identities) were more closely related to these communities than to the rest of Maryland. Such perceptions are aligned with the limited scholarship that has noted that hilly Western Maryland is more similar to the subregion of Northern Appalachia than to the rest of the relatively flat state of Maryland due to closely aligned economic, geopolitical, and cultural histories (Sangaramoorthy et al. 2016). The creation of a "regional" health profile that included several counties spanning three states instead of standard county and state-level comparisons posed challenges and debates within our team about the constitution of a valid "baseline" since such data were difficult to collect, measures proved inconsistent across states, and the process of demarcating regional contours was perceived as highly subjective. I advocated for using regional data, as this was something that was critical to our community stakeholders, and as a result, when possible, data for Allegany and Garrett Counties were compared to the health data of the region (Allegany and Garrett Counties in Maryland; Bedford, Fayette, and Somerset Counties in Pennsylvania; and Grant, Hampshire, Mineral, Preston, and Tucker Counties in West Virginia), as well as the State of Maryland for an overall baseline health profile.

During the next phase—the impact assessment—we developed a hazard-ranking methodology to evaluate the overall public health concern for eight hazards identified during the scoping process and literature review associated with fracking in Maryland and to provide a succinct overview of the impact of fracking-associated hazards on public health. The hazard-ranking methodology is akin to a scoring system, which seemed like a reasonable choice for our study, given that a similar scale was used in one of the only other fracking HIAs conducted to date. This approach also enabled us to provide an assessment despite limited data on the health and environmental effects of fracking. The hazard ranking included measures related to the presence of vulnerable populations, exposure, possible health effects, geographic extent, and effectiveness of a setback (i.e., distance between natural resources or buildings and fracking activity). Overall impact was determined by a color-coded ranking system (low, moderate, and high) that was generated based on the total for each hazard. Air quality, occupational health, and the social determinants of health were ranked as "high" concern; water quality, noise, traffic, and cumulative risk were ranked as "moderate" concern; and earthquake was ranked as "low" concern for their potential to negatively impact public health.

Several challenges arose during this phase. First, we suggested a two-thousand-foot setback, although this was not empirically determined; this suggestion was based on traffic-related air pollution literature, which showed the closest data we could find. However, the geospatial dimensions of fracking activities may be quite different from traffic from major roads, and additional measurements would be required to determine specific setbacks for fracking.

In addition, there were some concerns in applying the hazard-ranking criteria to such a broad range of impacts, especially those that did not pertain to natural environmental hazards such as those categorized as social determinants of health and healthcare infrastructure. For instance, the social determinants of health category included both public safety measures (e.g., industrial traffic and violent crime) and psychosocial and physical health outcomes (e.g., mental health, substance use, and sexually transmitted infections). Although the duration of and frequency of exposure, likelihood and magnitude of health effects, and geographic extent could be evaluated for each of these measures in a consistent manner, the definition of vulnerable populations varied across measures. Psychosocial and physical health outcomes could disproportionately impact vulnerable populations such as those with preexisting conditions or substance abuse issues, but public safety issues could affect all subpopulations evenly. Furthermore, setback regulations may not have any impact on psychosocial and physical health outcomes or public safety issues such as crime.

Likewise, healthcare infrastructure, and the use of a community's healthcare facilities and services, could not easily be assessed with our hazard-ranking criteria. Exposure in this scenario was established as population influx, particularly migrant farm workers engaged in high-risk activities, which we then determined would lead to increased demands on existing healthcare infrastructure. Healthcare infrastructure is disproportionately affected by those most likely to use services, such as the elderly, the disabled, those already in poor health, and children, although the entire community is potentially at risk. Similar to the social determinants of health, the effectiveness of a physical setback was not determined to mitigate issues related to healthcare infrastructure.

I used anthropological expertise to help my colleagues think through these limitations and provided possible alternatives in implementing such a ranking methodology. The development of this hazard-ranking methodology, including its limitations and alternatives, was published in *PLoS One* (Boyle et al. 2016).

Outcomes

Based on the scoping process and existing literature, we categorized fracking-associated hazards into eight broad categories: (1) air quality, (2) water-related (water quality, soil quality, and naturally occurring radioactive materials), (3) noise, (4) earthquakes, (5) social determinants of health, (6) healthcare infrastructure, (7) occupational health, and (8) cumulative exposure/risk. We then ranked each of these hazards using seven criteria. The scores were summed across the evaluation criteria to obtain an overall score for the hazards. Based on this overall score, we classified each hazard as:

+ high likelihood that unconventional natural gas development and production-related changes will have negative impact on public health;
+ moderately high likelihood that unconventional natural gas development and production-related changes will have negative impact on public health;
+ low likelihood that unconventional natural gas development and production-related changes will have negative impact on public health.

Four categories were classified as having high likelihood of negative impacts (air quality, healthcare infrastructure, occupational health, and social determinants of health); three were classified as having moderately high likelihood of negative impacts (cumulative exposures and risks, water-related flowback and production, and noise); and one as having low likelihood of negative impacts on public health (earthquakes).

Our final report included a comprehensive description of risks and potential public health responses to fracking using a baseline assessment of current regional population health, an assessment of potential public health impacts, and possible adaptive and public health mitigation strategies.

In various presentations and in the final report, our study underscored that, without adequate safeguards, drilling for natural gas using fracking operations could harm the health of residents, workers, and communities in Western Maryland. Our report, along with other commissioned reports on economic and environmental appraisals, were used by state agencies to present a final assessment to policymakers in accordance with the executive order. In late 2014, these agencies concluded in their final report that with adequate regulation and monitoring, "the risks of Marcellus Shale development can be managed to an acceptable level" (Maryland Department of the Environment and Maryland Department of Natural Resources 2014). Weeks before he left office, Governor O'Malley supported moving fracking forward with strict regulations to mitigate against air and water pollution. However, the Maryland legislature later passed a moratorium on fracking until October 2017. In April 2017, the new governor, Larry Hogan, signed a bill establishing a ban on fracking in Maryland. Since their release, our report and subsequent publications have been used and continue to be used by citizen groups, community-based organizations, and policymakers to make cases for and against fracking.

The project represents several innovations. The first was the utilization of a health impact assessment, the first of its kind to use participatory research to foster a relatively high degree of control over research by community members and stakeholders. It was meant to equalize power within the research process, which can enrich both the quality and outcomes of such studies. Second was the development of a hazard-ranking methodology to assess potential public health impacts, which is a valuable tool that allowed us to systematically evaluate each hazard related to fracking and provide recommendations to minimize the hazards. Both the assessment and the ranking methodology can be easily adapted by other communities facing similar situations, and it can be used in other settings that entail making decisions with limited information.

Furthermore, anthropological analyses led to findings that indicated that fracking contributed to a disruption in residents' sense of place and social identity, generating widespread social stress. We found that community residents welcomed the potential economic growth brought about by fracking, but fracking also generated rapid transformations in meanings of place and social identity, increasing people's anxieties about environmental and health impacts.

The Anthropological Difference

My official role in this study was as a coinvestigator. I was involved in all aspects of the project: facilitating public stakeholder meetings in Western Maryland, conducting observations of fracking sites and moderating focus groups with community members affected by fracking in neighboring West Virginia, analyzing health data, writing reports and recommendations, and publishing findings. In this collaboration, I was a full participant involved in the research process itself. Therefore, I did not conduct separate studies of the project, the scientists involved, or community members.

However, as a medical anthropologist and public health researcher without content expertise in environmental health, my role was also inherently one of a participant observer, trying to understand and reflect on the specific factors related to an emergent form of energy extraction and the subsequent study of it. It was often necessary to reflect on how concepts of risk and exposure are constituted within interactions between human bodies and changing environmental landscapes, especially in a context where knowledge about fracking is still not considered "universal." Yet these notions are (re)produced in familiar and new ways in places with long histories of extraction.

The method used, an HIA, is likewise an emergent tool in public health and public policy planning activities related to land use. There is substantial variation in the content of HIAs and the processes by which they are produced. HIAs represent one mode of operationalizing and institutionalizing calls for the democratization of science. The use of HIAs to understand the potential health impacts of fracking also underscores the anticipatory dimensions of public health science, which, in this case, are situated in predicting human health risks and benefits in the face of rapid environmental change. Our HIA is one of only a few to be conducted on oil and natural gas activities; this will have implications for activities related to energy extraction, particularly in places where such activities are deeply contested.

This project contributes additionally to several discussion points on the landscape of public and applied anthropology. First, it demonstrates the ability of anthropology and anthropologists to effectively study contemporary social issues through the interdisciplinary engagement of knowledge production as both full participatory actors and reflective outsiders. In considering the unparalleled urgency and reflexivity that accompany the politics of extraction, anthropologists must attend to multiscalar, multistakeholder, and interdisciplinary approaches in research and practice. These multiple entanglements can help us situate the structures and processes informing knowledge production around fracking within broad debates regarding transformations in the relations between science, society, and policy. It can also move us toward more engaged public discussions about risk and exposure studies, democracy and governance in science, scientific transparency and accountability, land use and rights, and social justice, which seem particularly critical at this political moment. Finally, such collaborations have the potential to shift our research focus to both scientists and research tools, which would enrich our understandings of the contested and continually shifting terrains of fracking. To this end, I published a solo authored paper discussing my firsthand experiences as a medical anthropologist and public health researcher on this project in *The Extractive Industries and Society* (Sangaramoorthy 2019).

Epilogue

As predicted at the time of this study, fracking has led to dramatic increases in US domestic oil and gas production and has reduced the need for the United States to import oil. US net imports of oil are declining after a steady thirty-year rise. This reduction coincides with a major increase in domestic oil production, due in large part to the expansion of fracking. Total US crude oil production roughly tripled in the decade spanning 2010 to 2020, while during the same time period the amount of total US oil consumption provided by imports fell considerably. While the United States remains dependent on foreign oil, this level of dependence is significantly less than before because fracking has allowed the United States to provide over half of its fuel needs.

The rise of crude oil production over the past decade allowed the United States to become a net exporter of crude oil toward the end of 2019, the first time in its history that it was exporting more than it was importing. The United States maintained high exports of crude oil as of January 2020. However, the COVID-19 crisis and resulting low oil prices led to reductions in US crude oil production, which could adversely affect exports. Experts predicted that the United States would again become a net importer of crude oil and petroleum products in the third quarter of 2020, remaining a net importer throughout the majority of 2021. However, this trend not only depends on developments in US crude oil production but also on US oil demand. Government stay-at-home orders lowered many Americans' rates of daily driving and travel overall, leading to a drastic reduction in the demand for gasoline.

Moreover, countries, regions, cities, and communities around the world are increasingly looking to prohibit or place moratoriums on fracking through various legal and administrative mechanisms. Maryland became the first state with oil and natural gas reserves to legislatively ban fracking, and more states were looking to address the risks associated with fracking through legislative actions. In Maryland, prohibitions or moratoriums on fracking at the municipal level were key to securing political and legal support at larger, regional jurisdictions. Furthermore, social mobilization by grassroots organizations—focused on climate concerns such as methane leakage from well sites, pipelines, and processing facilities; burning fossil fuels; and negative community impacts—have helped amplify and legitimize antifracking movements at the local, national, regional, and global level. As the future of fracking remains uncertain, projects and collaborations such as this are urgent and necessary to effectively broaden our understandings of ongoing matters of knowledge production and resulting policy decisions on contested and politically divided matters such as fracking.

Thurka Sangaramoorthy is a cultural and medical anthropologist and public health researcher with twenty-two years of experience in conducting community-engaged ethnographic research, including rapid assessments, among vulnerable populations in the United States, Africa, and Latin America/Caribbean. Her work is broadly concerned with power and subjectivity in global economies of care. She has worked at this intersection on diverse topics, including global health and migration, HIV/STD, and environmental disparities. She is the author of two books: *Rapid Ethnographic Assessments: A Practical Approach and Toolkit for Collaborative Community Research* (Routledge 2020), and *Treating AIDS: Politics of Difference, Paradox of Prevention* (Rutgers University Press 2014). She is cochair of the American Anthropological Association's Members

Programmatic Advisory and Advocacy Committee and a board member of the Society for Medical Anthropology. She serves as associate editor of *Public Health Reports* and is an editorial board member of *American Anthropologist*. She received her PhD from the University of California, Berkeley and San Francisco in 2008 and her MPH from Columbia University in 2002. She is currently associate professor of anthropology at the University of Maryland.

References

Boyle, M. D., D. C. Payne-Sturges, T. Sangaramoorthy, S. Wilson, K. E. Nachman, K. Babik, Christian C. Jenkins, J. Trowell, D. K. Milton, and A. Sapkota. 2016. "Hazard Ranking Methodology for Assessing Health Impacts of Unconventional Natural Gas Development and Production: The Maryland Case Study." *PloS One* 11(1): e0145368.

Maryland Department of the Environment and Maryland Department of Natural Resources. 2014. "Marcellus Shale Safe Drilling Initiative Study, Part III." Annapolis, Maryland: State of Maryland. https://mde.state.md.us/programs/land/mining/marcellus/documents/final_marcellus_shale_report.pdf.

Sangaramoorthy, Thurka. 2019. "Maryland Is Not for Shale: Scientific and Public Anxieties of Predicting Health Impacts of Fracking." *The Extractive Industries and Society* 6(2): 463–70.

Sangaramoorthy, T., A. M. Jamison, M. D. Boyle, D. C. Payne-Sturges, A. Sapkota, D. K. Milton, and S. M. Wilson. 2016. "Place-Based Perceptions of the Impacts of Fracking along the Marcellus Shale." *Social Science & Medicine* 151: 27–37.

PART III

~:~

Cultural Preservation

CHAPTER 7

The Denver Museum of Nature & Science Repatriation Initiative

STEPHEN E. NASH AND CHIP COLWELL

Project Background

Native American groups have expressed their concerns for decades about the long history of looting of their graves, cultural items, and other material heritage. In 1990, the US Congress finally took action and enacted the Native American Graves Protection and Repatriation Act (NAGPRA). The act established the rights of Native American tribes to assert claims to ancestral remains, funerary and other sacred objects, and items of cultural patrimony repatriated from museums and federal agencies.

Not long after NAGPRA was signed into law, the Denver Museum of Nature & Science (DMNS) held dozens of consultations with Native American tribes and began to return cultural items and human remains to them when and if repatriation claims were submitted. By the end of the 1990s, however, the DMNS had fallen out of legal compliance with NAGPRA. Those troubles reached a climax in 2002 when a Native American community leader sent a letter of complaint about the DMNS to the US secretary of the interior (who oversees NAGPRA compliance).

Four years after that complaint was filed, the DMNS Department of Anthropology underwent a near-total staff turnover. Isabel Tovar, a new collections manager, was hired in February 2006. Dr. Stephen E. Nash was hired in October 2006 as curator of archaeology and museum department chair. Dr. Chip Colwell joined the team in mid-2007 as curator of anthropology and NAGPRA officer. Along with Dr. Steven R. Holen, another curator of archaeology, the anthropology team began to rethink its approach to NAGPRA in particular and repatriation in general.

They decided to boldly confront the museum's collecting history, for they did not believe it was ethically appropriate for the museum to just hold on to what it had, simply waiting for the Native American tribes to approach the museum about repatriating their own cultural heritage, ancestors, and belongings.

After all, it was the museum's own policies and collecting practices that had led to the institution's repatriation crisis in the first place. Why should the burden to rectify that situation fall on the tribes? The team felt strongly it should be the museum's burden, and opportunity, to make things right. The team decided to start by picking up the phone—proactively reaching out to and talking with the tribes to whom the collections and ancestors belonged.

Thus, in 2007, the museum's newly reconstituted Department of Anthropology established the Repatriation Initiative, a comprehensive and systematic effort to address the museum's backlog of repatriation claims and, perhaps more importantly, to proactively address the issue of repatriation from a broader, ethical perspective. That effort launched the Denver Museum of Nature & Science to the forefront of the museum decolonization movement and debates surrounding the care and return of cultural items and human remains. The Repatriation Initiative used anthropological understandings of sacred and inalienable property, ethical values surrounding the dead, collaborative methodologies, and restorative justice to proactively grapple with the tangled history of museum collections.

The team penned an ambitious and audacious mission statement: *We seek to curate the best understood and most ethically held anthropology collection in North America.* "Best understood" meant having total intellectual control over the collections. Too many major museums have vast, uncatalogued collections and literally do not know what they curate or explicitly why they curate the items they do. Nash and the team wanted to completely document the DMNS collection for the first time in its history. After all, why should a museum expend resources if it did not clearly understand the collection's identity, value, history, and importance? "Most ethically held" meant that the team wanted to curate only those objects that were ethically and legally obtained—meaning they were collected with consent from Indigenous communities and in compliance with US and international laws. Too many museums have collections that were acquired in ethically compromised ways, including deceptive practices and outright theft. Colwell and the team wanted to cull the collections of such ethically challenged materials. Finally, the team wanted to ensure that the collection served to foster positive relationships with communities from where they came. Too many museums have collections of Native American material culture and almost no formal relationships with tribes, elders, and cultural experts.

Project Description

From the start, the team realized the mission statement was unachievable. Collections are large; histories and provenance can be murky, and tribes have many other pressing needs beyond the difficult work of repatriation. Nevertheless, the team felt the aspiration statement would guide their work on a day-to-day basis and inform their strategic planning over the long term. The team also hoped that by publicly stating and working toward such an aspiration, the museum might lead the way for other institutions.

In early 2008, the DMNS board of trustees revised the institution's ethics and collections policies; the anthropology team rewrote the statements pertaining to their collections to set the tone for their new approach. The new ethics policy explicitly stated that the museum would not accept illegally collected objects, that repatriation claims would be evaluated on the claimant community's own standards, and that the dignity of claimants mattered.

The NAGPRA section was straightforward, assigning operational responsibilities to ensure transparent and consistent processes in the museum's compliance-related work. The anthropology team recognized, however, that the collection involved international and other repatriation issues beyond the purview of NAGPRA. It therefore wrote into the new policy a broad process for the consideration of international repatriation claims based on the principles of "respect, reciprocity, justice, and dialogue."

To summarize, the museum agreed, in written policy, that it would not accept illegally acquired objects or those that were received under circumstances that encourage irresponsible destruction. It agreed that decisions regarding repatriation claims would be based not on Western museum and scientific standards but on the legal and ethical frameworks of a claimant's own community. The museum's repatriation work would be guided by publicly stated, morally driven virtues. Cross-cultural respect would be paramount in any evaluation. To some of the team's colleagues, both inside and outside the museum, this was (and is) radical stuff. But the trustees approved these policies in 2008, and they remain official museum policy.

At roughly the same time that the ethics and collection policies were being codified, the museum's Research and Collections Division decided to write and publish its first Long-Term Collections and Research Plan. That document included histories, summary overviews, and critical evaluations of each of the museum's twenty-four major subcollections, as well as five-year research and collections plans written by individual curators. At the department level, the anthropology team documented their new approach as follows.

"The new guiding principles of the (anthropology) collections at the DMNS will be respect, reciprocity, justice, and dialogue. *Respect* is honoring people and the things that make up their social lives and showing deep consideration of their personal autonomy and collective welfare. *Reciprocity* is creating relationships that are based on parity, the cooperative exchange of ideas and things. *Justice* is repairing past wrongs and treating all people fairly. *Dialogue* is committing to open, democratic, and sustained conversation.

"These principles do not entail the abandonment of "traditional" anthropological research but rather a new commitment to the ideal of benevolence—acknowledging anthropology's complicated legacy—that the discipline can and should do social good. The scientific use and long-term preservation of the collection will be pursued while embracing the respectful treatment of Native Americans, the mutual benefit for myriad stakeholders, and the evenhanded treatment of all people through open and sincere dialogue" (Colwell et al. 2008:39).

With the anthropology department thus remade, new ethics, collections, and repatriation policies in place, and long-term collections and research plans fully documented, Nash, Colwell, and the rest of the team set out, through the Repatriation Initiative, to bring the DMNS back into compliance with NAGPRA. They sought to go further by embracing the spirit, not just the letter, of the law. That meant they would go beyond NAGPRA's basic requirements to advance an anthropologically and ethically informed agenda to proactively collaborate with tribes and other stakeholders to address the often-odious legacies of museum collecting activities over the last century and more. The team pledged to address international repatriation issues as well.

Implementation and Anthropologists' Roles

Work proceeded on two fronts. First, as of 2006, the DMNS had a number of outstanding NAGPRA claims for sacred and communally owned objects. These claims had been submitted and in some cases were already found to be valid by museum officials, but they had not yet been acted upon. This part of the effort was relatively straightforward: simply reevaluate the legal basis for each claim under NAGPRA, make a decision, and follow through on it. Between 2006 and 2008, the team completed thirteen repatriations of forty-one objects—hardly enough to empty the storerooms, much less end science as we know it, as some shrill archaeologists and curators feared would happen under NAGPRA (for example, see Meighan 1992 and Turner 1986).

Second, the team focused on the Native American human remains in the collection. Some of these cases were also straightforward because NAGPRA claims had been previously submitted. Again, all the team had to do was (re)evaluate the claims, make decisions, and follow through. Holen had begun this important work in 2004, when he published the museum's first Notices of Inventory Completion. These are summaries of culturally affiliated human remains and associated funerary objects that get published in the *Federal Register*, the US government's public newspaper. Between 2004 and 2007, Holen published eight notices describing the remains of eleven individuals. Once the notice was published, control over the remains of these individuals was given over to their descendant tribes. By 2008, the museum was back in full compliance with NAGPRA.

With the museum in compliance, the team turned its attention to addressing the remaining Native American ancestors in the collections. All of them had previously been determined to be "culturally unaffiliated," which meant they could not be connected to any living tribe or descendant, most of which were thus subject to NAGPRA section 43 CFR 10.11, a section that provides guidance on how to determine the disposition of human remains that could not be affiliated with a federally recognized tribe or lineal descendants. The goal of this project phase was not to return the remains per se but rather to enter into meaningful consultation with all interested tribes and parties in such a way that a collective decision about the future of these remains could be made. Significantly, when the team began this work, section 43 CFR 10.11 was held "in reserve," meaning the section had yet to be written and formalized into law. Nevertheless, the team felt it had an obligation to proactively explore how it could move forward in addressing the problems raised by curating these human remains. When the final draft of 43 CFR 10.11 was promulgated in early 2010, the curators, in the midst of their efforts, were uniquely positioned to contribute to the public debate about the merits and shortcomings of this new part of the law.

Between 2008 and 2010, the team applied for and received three National Park Service (NPS) grants, totaling nearly $200,000, to address the future of 67 unaffiliated human remains subject to 43 CFR 10.11. They used the museum's (then-)novel satellite video teleconferencing technology as a basis to facilitate consultation with 142 tribes across the United States. These consultations led to formal disposition (the legal term for repatriation of unaffiliated remains) agreements, which involved the return of all 67 individuals to tribes for reburial in four geographic areas: West Coast, Southwest, Plains, and Northeast.

With this work complete, the DMNS only had the remains of 15 Native American individuals left to address. These last 15 were not subject to section 43 CFR 10.11 because, although the museum believed them to be "Native American" under the law, they had no geographic information and thus were subject to 43 CFR 10.15(b) of NAGPRA—a section of the law intended to address all other human remains and items that fell beyond the culturally affiliated and unaffiliated provisions. In 2012, the museum received its fourth NPS grant under the Repatriation Initiative. At the time, only a small number of museums had even attempted to return human remains subject to 43 CFR 10.15(b), so the team developed a new approach that began with key regional partners and eventually reached out to all 565 of the then-federally recognized tribes, as well as all relevant Native Hawaiian organizations and Native Alaskan groups, to seek their input. If all proceeded according to plan, the ancestors would be reburied with collective approval and specific leadership provided by regional tribes (see below).

The Repatriation Initiative was designed to work in conjunction with another related project, the DMNS anthropology department's Native American Sciences Initiative (NASI). Also established in 2008, the NASI sought to reformulate the museum's engagement with Native American communities, particularly seeking to provide mission-specific research and educational opportunities to Native Americans. The NASI is therefore an important complementary program because repatriation is often a backward-looking endeavor (trying to fix historical problems), while these outreach and research efforts are forward-looking (trying to build a new future). Specifically, the NASI included five components:

+ *Native American Annual Scholarship Program:* The museum awards annual scholarships to Native American high school, college, and graduate students who have demonstrated leadership, academic achievement, and an interest in science.
+ *Native American Science Career Day:* The museum hosted a day-long event in which notable Native American scientists and healthcare professionals come together with Native American middle school students to discuss science-related careers.
+ *Native American Internship Program:* The museum hosts annual, paid internships for up to three Native American college or graduate students each year, with potential funding for up to three years per student.
+ *Indigenous Fellowship Program:* The museum sporadically hosts Native American artists, elders, curators, scholars, and other professionals to study the sixty-thousand-piece anthropology collection or participate in some other aspect of the museum's work.
+ *Indigenous Film Program:* In partnership with the Indigenous Film and Arts Festival of Denver, the museum hosts a monthly viewing and discussion of a Native American–made film, often with the director, producer, or actors present.

A final component of the Repatriation Initiative is the effort to explore how repatriation can work outside of NAGPRA's mandates, as well as to consider the broader ethical stakes of repatriation debates for museums. Two projects exemplify this aspect of the team's work.

First, the museum sought to return thirty remarkable memorial statues to Kenya called *vigango* (singular: *kikango*). Carved out of wood in the form of decorated and abstract human males, with long, rectangular bodies and circular heads, *vigango* are publicly held memorials erected near the graves of notable men in the community. *Vigango* are more than just grave markers in the Western sense. The nine tribes of the Mijikenda, who carve *vigango*, believe they are living objects and the physical embodiment of a dead person's soul. Like totem poles in the northwest coast of North America, *vigango*, once erected, are to be left alone to decay through natural forces. Although made by individuals, *vigango* serve to protect entire communities of the Mijikenda culture.

The team used Weiner's (1985) concept of "inalienable possessions" to argue that, without an entire community's express consent, the *vigango* were by definition stolen, for they are inalienable. Most assuredly, *vigango* are not works of art to be held by or displayed in museums. The team knew they should return the *vigango* to the Mijikenda, even though they were not legally bound to do so. (NAGPRA does not apply to objects from Kenya because, among other things, the US government has no jurisdiction over Kenyan property and people, and rightfully so. The flip side is also true—the Kenyan government cannot simply pass a law declaring that foreign entities like US museums have to repatriate *vigango*.) The team struggled unsuccessfully to find anthropological colleagues or other museum and heritage professionals in Kenya with whom to collaborate and also failed to identify the specific communities in southeastern Kenya from which the *vigango* had been stolen. Nevertheless, the team's work on the *vigango* issue raised the visibility of the ethical and moral nature of repatriation work within the museum and beyond.

For the second project, in the summer of 2009, members of four grassroots 9/11 family advocacy groups reached out to several museum professionals, including Colwell, about the National September 11 Memorial and Museum being built at Ground Zero in New York City. Based on lengthy discussions with the 9/11 family members, several key problems emerged concerning how the new museum was proposing to help care for thousands of fragments of unidentified human remains. Drawing on his experiences with the repatriation debates as they have impacted Native American communities and broader anthropological and cross-cultural views of death and dying, Colwell became an informal advisor to the four 9/11 family groups. Although the groups and Colwell had little success shifting the 9/11 museum's plans, their efforts helped create a public dialogue about these controversies and problems.

Public awareness and scholarly engagement have been a vital part of the DMNS Repatriation Initiative for several reasons. First, the anthropology team believes its unique experiences can contribute to better public policy. Second, the public has a stake in how our nation's museums present the past and sustain living cultures. Publications resulting from this project vary from academic articles to op-ed contributions. Also, in their role as editors of the journal *Museum Anthropology* from 2009 through 2012, Nash and Colwell edited a special issue on the theme of NAGPRA's twentieth anniversary. By speaking openly—contributing to the academic literature and public debates—the Repatriation Initiative has sought to illuminate the profound impacts of repatriation on both museums and descendant communities.

Outcomes

The innovative and forward-looking Repatriation Initiative was a wide-ranging and groundbreaking project that illustrates how the tools of applied anthropology can work within museum anthropology. This pioneering, systematic, and comprehensive effort creatively confronted, head-on, one of the most difficult and polarizing issues facing museums in recent decades—providing solutions to past problems while establishing the foundation for new and better relations with Indigenous communities in the future. The specific and tangible accomplishments of this program through 2013 included:

+ establishment of formal ethics and collections policies and research and collections plans that embrace not just the letter but the spirit of repatriation law through the principles of respect, reciprocity, justice, and dialogue with all potential claimants;
+ successful implementation of three NPS grants totaling nearly $200,000, using novel satellite video-conferencing technology to consult with 142 tribes, leading to disposition agreements for 67 unaffiliated human remains subject to section 43 CFR 10.11;
+ acquisition of a fourth NPS grant of nearly $40,000 to address the future of 15 human remains, leading to repatriation and reburial in 2015;
+ successful implementation of the Native American Sciences Initiative, which has provided educational opportunities and financial support for Native American students, artists, professionals, and community members;
+ proactive grappling with the theft of and efforts to return 30 *vigango* from the Mijikenda of southeastern Kenya;
+ assistance to four 9/11 family advocacy groups in articulating their concerns about the care of unidentifiable human remains in the 9/11 museum complex at Ground Zero;
+ substantial contributions to the scholarly literature as well as active participation in public dialogues on these contentious matters.

One lesson learned through all of this was how legal frameworks mattered far less than the goodwill of museum administrators and tribal colleagues. While NAGPRA provided a straightforward process for uncontentious claims, it became clear to us over the years that many scenarios fall through the law's yawning chasms. To create a bridge over those gaps requires institutional and personal commitments about which the legislation says nothing.

For instance, we saw how the museum's president and its vice presidents over the last dozen years were genuinely unsettled to learn that the museum held stolen objects and that many Native communities felt our beloved institution violated their dignity and human rights. They did not hesitate to support the anthropology department in trying to set things right, to make amends and find common ground. They were not directed by the law in this desire to fix what was morally broken; it was their commitment to community and basic human decency.

The Anthropological Difference

The Repatriation Initiative specifically sought to bring anthropological viewpoints to bear on the questions of museum collections care. For human remains, the team specifically sought to situate the possession of Native American ancestors in the context of broad cross-cultural values of death, as well as to respect specific cultural practices and religious beliefs. To be blunt, the team viewed human remains not as specimens to be curated in perpetuity but as ancestors of various Native American communities, none of which had granted informed consent for their ancestors to be curated. In contrast, it is easy to understand how, for example, geneticists studying ancient DNA often struggle to find common ground with Native communities because their starting point is rarely traditional cultural beliefs and the historical context of scientific colonialism.

Our anthropological perspective allowed the museum to consult with hundreds of tribes with the general goal of addressing the respectful care of human remains while simultaneously following the particular goals and beliefs of individual tribes. For sacred and communally owned objects, the team used anthropological understandings of cultural items that could work within the confines of NAGPRA as well as outside of its purview. This allowed the museum to have flexibility to negotiate with all potential claimants whether or not repatriation law would strictly apply, as was the case with the *vigango* funerary statues from Kenya (see below).

Based on Colwell's research on collaborative methodologies, the department used a consultation model that went beyond legalistic strictures. Consultation at the DMNS placed, and continues to place, as much emphasis on process as on results—based on anthropological insights on the importance of relationship building (leading to trust, respect, and honesty) and strong cross-cultural partnerships. Just as significantly, the museum staff see repatriation as a form of social justice required for true reconciliation between tribes and museums. Although they recognize that returning stolen items or ancestral remains is neither punishment nor reparation, they see repatriation as an important step toward restorative justice, a way of coming to terms with the darker side of anthropology's history.

Epilogue

The DMNS Repatriation Initiative led to the reburial of 97 sets of human remains, 317 associated funerary objects, and 11 unassociated funerary objects, as well as to the repatriation of 231 sacred objects and objects of cultural patrimony. The museum is now out of the human remains business—it will no longer curate human remains in the absence of informed consent. It is also a recognized leader in the museum decolonization movement. Since submitting the successful Praxis Award application in 2013, a number of projects have been completed.

Culturally Unaffiliated Native American Remains without Geographic Information

Following the consultative process established under the NPS NAGPRA grants, the museum completed repatriations and reburials of all Native American human remains under its legal control. This included the difficult but important work of reaching out to every federally recognized tribe, Alaskan Native corporation, and Native Hawaiian organization, seeking their advice and consent on human remains that were "Native American" but without any geographical context. The only Native American ancestral remains left in the museum have been repatriated to two culturally affiliated tribes who have yet to find a suitable reburial location.

Non-native American Human Remains

The museum had in the collections the remains of twenty-seven individuals who the team believed were not "Native American" under NAGPRA, so the law did not apply in this context. Rather than let these unstudied, poorly provenienced remains sit on shelves, the team in 2015 held what they affectionately called the Bad Bar Joke Conference: they convened a rabbi, a priest, an imam, an agnostic, an atheist, a physical anthropologist, an archaeologist, a lawyer, a Cherokee tribal member, a professor of religious studies, and various and sundry museum staff. They collectively addressed the question of what to do with these remains, morally, legally, and ethically. In the end, attendees decided to bury the remains in a natural (i.e., no boxes, no chemicals) burial plot with a nondenominational ceremony. The team followed through with that pledge in two burial ceremonies held in late 2015 and mid-2016 in Crestone, Colorado.

Vigango

The *vigango* finally made it to the National Museums of Kenya in Nairobi in 2019. From there, they went to the Fort Jesus Museum in Mombasa, Kenya, near the Mijikenda's many sacred forests, from which the *vigango* were stolen. The effort to repatriate the *vigango* took many years and proceeded in fits and starts for a range of bureaucratic reasons. In the end, however, Nash visited the Mijikenda in October 2019, to celebrate with them the long-awaited return of their ancestors. Disturbingly, the total number of *vigango* still held by US museums is at least four hundred; it is hoped that those institutions will follow the DMNS lead in repatriating these culturally important objects.

The 9/11 Museum

Colwell continued his work with those 9/11 families who objected to the 9/11 Museum and Memorial's efforts to incorporate their loved ones into the museum experience. Unfortunately, all efforts failed, and the human remains room was incorporated into the museum's exhibition gallery.

Native American Sciences Initiative

The NASI was designed as a corollary to the Repatriation Initiative, created because the team felt a strong moral obligation to the source communities for the DMNS anthropology collections. Over the last dozen years, the NASI has directly benefitted various communities and talented individuals through scholarships, internships, and fellowships.

The museum has awarded $68,000 in scholarships to 30 high school, college, and graduate students representing nearly a dozen tribes. It has granted $110,000 in internships to nearly a dozen graduate and undergraduate students (two former interns are now university professors; one is a tribal historic preservation officer). It has hosted professional artists, elders, educators, and other professionals from various tribes. It continues to host the monthly Indigenous Film Festival at the museum.

Repatriation is far more than a bureaucratic process, which is why the museum's Repatriation Initiative must be considered with its Native American Sciences Initiative. Repatriation involves a long chain of events that unfold over many years—from shaping policies to holding meetings, from writing endless emails to sending letters, from making difficult phone calls to navigating arguments, and from sharing meals to shedding tears. All these activities lead to the repatriation and reburial of Native American peoples and their possessions. For many Native Americans and the museum staff who do this important work, repatriations never quite end. Memories of reburied people linger; new relationships formed among the living continue.

That being said, the team knows that many of their museological and scholarly colleagues have whispered about their repatriation efforts. Many of the decisions that they have made were intentionally radical—made to demonstrate an alternative pathway for museums to confront their histories and reshape the field's future. Simply put, the team felt it was important for a major natural history museum to play a leadership role in repatriation and to demonstrate that a progressive approach to repatriation does not decimate a collection. Rather, it leads to better, more informed, and more inclusive anthropology, archaeology, exhibitions, art, and science.

Stephen E. Nash is director of anthropology and senior curator of archaeology at the Denver Museum of Nature & Science, where he has worked for fifteen years. He currently conducts archaeological fieldwork on Mogollon sites in west-central New Mexico (USA) and has conducted archaeological research in places ranging from Neanderthal sites in France to the majestic cliff dwellings of Mesa Verde National Park in southwestern Colorado (USA). He has written and edited seven books, the most recent of which is *Pushing Boundaries: Proceedings of the 18th Southwest Symposium*, scheduled to be published in 2022. From 1999 to 2006 he served as head of collections in the Department of Anthropology at the Field Museum in Chicago. He writes the Curiosities column at SAPIENS.org and performs science-based stand-up comedy with ScienceRiot. He received his PhD in anthropology from the University of Arizona in 1997.

Chip Colwell is the founding editor in chief of SAPIENS, the digital anthropology magazine of the Wenner-Gren Foundation. He received his PhD in anthropology in 2004 from Indiana University. From 2007 to 2020, he was the senior curator of anthropology at the Denver Museum of Nature & Science, and has held fellowships and grants with the American Academy of Arts & Sciences, the National Science Foundation, the National Endowment for the Humanities, and the J. William Fulbright Program. He is the author and editor of twelve books, most recently *Objects of Survivance: A Material History of American Indian Education* (with Lindsay Montgomery) and *Plundered Skulls and Stolen Spirits: Inside the Fight to Reclaim Native America's Culture*, which won six prizes, including the 2020 Society for Historical Archaeology James

Deetz Book Award. His essays and editorials have appeared in the *New York Times, The Atlantic, The Guardian,* and many other popular outlets.

References

Colwell, C., S. E. Nash, and S. R. Holen. 2008. Denver Museum of Nature & Science Long Term Collections and Research Plan. Unpublished manuscript on file, Denver Museum of Nature & Science Archives.

Meighan, C. W. 1992. "Some Scholars' Views on Reburial." *American Antiquity* 57(4): 704–10.

Turner, C. G. 1986. "What Is Lost with Skeletal Reburial." *Quarterly Review of Archaeology* 7(1): 1–3.

Weiner, A. B. 1985. "Inalienable Wealth." *American Ethnologist* 12(2): 210–27.

CHAPTER 8

~:~

Alan Boraas and Kahtnuht'ana Qenaga
Preserving and Renewing an Alaska Native Language

KERRY D. FELDMAN AND PHYLLIS A. FAST

Project Background

The motivating problem for this project is that the Kenai (Alaska) dialect of the Dena'ina Dené, or Athabascan language, is among the world's most endangered. No active speakers remain; however, primarily because of the renowned Dena'ina elder and scholar Peter Kalifornsky (Kalifornsky, Kari, and Boraas 1991), a large body of recorded and written material exists in the Kenai dialect.

For those not familiar with the Dené language family, of which the Kenaitze language is a member, it is one of the most geographically widespread language families in the world. Dené-Yeniseian is thought today to extend from the Russian Far East through Alaska and Canada to the US Southwest (spoken by the current Navaho and Apache peoples who moved southward in the thirteenth century), and to the southern US Pacific Coast.

The context of language loss for the Dena'ina involved three key events. In 1838–39, half of the Kenai Dena'ina died in a smallpox epidemic that swept through coastal Alaska. Traditional cosmologies expressed the idea that "everything happens for a reason," and the reason may be something someone did, said, or thought. Consequently, the emotional burden on the survivors was immeasurable. The Russian Orthodox Church expressed the idea that events happened because of "God's will," an idea that made significant inroads, with the church's Slavonic language becoming a tool to express spirituality at the expense of Dena'ina language and spirituality.

In addition, starting in 1881, the commercial salmon canning industry came to Cook Inlet in southwest Alaska, and within twenty years it dominated economic life there. The language of the workplace where many Dena'ina people began to work was English, and Dena'ina became severely marginalized as a language.

Perhaps the most significant event in language loss was the forced language extinction policy carried out by the American Territorial Schools in Cook Inlet until the 1960s. Students as young as eight years old had their mouths washed out with soap or were beaten for speaking Dena'ina. A generation grew up conflicted about and ashamed of their language. By 1974, there were only three individuals who admitted to speaking the Kenai dialect of Dena'ina. Two would die shortly thereafter, but one, tribal elder Kalifornsky, himself a victim of school beatings for speaking his language, learned to write his language and embarked on a dedicated and emotionally taxing nineteen-year agenda to write as many of the tribe's stories as he could remember.

The difficulty of Dené/Athabascan languages is legendary. As with all Dené languages, the verb form, consisting of nineteen or more prefixes and a stem, also a bound morpheme, is complex in two ways. First, use of any given prefix may dictate the addition or deletion of another prefix. Second, there are complex phonological changes, many specific to regional dialects, that further complicate learning the language.

Figure 8.1. Alan Boraas (*left*) with Kenaitze elder Peter Kalifornsky (*right*) reading from the book Boraas and James Kari helped Kalifornsky to publish in 1991: *Dena'ina Legacy: K'tl'egh'i Sukdu: The Collected Writings of Peter Kalifornsky.* Photo courtesy of Kenai Peninsula College.

Local anthropology professor Alan Boraas and James Kari (linguist, Alaska Native Language Center, University of Alaska Fairbanks) helped tribal elder Kalifornsky produce several books. His final book, *K'tl'egh'i sukdu (Remaining Stories): The Collected Writings of Peter Kalifornsky* (1991), won the Book of the Year Award from the Before Columbus Foundation in 1992. Kalifornsky died the following year at the age of eighty-three. Recognizing the importance of "thinking in our Native language," the Kenaitze Tribe embarked on a policy to enable its members and others to read and write Dena'ina and engaged Boraas in assisting in this project.

Project Description

The Kenaitze Indian Tribe (an Indian Reorganization Act [IRA] of 1934, federally recognized tribe) of Alaska, through its cultural programs director, Alexandra Lindgren, obtained project funding through a series of Administration for Native American grants and a Cook Inlet Tribal Council grant via the US Forest Service, with additional funding provided by the University of Alaska Anchorage and Kenai Peninsula College, where Boraas worked. The funding goal: literacy for tribal members and the broader community in a language that had never actively been written or read and that is structurally among the most complicated in the world.

The primary tools used for this language restoration effort were the writings of tribal elder Kalifornsky, assembled in *A Dena'ina Legacy: K'tl'egh'i Sukdu: The Collected Writings of Peter Kalifornsky*, via audio tapes of most of the stories in that book; *Morphology and Semantics of the Tanaina Verb* (Tenenbaum 1978); *Dena'ina Topical Dictionary* (noun dictionary) (Kari 2007); and an unpublished electronic draft of James Kari's verb theme dictionary, as well as Boraas's thirty-seven years of working with and on behalf of the Kenaitze Indian Tribe, IRA, who were the clients for the project.

At the time of the development of the language-learning website project, no members of the Kenaitze fully read, spoke, or wrote their native language.

Boraas, carrying forward the holistic methods of Franz Boas, learned this difficult language and how to teach it. He learned it at the feet of Kalifornsky, with whom he worked for many years. The complexity and interconnectivity of the language is such that it is difficult to build a sequential, progressively more complex curriculum as is normally done in language learning. The solution employed in this project was to use the functions of the internet and a resource website to provide text with audio and utilize HTML hyperlink features to click back and forth among web pages so that a learner can understand the structure of a Dena'ina sentence from an actual speaker.

The implications of understanding a native language, following the Boasian dictum—if you are going to understand the culture, you must understand the language—are quite relevant here. Two examples illustrate its significance for Dena'ina. First, much of cognitive anthropology traces its intellectual development to folk taxonomies and schema theory resting primarily on the nominative naming of the world (emphasis is on nouns) and its resultant cultural representation. Not so with Dena'ina, which is verb-based, and verbs might function as nouns. Boraas wrote, "Moreover, the Dena'ina verb is not only a verb in the English sense of the term, indicating action or state of being, but contains a great deal of additional information such as who is involved in the speech event (pronouns) and a system to classify nouns as belonging to certain conceptual categories. A verb is frequently a sentence in itself." For example, *nuntnghel'ił* means "I will see you again."[1]

Cognitive anthropology might have a significantly different history if it emerged from an Athabascan language. The irony should not be lost on cognitive anthropologists; the implicit assumptions of that which they study, human cognition, are rooted in the nominative nature of the Germanic and Indo-European language in which they speak and write. Boraas was aware of these complexities and of the challenge they present to cognitive anthropological theory.

Implementation and Anthropologist's Role

Boraas, a trained four-field anthropologist, acquired a basic understanding of linguistics, HTML and web work, and how to construct a language website. As noted, he also learned the complex Dena'ina language and related cognitive anthropology theory. The creation of this resource and language-learning website culminated thirty-seven years of his collaborative anthropological association with the Kenaitze Indian Tribe, IRA. Boraas was the only anthropologist working on this project; he had one assistant, legally blind but with acute hearing ability, to help sort through the unusual sounds of Dena'ina and visually represent them for a reader of the website. Boraas also hired a web designer and learned to code HTML himself.

Anthropological theory grows out of immersion in, and later reflective examination of, the anthropologist's engagement with (praxis regarding) lived lives. Without our anthropological theories and methods, our practice to better the lives of others would be little different than social work or neoliberal humanism. The latter are admirable but are not what we have to offer for bettering the lives of others. "Bettering" the lives of others requires acknowledging and respecting their Otherness, not simply enabling them to be more "like us" and thus "successful" as "we" define success.

With this understanding, we move to a further consideration. We felt it necessary to preface our next paragraph with the above so that a reader understands why we introduced postmodern concepts into what appears to be a "practicing" volume. We must examine the postmodern deconstruction theory of Jacques Derrida (Derrida 1978).

Although Boraas taught at a rural community college in Alaska, he was a tripartite faculty member required to conduct research and was cognizant of how the intellectual awareness of the Western world related to his project on behalf of the Kenaitze. One version of Derrida's theory regarding the need for "deconstruction" of "texts" that influenced Boraas's work is that inherent in all binary opposites, thinking is the tyranny of the mind that one opposite is superior to the other. Deconstruction forces to consciousness the implicit superiority of binary oppositions such as male/female, civilized/primitive, or democracy/tribal and the political manipulation that results from the uncritical application.

In the Dena'ina language, singular is one or two, and plural is three or more. Deconstruction, in a sense, is already done by the grammar, Boraas noted, making binary opposition more ambiguous in Dena'ina than in European languages. These and many other patterns of thought are what Dena'ina people gain by an understanding of their language through literacy.

Outcomes

Through the efforts of Alan Boraas, the Kahtnuht'ana Qenaga (Kenai Peoples Language) resource website provides tribal members a means for learning how to read, write, and speak the Kenai dialect of Dena'ina wherever they now reside, whether in the United States or elsewhere in the world. This extraordinary project includes orthography, vocabulary, grammar, story translations, and ethnogeography, integrating words, images, and audio recordings from the last speakers of the Kenai dialect.

Another component was the insertion of ethnogeography into the project website, which is intended to mirror the mind of a traditional Dena'ina. Such a person would have had a mental map of his/her territory organized by place names. Since places exude information about events associated with a place in their traditional culture, they also became a moral landscape of good and bad events expressing values and identity.

The Anthropological Difference

This project of Boraas's, and indeed his larger professional life, reflect the goal of fostering the practice of anthropological theory, methods, and ethics to better the lives of others. Not just "do it" for "them" but *with them*—in this case, with an Alaska Native Tribe determined to regain their cultural identity and confront the globalization of the twenty-first century with their own world-view that is enshrined in their language.

On the theoretical level, the structure and organization of this project is an application of the still-controversial Sapir-Whorf hypothesis that language influences thought (Sapir 1929; Whorf 1940). While controversial, it was un-derstood to be true by Kenaitze tribal leadership and Boraas: language does influence thought, in this case at the grammatical level, and it is that under-standing that sustains the revitalization of their language.

Methodologically, this project utilized the kind of collaborative research and praxis referred to in anthropology as "participatory action research." Bo-raas worked with the client group on a project they envisioned, relying on language texts provided by Kenaitze elders who spoke the language that he and a linguistic colleague (James Kari) had recorded years earlier. Boraas learned the Dena'ina language, one of the most difficult languages in the world, adhering to the fundamental insight of Boas regarding the need to know the language of people if one wishes to know their cultural worldview deeply.

Place names are significant in the culture and traditional worldview of the Kenaitze. Prior to being asked to develop the resource website for their lan-guage, Boraas spent many years hiking the mountains and valleys of their geo-graphic area to see, photograph, and experience those peaks, rivers, and locales. In winters he engaged in cross-country skiing trips and winter camping to ex-perience them during the long Alaska winter, as the Dena'ina would have en-gaged in winter hunting and trapping. Gaining the trust of the tribe to develop a website for their language renewal effort (establishing rapport) occurred over three decades of participant observation among them, resulting in honorary tribal membership for Boraas in 2000.

Conclusion

Some results of Alan's work after the submission of the initial award applica-tion are as follows.

He presented a powerful paper, "People of the Verb: Observation on Language-Mediated Habitus among the Dena'ina of Alaska," at the Athabas-can Identity Symposium, Alaska Anthropological Association Conference, Fairbanks, Alaska, 17 March 2007. He lectured widely about this project, in-cluding "The Moral Landscape of the Dena'ina of Cook Inlet, Alaska," a talk given at the Indigenous Peoples and Place Seminar, Arizona State University, Tempe, 31 March 2009.

Kenaitze Dena'ina cultural identity and pride have been significantly enhanced by this project, younger Dena'ina have an accessible medium for learning their language, and mutual respect is enhanced among intergenerational tribal members who participate in summer language workshops that were conducted by Boraas in conjunction with linguists and Dena'ina elders. More than sixty Dena'ina participants have been involved in summer workshops related to this project, and Kenaitze Athabascans within and outside of Alaska now look to this extraordinary website as a means of connecting with their traditional cultural worldview.

One of Boraas's young Dena'ina protégés, Aaron Leggett (from another Dena'ina village, Eklutna, 120 miles from Kenai) can now read, write, and speak basic Dena'ina. He recently completed a bachelor's degree in anthropology at the University of Alaska Anchorage. His goal is to become a practicing, professional anthropologist; others will follow. Aaron holds the position of curator of Alaska history and culture at the Anchorage Museum at the Rasmuson Center. Boraas turned over to Aaron and all Dena'ina the tools needed to reclaim and renew their culture.

Our friend and distinguished colleague, Alan Boraas, died 4 November 2019, following a stroke. The director of the Kenai Peninsula College wrote, "It's not a legacy that he has left just at KPC. It's a legacy to the state, the borough, so many people. What he did with native languages and cultural research . . . it goes way beyond the realm of the college." He was posthumously named a University of Alaska Anchorage emeritus professor at his Celebration of Life. As this book went to press, there was a bill before the Alaska Legislature to rename College Road to Alan Boraas Road, and it is expected to be approved.

You can hear Boraas's engaging and challenging lecture "Yaghanen, the Time Before," a discussion about the lives of the Dena'ina people who have lived and thrived in the region for a thousand years, presented to the Kasilof Regional Historical Association, at https://www.kdll.org/post/spring-2019-yaghanen-time.

Alan Boraas enthralls us in a talk with his grasp of the Dena'ina culture. His and the Tribe's extraordinary language website can be accessed at https://web.kpc.alaska.edu/denaina/.

Kerry D. Feldman completed his MA and PhD in anthropology on a National Institute of Mental Health Fellowship at the University of Colorado, Boulder; dissertation topic: squatter settlements Davao City, the Philippines (1973). He served as social science consultant for the Davao City medical *katiwala* project, which developed into a new medical school to serve inner city squatter health needs. He specializes in urban anthropology, anthropological theory and research methods, applied anthropology, anthropology through literature, and

Alaska. He cofounded with Jack Lobdell the Alaska Anthropological Association in 1974. Today, he writes and publishes literary and historical western fiction and is professor emeritus of anthropology at the University of Alaska Anchorage.

Phyllis A. Fast received a BA in English from the University of Alaska Fairbanks, an interdisciplinary MA in anthropology and English on Alaska Native Literary Forms from the University of Alaska Anchorage, and a PhD in social anthropology from Harvard University (1998). Fast also was a gallery artist in Anchorage. Before her death in 2019, she was a professor of anthropology and liberal studies at the University of Alaska Anchorage. She is the author of *Northern Athabascan Survival: Women, Community, and the Future*. Her aunt was the first Alaska Native woman to graduate from the University of Alaska in Fairbanks (1935). Her grandfather, Arthur Harper, was one of the first to discover gold in the Yukon Valley, and, with Jake LaDue, he built Dawson City. Walter Harper, her Athabascan great-uncle, was the first person to reach the top of Mount Denali (1913). She received professor emerita status from UAA upon her retirement.

Notes

Editors' Note: Per submission options for the Praxis Award, the original application was submitted by the authors on behalf of Alan Boraas. Coauthor Phyllis Fast has since passed away. Alan Boraas himself also passed away in 2019. Kerry D. Feldman provided the revisions and updates to this chapter.

1. For more detail about the structure of the Dena'ina language, visit the resource website at http://qenaga.org/language.html.

References

Boas, F. 1940. *Race, Language, and Culture*. Chicago: University of Chicago Press.

Boraas, A. n.d. "An Introduction to Dena'ina Grammar: The Kenai (Outer Inlet) Dialect." http://web.kpc.alaska.edu/denaina/documents/denaina_grammar.pdf.

Derrida, J. 1978. *Writing and Difference*. Translated by A. Bass. Chicago: University of Chicago Press.

Kalifornsky, P., J. Kari, and A. Boraas. 1991. *A Dena'ina Legacy: K'tl'egh'i Sukdu: The Collected Writings of Peter Kalifornsky*. Fairbanks: Alaska Native Language Center.

Kari, J. 2007. *Dena'ina Topical Dictionary*. Fairbanks: Alaska Native Language Center.

KDLL 91.9 FM. 2019. "Yaghanen, the Time Before." Retrieved 5 August 2021 from https://www.kdll.org/post/spring-2019-yaghanen-time#stream/0.

Kenai Peninsula College. n.d. Kahtnuht'ana Qenaga (Kenai Peoples Language). Retrieved 5 August 2021 from https://web.kpc.alaska.edu/denaina/index.html.

Sapir, E. 1929. "The Status of Linguistics as a Science." *Language* 5: 207–14. Reprinted in *The Selected Writings of Edward Sapir in Language, Culture, and Personality*, edited by D. G. Mandelbaum, 160–66. Berkeley: University of California Press.

Tenenbaum, J. 1978. "Morphology and Semantics of the Tanaina Verb." PhD diss., Columbia University, New York.

Whorf, B. L. 1940. "Science and Linguistics." *Technology Review* 42: 227–31, 247–48. Reprinted in *Language, Thought, and Reality: Selected Writings of Benjamin Lee Whorf*, edited by J. B. Carroll, 207–19. Cambridge, MA/New York: The Technology Press of MIT/Wiley, 1956.

CHAPTER 9

~:~

San Diego's Little Saigon
Using Anthropologically Informed Outreach to Create a New Public Space

STEPHEN WEIDLICH

Project Background

With the fall of Saigon in 1975, thousands of Vietnamese citizens were forced to leave their homeland in search of safer and more prosperous futures. Many came to the United States and settled in neighborhoods along the West Coast. One of these initial gateway neighborhoods is now the location of the Little Saigon district, a six-block commercial area located along El Cajon Boulevard, a historic thoroughfare between the communities of Talmadge and Teralta East in the City of San Diego, California.

According to the 2010 US Census, the City of San Diego is home to more than thirty-five thousand Vietnamese residents, and much of the original immigrant community is still present along El Cajon Boulevard. Many have invested in the community over time, and a majority of the commercial and retail properties were owned by individuals of Vietnamese descent. Despite a history of investment and community participation, however, the neighborhood has lacked a cohesive identity and culturally relevant public space. The Little Saigon Design Guidelines developed by the project team described in this chapter sought to address these challenges and provide the connective threads to unite the public realm around these Vietnamese restaurants, markets, and retail shops.

Conducted in 2011–12, The Little Saigon Design Guidelines project was a collaborative effort between the Little Saigon Foundation, the El Cajon Boulevard Business Improvement Association, City of San Diego leadership, and a team from AECOM, an engineering and infrastructure design company with a focus on landscape architecture composed of designers, outreach specialists, and myself—a cultural anthropologist. Through comprehensive and innovative outreach techniques, the team developed and facilitated a planning process that placed a cohesive design vision for the Little Saigon district within reach for the community at large. Once fully realized, the plan would inform the design of in an iconic destination promoting cultural, social, and economic prosperity.

The planning and outreach processes explored how social and cultural influences could be manifested most powerfully through designing and, ultimately, establishing an identity unique to the Little Saigon district. For the plan to reach its full potential, it was vital to have the community participate in the vision and planning process. An early site tour with members of the Little Saigon Foundation and the project team laid the groundwork for the project goals and overall aim of the project. Outreach events served to explore and record the ideas, goals, and concerns about the neighborhood and about enhancing the identity of Little Saigon. During a community outreach event held during the annual Tet (New Year) Festival, planning and outreach specialists spoke with residents and visitors about their desires for the district. The questions and resulting feedback extended beyond more traditional concerns for lighting, safety, and cleanliness and began an ongoing discussion about cultural forms, colors, and iconography, and how these concepts could be authentically expressed in a streetscape environment.

Project Description

The overall objective for the Little Saigon Design Guidelines project was to assist the Little Saigon Foundation and the El Cajon Business Improvement Association in developing a set of public space design guidelines that could be used as a foundational planning document for the neighborhood. The Little Saigon Foundation is a nonprofit group focused on revitalizing community infrastructure and promoting Vietnamese culture and tourism in the community. The El Cajon Business Improvement Association is composed of over one thousand small businesses and was focused on improving economic vitality of El Cajon Boulevard, on which Little Saigon is situated.

Once completed, both nonprofit entities hoped that the design guidelines could be used to influence the establishment of a more visually cohesive Little Saigon ethnic business district within the City of San Diego and help guide the design and aesthetics of public space improvements, zoning, and planning within the neighborhood. The president of the Little Saigon Foundation stated at an early project meeting, "The key element here is identity and ownership. . . . By branding a business sector as a 'Little Saigon' district, we give everyone in that area a sense of pride and ownership."

The Little Saigon Foundation had met previously with other landscape architects and planning consultants on these issues, and some preliminary ideas
had been suggested. However, many of these ideas consisted of a singular gateway design element (i.e., a large sign), and civic leaders were unimpressed with
the perceived lack of creativity and public involvement in the previously developed design documents. Little Saigon Foundation leaders believed that the design guidelines should take into consideration the perspectives of community
members and other stakeholders; however, community leaders were finding it
difficult to obtain diverse perspectives on the future of the business district
due to a limit in time, personnel, and funding. Ultimately, the Little Saigon
Foundation and El Cajon Business Improvement Association reached out to
my employer at the time, AECOM, for assistance.

AECOM had an internal program that supported its employees' participation in pro bono efforts in the local community and around the world, and the
opportunity to assist the Little Saigon Foundation was an excellent match for
the mission of AECOM's pro bono program and the skillset of the local landscape architecture staff. In initial meetings between the Little Saigon Foundation and AECOM, foundation representatives stressed that meaningful public
involvement was an element missing from earlier attempts to develop design
guidelines and that they were struggling with the development of outreach approaches that could engage a diverse public that had been historically underserved by traditional communication strategies like public meetings. It was at
this point that the AECOM landscape architecture staff reached out to me, a
cultural anthropologist and ethnographer, and other members of our professional public outreach staff within the company. As part of the outreach team
for the project, I assisted with the overall outreach approach, participated in
project meetings with Little Saigon Foundation members, and coordinated and
implemented the participatory photography workshop that formed the cornerstone of the project's outreach effort.

Implementation and Anthropologist's Role

The AECOM landscape architecture team and the public outreach team
worked in the same office and had historically participated on the same projects. It was not uncommon for both teams to be involved in large projects like
massive highway realignments or planned community developments. Typically,
the landscape architecture team would develop various design alternatives
based on the engineering needs of the client within the limits of the landscape
and budget, after which the public outreach team would solicit feedback from
community members on the alternatives as to what could be changed or improved. Depending on the scope of the project, this cycle would repeat until

the alternatives were finalized and carried forward for more in-depth environmental review.

While this standard approach had resulted in a number of well-received infrastructure and community development projects, members of both the landscape architecture team and the public outreach team had always thought that design alternatives might be better served if public input was brought in earlier in the process. Members of the public outreach team, including myself, would respectfully tease our design colleagues that they would typically close themselves off in a room and, after a week or two, designs would miraculously emerge, fully formed, with no outside input. In discussing this process with members of the design team, we discovered a clear conflict: On one hand, they were trained professionals hired for their sense of artistic vision for the space. Many had also been part of processes where too many outside opinions had served to dilute more dynamic or innovative ideas or, worse, where members of the public had strongly requested something technically infeasible and felt betrayed when their ideas were not incorporated into initial plans. On the other hand, members of our landscape architecture team strongly believed that early public outreach could be beneficial, especially for projects where there could be cultural unfamiliarity between our designers and the community. It was rare, however, for a client to invest in this early outreach effort, despite there being interest and a clear need.

The request for assistance from the Little Saigon Foundation had been originally routed to our landscape architecture team. As noted above, there was intense interest by the Little Saigon Foundation to incorporate the views of the community in the design process during the early stages. It is not an exaggeration to state that many staffers—both designers and outreach team members—reacted with "Finally!" to hearing the news of this request. We believed that this project could be an excellent opportunity to finally demonstrate a different approach to urban landscape design, carefully taking into consideration community input early in the process. Additionally, as our project was pro bono, we were given substantial freedom in the development of our approach and could incorporate a number of new methodologies that had historically been considered cost- or time-prohibitive by paying clients.

During early meetings, the project team decided that an excellent way to get early input on guiding themes and preliminary design ideas would be to solicit ideas from neighborhood visitors during the annual Tet Festival. We believed that outreach during this event would provide the opportunity to get a range of ideas from all kinds of stakeholder groups, including neighborhood residents, business owners, and visitors, as well as a cross-section of various ethnic, gender, and socioeconomic groups. We created a number of displays identifying the Little Saigon business district along El Cajon Boulevard as well as large notepads for members of the community and visitors to write down their ideas regarding their own visions for Little Saigon. Volunteers from the Little Saigon

Foundation were on hand to provide English/Vietnamese translation services for members of the community, while English/Spanish bilingual AECOM staff were also present. The project team and I used the following discussion questions to elicit input from attendees at the Tet Festival:

+ What would you like to see improved?
+ Are there aspects of the neighborhood that you like? What is being done right?
+ What would like to see more of/less of?
+ What do you want the Little Saigon district to be like in twenty years?

Our booth was centrally located near the main performance stage, where substantial foot traffic passed throughout the day, leading to the project team capturing a wide range of perspectives from residents, business owners, and visitors. Between traditional dancing and singing performances, visitors to our outreach booth provided ideas that the landscape architecture team later categorized into the following issue areas:

+ Safety and Security
+ Art, Color, and Aesthetics
+ Cultural Influences
+ Circulation and Wayfinding
+ Gathering Spaces
+ Identity Building
+ Greenery

Following the Tet Festival outreach event, the public outreach team and I developed a participatory photography workshop to engage a more targeted subset of community members. The public outreach team and I had been developing a participatory photography workshop methodology prior to our involvement in the Little Saigon Design Guidelines project, but we had not had the opportunity to implement it. Once we considered the unique challenges of outreach associated with the Little Saigon project, we decided that a participatory photography workshop could be an excellent fit. We believed that a participatory photography workshop would be an engaging activity for community residents and business owners and would lead participants to interact with their neighborhood with an eye toward aesthetics and design; this would lead to a more fruitful discussion during the focus group/workshop setting for the landscape architecture team. Additionally, the public outreach team and I believed that a participatory photography exercise would provide all workshop participants with the capacity to engage in the input process regardless of their relative English-language proficiency.

The format, which loosely followed the "Photovoice" workshop format used with great success elsewhere,[1] required participants to explore the Little Saigon district and photograph those aspects of the community that meant something to them or to respond to set of prompts provided by the outreach team and me. After taking these photos, the process required that participants reconvene and discuss the photographs they had taken, exploring the reasons why they captured a particular image, and examine the potential public space design implications of the captured imagery. Our initial meeting focused on the project objectives, photography fundamentals, and ethics for taking photographs in public spaces. We also discussed some of the more concrete challenges associated with photography workshops, including what kind of camera to use, where to get film, whether cell phone cameras were adequate for the project (a point of debate in 2012), and how to transmit final photographs to the project team for organization. Finally, we prompted the participants with the following questions to consider as they took photos throughout the community:

+ What do you like about your community?
+ What aspect of your community are you the proudest of?
+ What should there be more of to make a Little Saigon district?
+ What should there be less of to make a Little Saigon district?
+ If you were showing around someone from out of town and they wanted to see "Little Saigon," where would you go, and what would you do?

One of the benefits of participatory photography that the project team and I appreciated, as a technique, was that it actively involved community members as part of the research team, providing them the ability to influence the project design and take ownership of the project process—which was a primary objective of the Little Saigon Foundation and its partnership with the AECOM team. While using photographs to elicit information is not a new concept (for example, see Collier 1957), the process of directly involving the community in the generation and analysis of photographs meaningful to them has become more common recently as a community-based social science tool. This methodology has proven successful in the past because of its accessibility of the process across all ages, education levels, and cultures. Also, the process is helpful in capturing visual ideas, influencing policy, and emphasizing individual and community action.

After the initial meeting, participants were given two weeks to take pictures throughout the neighborhood and submit them to the project team. The public outreach staff and I worked together to collect the photographs and print them out for the second meeting, a focus-group session during which the photographs would be discussed. The project team and I took the printed photos and organized them by participant on tables throughout the room. Many participants took dozens of photographs, and we quickly realized early in the collection process that it would be impossible to discuss all of the photos in one afternoon session. To focus the discussion, I asked participants to select three of their photos to present and discuss with the group. Then, participants were asked to select a photo from someone else's collection that—despite not being taken by them—made them consider something new that was worthy of discussion. This process resulted in the selection of four photographs per participant for discussion, which was more manageable. During the next phase of the workshop, we projected the photographs on a large screen, and I facilitated a discussion about each photograph, first asking the photographers why they selected the images to discuss. I then opened the discussion to the group and tried to focus on how the ideas captured in the image could inform the design of a public space. Throughout the session, members of the public outreach team and landscape architecture team took careful notes.

While the group discussed the selected photographs, members of our outreach team printed multiple smaller copies of the selected photographs, creating a full set for each participant. I then asked each group member to use the photographs in a pile sorting exercise. Pile sorting is a systematic, qualitative data collection technique by which participants take items in a particular domain (e.g., plants, illnesses, locations, etc.) that are printed on small cards and organize them into discrete piles based on their relationships with one another; like is placed with like.

Figure 9.1. Little Saigon Design Guidelines project participants sort through photographs of individual community features as part of a project research exercise. © Stephen Weidlich.

Generally, participants are not directed as to how many piles they should make. After the cards are sorted, the anthropologist typically asks the participants to explain their thoughts behind their sorting decisions. This process is repeated across multiple participants, and the cards and piles are recorded for each person. Eventually, patterns should emerge as to which cards tend to be placed into the same piles by multiple participants. Statistical software can be used to quantify the relationships between various card items, with those cards regularly falling into the same pile across multiple participants showing a stronger statistical relationship with one another than with other card items. Combined with interview data and other information, the researcher can explore connections between those items most closely related quantitatively, potentially uncovering overarching cultural concepts that relate certain domain items with one another (for more information, see Weller and Romney 1988).

I had used pile sorting exercises in previous projects, and I found the technique beneficial in a few ways. First, I had found that pile sorting was an engaging technique for participants. In general, participants enjoyed physically manipulating the various cards, and the concept of placing cards with similar items together usually made intuitive sense. Second, I had found the process to be a relatively rapid way to systematically research the relationships between items in a domain across multiple respondents when time and other resources were limited. Finally, I had found that the mathematical analysis conducted to quantify the relationships between domain items to be readily accessible by clients, who also appreciated a systematic approach to qualitative data collection.

This project was the first time I had attempted to use photographs instead of words written on card stock. However, I believed that it was possible to gain a deeper level of understanding of the concepts illustrated in the photographs (which could be abstract) if participants were able to group similar photographs together. After describing the process and the purpose of the exercise, I met individually with participants, recorded their piles, and quickly interviewed them regarding their piles and the mental processes each participant had as they sorted the photographs. After the focus group sessions, I aggregated the pile sort results for each participant and calculated their statistical relationships with other photographs using Anthropac software. The resulting x/y values were used to create a graphic representation of the quantitative similarities and differences between the individual photographs, with thematically similar photographs (i.e., those photographs grouped together by multiple participants) located closer to one another in two-dimensional space. Although the number of participants was relatively small for this methodology, a few clear clusters were present in the analysis. These included:

+ photographs identifying aspects of the community that should be accentuated in the design document;
+ photographs identifying aspects of the community that could be improved;

+ photographs detailing the individual people and items that make the Little Saigon district stand apart from other communities.

The outreach team and I expected the first two categories to be clear in the data, as the prompts provided to participants requested these kinds of pictures. However, the third cluster was unique, as these photographs served as a way for participants to show details of the community of which they were most proud, including civic pride, friendship, and perseverance. The landscape architecture team found the discussion surrounding the photographs in the first two clusters to be largely intuitive, as the ideas expressed echoed many of the sentiments captured during the Tet Festival outreach event as well as the team's own ideas from a professional planning perspective. However, the landscape architecture team found this third cluster to be particularly insightful into the design guidelines development process because they touched on more abstract concepts that had not been expressed in other venues.

Outcomes

The design guidelines for Little Saigon provided the framework for creating a unique cultural district experience. The community engagement and stakeholder meetings, including the participatory photography workshop, produced a set of guiding themes that informed and influenced the development of the design guidelines.

The final document explored the creation of a cultural district within the public realm, a portion of the streetscape that is contained within the public rights-of-way. Streetscapes comprise a series of primary elements that collectively define the overall street compositions. These elements influence the visual, spatial, and psychological perceptions that are associated with a "district" experience. The document explored and provided guidelines for the following major streetscape elements:

+ Street Structure
+ Hardscape Improvements
+ Softscape/Landscape Improvements
+ Street Furniture
+ Lighting
+ Signage and Wayfinding
+ Public Art

The design guidelines encompassed an array of social, cultural, and design-related issues focusing on each subject with enough detail to spark community excitement while clearly conveying the steps necessary to make this district a reality. A vital component of the process was stakeholder engagement and community outreach. The feedback gathered from the community meetings, onsite outreach, and participatory photography sessions directly drove design decisions. Each comment and suggestion was taken into account, explored, and applied to further investigation by the design team. As discussed by multiple outreach participants, the district should be a direct representation of cultural identity, and the project team placed primary importance on the community informing the district's development and creation. By taking community desires and concerns and applying them to the design guidelines for the district, the project team established the framework for a cultural district that embodied the vision of the people. The guidelines laid the groundwork for a pedestrian-friendly, safe, and enjoyable experience for residents and visitors alike while providing a framework for future economic, cultural, and social revitalization of this important cultural district.

A broad range of community partners was instrumental in crafting the vision for a revitalized Little Saigon. These voices included Little Saigon residents, merchants, community leaders, business owners, and representatives of government and nonprofit organizations, as well as local residents who live outside the neighborhood but often visit Little Saigon's markets and unique retail offerings.

Public participation activities were designed and carried out in a collaborative process with the stakeholder committee, which included the Little Saigon Foundation, the El Cajon Business Improvement Association, and additional community members and business owners. The stakeholders committee provided key input on the best way to engage community members, particularly those who may not typically attend a formal public meeting. A range of on-the-ground community engagement activities were developed to allow multiple ways for stakeholders to provide input. This was truly a community-driven, collaborative process, with local business owners providing food at events, consultants donating their time, and volunteers providing interpretation services to maximize opportunities for multilingual participation. The final design guidelines were presented at a community meeting at which the Little Saigon Foundation president stated that "the design team was part of us"—an extension of the Vietnamese community.

The Anthropological Difference

After an early meeting with the Little Saigon Foundation, members of the landscape architecture team felt that the cultural considerations of the Vietnamese community deserved focused, professional attention and made a special point to involve me, an anthropologist, with the other public outreach team members. While my job duties at the time were generally oriented on conducting outreach and consultation programs with Native American stakeholders in the region, I would regularly describe my academic and professional expertise to engineers and designers as being a "cultural translator." Specifically, I would take the concerns and ideas from a group of stakeholders, combine what I heard and saw with a historical and ethnographic context, and present my research in such a way that engineers and designers could understand what they should or should not do to be sensitive to the community concerns. The landscape architecture team felt that my skills would be useful on this project, and I wholeheartedly agreed.

I found that everyone on the team had a full and earnest commitment to cultural sensitivity and inclusion despite a general lack of familiarity with the Vietnamese community or major aspects of Vietnamese culture in general. Additionally, I found that many of the other public outreach specialists had some well-established approaches to working with communities with various levels of English proficiency that could be employed here, even if there was a lack of experience working with Vietnamese immigrant communities. With an eager, prepared, and conscientious team in place, I sought to define my own role.

I found that I was most helpful providing overarching guidance on the approach, regularly asking the landscape architects, rhetorically, "Who knows the community best?" when stressing the need for meaningful outreach strategies. I was able to bring an anthropological perspective to project team meetings during which we discussed how the public could be meaningfully involved in the development of the design guidelines and the various mechanisms through which diverse public opinions could be used to inform the various design elements. I also took on the responsibility of doing the historical and cultural research on the Vietnamese history of the community, including the aspects of Chinese history, language, and folklore present in the Vietnamese culture as a result of thousands of years of imperial rule and transculturation; the influence of French colonialism on Vietnamese culture, including cuisine; and the complex relationship between Vietnamese immigrants, memories of the Vietnam War, and the current political and economic developments in Vietnam itself. This research and historical perspective became particularly important when fielding questions from the architects and designers. For example, one project team meeting on signage turned on questions such as, "Why do some of the signs in the neighborhood have Chinese characters, while some signs use the Latin alphabet with diacritics?" and, "Why is a traditional banh mi sandwich made with a French baguette?" and, "Why is the Vietnamese flag from 1975 flown around the community instead of the current one?"

In addition to providing an ethnohistorical perspective, I also reinforced the already present appreciation for cultural sensitivity and relativism from the project team, highlighting the need to take into consideration input not only from Vietnamese residents in the community but also from the sizeable Somali and Latino communities in the area. I also stressed the possible social, linguistic, and cultural limitations community residents may have providing input on urban design concepts. Finally, I was able bring a different methodological toolkit to this project than might otherwise have been the case. Specifically, I had used photo elicitation interview techniques in the past and had found them incredibly productive. By encouraging the use of different engagement methods, such as participatory photography, the project team was able to build on rich community input to create guidelines that have deep roots in the place and its people.

Epilogue

Happily, community development efforts continue. The Little Saigon Design Guidelines document was just the first step in making a new public space focused on the culture and history of the Vietnamese community in San Diego a reality. The effort took many ideas from the community and created a set of concrete, long-term goals and near-term attainable projects for the city to consider. Immediately following the submittal in 2013 of the Little Saigon Design Guidelines to the Little Saigon Foundation and the El Cajon Business Improvement Association, community organizers were able to work with the San Diego City Council to have the area officially designated the Little Saigon Cultural and Commercial District. Having a physical document informed by a wide range of community members and residents made the concept of a Little Saigon district a substantially more concrete possibility, and it was the first formal designation of its kind in the City of San Diego, establishing the model for the creation of ethnic business clusters in the city. Marti Emerald, the San Diego councilwoman who represented the area at the time, discussed the establishment of the district: "This is not only an expression of the diversity that makes San Diego and, in particular, City Heights [the larger neighborhood in which Little Saigon is located]. It also speaks to the unity in a community that respects the differences that we share, and learns from them and acknowledges that all of these different cultures, all of these different communities coming together enriches all of us" (San Diego Union Tribune 2013).

Since the formal establishment of the district, members of the Little Saigon Foundation and other community leaders have worked to create incremental improvements, establishing the district's brand within the city, implementing some of the simpler design ideas outlined in the document, and focusing some of the broad recommendations of the planning document on specific design elements for construction in certain district areas.

In 2015, the Little Saigon Foundation did another series of public fora and workshops and developed a "10 Year Vision Plan" document that focused on the creation of an "open-air museum" that would explore the history and culture of Vietnam and the immigrant experience throughout the public realm. Different design elements included a space for a large Vietnamese heritage flagpole (at a height of sixty-five feet, it was estimated to be potentially seen from over a mile away), mythical animals from Vietnamese folklore incorporated into lighting features and other public infrastructure, sculptures devoted to documenting the immigrant experience, and a reconstruction of the gateway to the citadel of the last Vietnamese emperor as a central gateway showpiece. Following the ideas in that document, community leaders began working on formal engineering documents to gain permits for the flagpole.

In 2018, the Little Saigon Foundation coordinated with traveling artists to create a "vintage large-letter postcard-inspired" mural on the outside of one of the neighborhood's established Vietnamese grocery stores. This was part of a larger public art effort by the San Diego Art Institute to install ten to twenty murals, sculptures, decorated light/utility boxes, and other media created by local artists to capture and commemorate stories collected by a local arts center as part of their "Little Saigon Stories" project. The Little Saigon Stories project was focused on training Vietnamese American youth to capture the experiences of Vietnamese refugees and document the firsthand experiences of migration and resettlement among those residents who currently live in the Little Saigon district. The stories were ultimately curated as part of a Little Saigon Mobile Museum, which served as a place for cultural events, youth-based programs, and oral history interview sessions.

The level of commitment to realize the creation of Little Saigon by community organizers and planners has continued in the years since the Little Saigon Design Guidelines were formally submitted. The community's grand vision to create a district that honors and celebrates Vietnamese cultural history has been shared with the public, governing agencies, nonprofit organizations, and political leadership. The guidelines were an important early step to convey the community's vision for the neighborhood in a way that has inspired action and support over the years since its completion. Ultimately, the project team hopes that the culmination of these efforts will result in public and private investment and the physical manifestation of an enhanced and revitalized Little Saigon.

Stephen Weidlich is a strategic planning manager and the research and data analyst at the King County Department of Public Defense, based in Seattle, Washington. He leads and organizes the data analyses and research initiatives sponsored by the department, including research into attorney caseload, collateral civil consequences for accused clients, police misconduct, and racial disparities in case dispositions. He received an MS in anthropology from Florida

State University in 2007. Prior to his work at King County, he was employed at AECOM, where he managed and contributed to a wide range of projects for the US National Park Service, Bureau of Land Management, National Marine Fisheries Service, California Department of Transportation, and the Little Saigon Foundation in San Diego. He is a fellow in the Society for Applied Anthropology and regularly presents at its annual conference on issues surrounding fisheries and fishery management in the North Pacific.

Notes

1. See http://www.photovoice.org/ and other resources related to the search term "Photovoice" for more information on the methodology and its use around the world.

References

Collier, John K., 1957. "Photography in Anthropology: A Report on Two Experiments." *American Anthropologist*, 59: 843–59.

San Diego Union Tribune. 2013. 'Little Saigon' official in City Heights. June 4, unattributed article. https://www.sandiegouniontribune.com/news/politics/sdut-little-saigon-district-created-city-heights-2013jun04-story.html, accessed December 16, 2021.

Weller, S. C., and A. K. Romney. 1988. *Systematic Data Collection*. Newberry Park, CA: Sage Publications.

PART IV

Health Promotion and Management

CHAPTER 10

~:~

Pastors at Risk

Toward an Improved Culture of Health for United Methodist Clergy in North Carolina

CATHLEEN E. CRAIN, NATHANIEL TASHIMA,
AND TERRY M. REDDING

Project Background

For generations, the occupation of Christian clergy in the United States provided one of the healthiest careers available, according to federal statistics. However, as the new millennium dawned, clergy were among the occupations highest in national rates for diabetes, heart disease, and depression, among other indicators. All around clergy members, society had been changing from the comfortable era of the 1950s, and the role of pastor itself had evolved to be extremely stressful, time-consuming, and unpredictable as church religious leaders took on increasing burdens of administration, fund-raising, counseling, and balancing family and church life.

Compounding this was the loss of congregants needed to support the traditional, mainstream churches. Some former members joined more evangelical congregations. Others simply walked away from religion altogether, leaving many small and medium towns with lovely, spacious buildings attended and supported by only a handful of congregants. In addition, skyrocketing insurance costs were having a dramatic effect on church budgets.

However, in North Carolina, the United Methodist Church (UMC) has a powerful ally. The mounting health insurance costs caused in part by the rapidly declining health status of church clergy led The Duke Endowment to fund a special program called the Clergy Health Initiative (CHI) in 2007 through a partnership with the North Carolina and Western North Carolina UMC Conferences (conferences are UMC administrative districts, similar to a diocese in the Catholic Church) and the Duke University Divinity School.

Project Description

While noting the importance of whole wellness, the CHI initially centered on improving clergy health as measured by physical health indicators (e.g., weight, blood pressure, cholesterol); the biomedical approach to health was initially directed to the pastor as an individual and focused on physical health. A more holistic approach was anticipated later in the program.

LTG Associates was engaged as the external evaluator to provide The Duke Endowment and the CHI with an unbiased perspective on the process and effects of the CHI and the health intervention, which came to be called the "Spirited Life." The LTG team, led by managing partners Nathaniel Tashima and Cathleen Crain, was awarded the contract and began work on the CHI in early 2009. The team was joined later by Terry Redding, senior research associate, who became the project director.

The design of the process evaluation was always intended to be iterative, that is, living, changing, and responding to what we learned from the initiative's stakeholders as the program progressed over the course of five years. The following are early paragraphs from LTG's initial proposal:

> While the outcome evaluation will consider changes in health status of clergy, it cannot fully explore and explain the facilitators and barriers to the success of the CHI in the context in which the United Methodist pastors and the program functions. Both the program and the pastors' function within a complex cultural framework and the process evaluation must respond to that complexity. The process evaluation will complement the outcome evaluation and will answer the master questions:
>
> + Does the culture of health change as a result of the CHI?
> + What are the factors that influence the process and outcomes of the CHI?
> + What are the key strategies that account for the changes?
>
> In the formative phase of process evaluation planning, defining the evaluation questions with input from core stakeholders is essential. The process evaluation will explore the course of the CHI through the experiences of the different stakeholders, each of which will affect the course and outcomes of the CHI.
>
> In order to understand how the CHI was implemented, the meaning of the CHI to the stakeholders, the context for the CHI, and the experience of participation, each group of stakeholders will be engaged over the life of the process evaluation. This long-term engagement will create an ongoing dialogue that will allow an exploration of continuing and emerging issues.

As the external evaluator, under contract to The Duke Endowment, LTG was truly external both to the Church community and to the Duke Divinity School, the home of the intervention. As seen in the above excerpt, LTG envisioned a design that would ensure that each of the stakeholders' interests was understood and that all voices were heard through the evaluation.

The team addressed a variety of challenges in developing the approach and being positioned to be effective. The first challenge was as an outsider understanding the structure of both the Church and the intervention, learning the languages and values of each, and working deftly within them. Developing an emic understanding of the UMC cultures within the state's two conferences and being able to describe the CHI intervention experience from the perspectives of the various stakeholders was the critical starting point for our work. A companion challenge was for the team to be sufficiently trusted and to establish rapport with all of the stakeholders so that they would speak freely during our interactions. And, as with most evaluations, those most responsible for the outcomes of the intervention were the most concerned with the process and outcomes of the evaluation and gaining the stakeholders' trust was an ongoing challenge.

The work included an external evaluation of the pilot program and the intervention itself, which consisted of three staggered clergy cohorts, as well as another CHI pilot program that targeted the Pastor-Parish Relation Committees, consisting of local church members that work with the pastor and hold great sway over the pastor's employment. The entire intervention over the five years of clergy experience became known as "Spirited Life," and over one thousand clergy participated across North Carolina.

Our involvement in the CHI's developmental stages allowed us to present the anthropological perspective regarding the importance of understanding the clergy's sociocultural context by focusing on cultural values and language, and through considering the range of affected and affecting stakeholders, thereby taking a holistic approach to clergy health. We understood the pastor to be an individual, influencing a church community as a faith leader through word and deed. We also recognized and accounted for pastors as individuals who lived and functioned within a personal community of family, friends, and their congregants, all of whom affected and were affected by the pastor. We addressed pastors as professionals working within a faith organization with its own philosophy and culture.

Implementation and Anthropologists' Roles

Our evaluation design began with an exploration of the shape of the Church structure, the roles and expectations for all related stakeholders within that structure, the definition of wellness for pastors, the definition of wellness for other initiative stakeholders, the challenges to wellness experienced by pastors, and the rationale behind the shape of the initiative and its goals, objectives, and activities. From this formative work we were able to begin sketching the outline of the cultures that were involved in the CHI, their visions of the issues, and how to address whether these were or were not in agreement. From this early work during the initiative's pilot phase, we were able to shape the master form for the evaluation for the next five years. Our core methods included observations, semistructured interviews, intercept interviews at various events, surveys, and focus groups, with a few freelisting and pile sorting exercises as well (Bernard 1995; Patton 2002). An important part of our approach was to build in continual opportunities for data collection through attending Church functions, conducting ongoing in-person and telephone interviews, and engaging with clergy, lay leadership, and congregants in their churches and communities. We attended "Annual Conferences" (annual meetings of church leaders and clergy), church meetings, and church socials. We ate fried chicken and apple pie and drank sweet iced tea. We chatted with the church ladies, talked with church trustees and other leaders, interviewed pastors and their families, and observed the church, congregational, and community contexts.

This close and continual engagement helped to elicit emic descriptions of the UMC culture and its stakeholders. These descriptions were utilized to inform our evaluation design and to shape the language that was used in fieldwork and in reports to mirror that of the various stakeholders. This use of appropriate language was critical as the findings had to be clear and usable by the stakeholders themselves. Finally, we also built in nearly continual opportunities for sharing insights from the evaluation. The use of these methods, the continual data collection, and the reporting of information will be explored further below.

From the evaluation design's beginning, LTG recognized that the project stakeholders formed expanding communities within a larger Church structure. On completing the pilot evaluation, we were schooled by pastors as to both the challenges and rewards of their work and the implications for their wellness. In our subsequent evaluation activities, we utilized both our early learning about the cultures at play and the views of the pastors to shape our activities. In our early reporting we were able to say that clergy members' health did not exist in a vacuum and that various factors must be considered that relate to a pastor's occupation (e.g., frequent relocation,[1] the "on call" nature of the job, responsibilities to different stakeholders in the local and conference Church communities), as should the important actors in clergy support networks (e.g., spouses, family members). Thus, the evaluation design grew in understanding of and accounting for the perspectives and experiences of all of the cultural actors. Only with this full view did we believe that we would be able to understand the drivers and trajectory of pastor wellness and what within the Church culture enabled or impeded wellness. Additionally, we believed that the potential for the culture of health to change for pastors also had the potential to change the culture of health for all stakeholders.

As we learned, we were able to emphasize that physical health is only one component of a more holistic vision of wellness and that other aspects of wellness such as spirituality should play an early and key role in the wellness support for spiritual leaders. This emphasis supported advancing the holistic wellness agenda that was envisioned in the design of the CHI. Although the pilot intervention program was designed to have flexibility in allowing the pastor and a health coach to discuss individual health needs, the pilot focused clearly on physical health. One pastor noted that being a pastor "is a very dangerous profession now," and many clergy expressed the importance of receiving support for the full continuum of wellness, including mind, body, and spirit. Indeed, a CHI study (Proeschold-Bell et al. 2013) conducted in 2008 found clergy at high risk for mental health issues, including depression and anxiety. LTG's initial report was provided to The Duke Endowment and to the CHI, and a briefing and consultation was held to discuss the findings. This report and the briefing helped to lay the groundwork for subsequent changes in the CHI design, moving from physical health to include psychological and spiritual health.

The following year, LTG's field results highlighted the importance of the Pastor-Parish Relations Committee (PPRC) to pastor well-being and the challenges experienced by many PPRC members in fulfilling their roles. We also addressed the nature of a local church culture and the challenges of a newly appointed pastor being allowed to enter and participate in the culture. The CHI developed a PPRC video training series for this key committee, which was piloted by the CHI and evaluated by LTG. The video series became an important part of training for PPRC members across the state, and the training has been credited by pastors with helping the PPRC members to understand the needs of pastors and support their wellness, and to actively welcome new pastors into the local church culture.

As LTG entered more deeply into the United Methodist culture, we sought to learn the language and values, particularly as they related to clergy life and wellness. Employing a mixed-methods approach with an ethnographic lens, we carried out data collection at all levels of the culture, most of it longitudinal to allow us to identify and understand process and outcomes of changes. Through all of these activities, the LTG team was able to construct an ongoing understanding of the changing and developing nature of the intervention as well as the experiences of a number of clergy, their families, and their congregations. LTG conducted continuing data collection focused on the Church itself, with particular interest in how the culture of wellness was defined and the ways in which it was supported or not.

As the Spirited Life got underway with the first of the three annual clergy cohorts, we attended workshop sessions (usually held for thirty to fifty cohort members over a long weekend) over several weeks and provided immediate feedback after each workshop to CHI training and support staff. Data were collected through clergy satisfaction surveys as the workshops concluded, and we recorded our own observations and intercept interviews over the weekends.

These feedback loops were important in adapting the Spirited Life workshops in real time from week to week as the workshops progressed with different groups within the cohort. Staff would return to their home office, discuss findings and experiences, and tweak the program for the following group at the next workshop session.

The workshops were a mix of group presentations and smaller breakout sessions in which facilitators explored lessons and wellness activities with clergy. When all participants were comfortable with the idea, we were allowed to sit in on these more intimate sessions. The small groups often provided rich and useful insights on how individuals were struggling with certain church members or ineffectual committees, the "toxic" culture of some congregations, and the lack of personal time needed to pursue their own wellness.

The workshops provided us, as participant-observers, with an understanding of the Spirited Life program and how each clergy participant experienced the rollout. It also provided the clergy and us an excellent opportunity to get to know each other and our purpose as external evaluators, which was valuable as we scheduled subsequent church visits and interviews. The opportunity was also rather atypical; it is not often that you have the chance to sit through an intense weekend with your respondents, while sharing meals, experiences, and stories, as a means of getting to know each other.

We often scheduled field visits to individual clergy and churches after these weekend workshops. At the heart of the visits were semistructured interviews, usually lasting from thirty to sixty minutes, with clergy, their family members, and church lay leaders. Among other topics, clergy were probed about their health habits and needs; lay members were probed about their knowledge of what keeps a pastor holistically healthy. We also had the chance to explore the churches and grounds and see the outside of the pastors' homes (which are provided and maintained by the respective church congregation). These observations were quite useful in understanding the emphasis (or lack thereof) a community and congregants put on maintaining both a comfortable and tidy church and pastor residence.

Church members were typically quite open about their sentiments, and it was not a given that a particular congregation was expected to accept and be happy with their pastor. It is the nature of the United Methodist Church that some member families, often going back several generations, feel ownership of the church that their forebears founded and see pastors as itinerant preachers who are seemingly at their disposal. One telling anecdote was an informal discussion early on over lunch with two long-time members of a small, rural church. One leaned in closely and said, "If we don't like the pastor, we call the District Superintendent and tell [him] to get that joker out of here."

Figure 10.1 illustrates the data collection over the life of the project. Of the 380 interviews conducted, almost half of the interviews were with clergy.

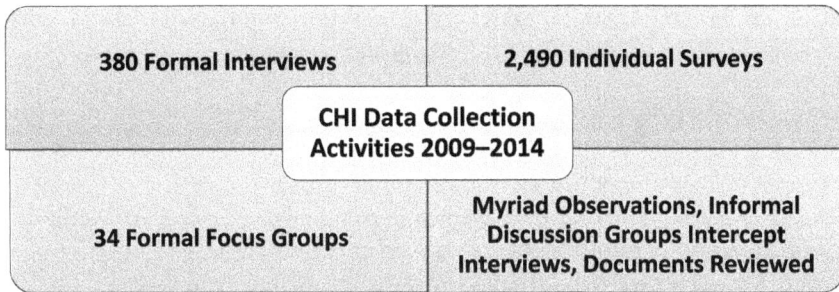

Figure 10.1. Data collection over the life of the Clergy Health Initiative evaluation. © 2000 LTG Associates, Inc.

We interviewed a variety of other stakeholders, often in multiple cycles, including UMC leaders (District Superintendents, who lead a regional group of pastors, and Bishops, who are in charge of the conference), CHI staff (health coaches and wellness advocates), pastors' spouses or adult family members, and lay people (PPRC chairs, congregants, and local church staff). In addition, we conducted intercept interviews (both structured and unstructured) and observations at events that were not included in this tally.

Showing up, being there, becoming familiar, and gaining trust all allowed us to become increasingly better at understanding the needs of the stakeholders and translating those needs into actionable information. As with many projects, the critical experience of face-to-face interaction was an important element in the success of LTG's work with the CHI.

Communicating with a core set of project partners was key to project effectiveness. For the first several years, staff from LTG, the CHI, and The Duke Endowment held monthly conference calls to discuss the progress of the work and for LTG to provide feedback from our data collection in near real time to the initiative's implementation. We also traveled to North Carolina (from our offices in suburban Washington, DC) for day-long meetings to discuss the progress and trajectory of the intervention with all of the core partners. Over the course of the evaluation, we developed fourteen data and analysis reporting documents, each of which involved briefing the core partners. Finally, we briefed the Bishops of the two UMC conferences, the dean and other senior leadership of the Duke Divinity School, and senior Duke Endowment staff on the findings of our work at a strategic planning meeting.

This stream of communication allowed the LTG team to deliver highly targeted messages regarding our findings from the field to core partners and to continue to reinforce key messages about the instrumental nature of addressing the full culture of mind, body, and spiritual wellness. These messages were designed to reflect the concerns of pastors, families, congregations, PPRCs, and district superintendents. We were careful, as was appropriate, to reflect the nature of the Church's Wesleyan philosophy and teachings.

Outcomes

The deep ethnographic dive we were able to take into the United Methodist Church culture in North Carolina allowed us to reflect the gaps in active support for clergy wellness and the opportunities presented by those gaps. The following are results and points of influence we were able to organize in response to the three main evaluation questions.

Did the culture of health change as a result of the CHI?

Through our work we were able to show that CHI efforts contributed to positive shifts in the United Methodist Church's culture of health for clergy in North Carolina. The CHI paved the way for creating an enabling environment, or sanctioned space, for clergy to care for themselves. Through the Church leadership's support of the CHI's efforts and attention to holistic wellness issues, and awareness created by the program among congregants as to the health of their pastors, clergy received permission to administer self-care and were empowered to do so, gaining agency in an occupation that many would characterize as a high-demand job.

A majority of clergy participants (72 percent) perceived improvements to their wellness, whether it was in mind, body, or spirit, or a combination. In addition, for a strong majority of clergy (80 percent), their approach to health and wellness changed.

Although the CHI's focus was primarily on clergy, it also influenced the wellness of clergy families. A majority of clergy families noted that they also saw some benefit, primarily with nutrition and exercise. Clergy families also noted that as the CHI positively affected clergy wellness, family life was enhanced. The CHI also may have positively influenced congregations and supported the development of a healthier church environment. Many of these findings would not have been revealed if an ethnographic design had not been at the base of the evaluation.

What Were the Key Factors That Influenced the Process and Outcomes for the CHI?

Several factors at the programmatic level of the CHI enhanced clergy engagement and ultimate success. The CHI's adaptability in modifying the intervention to meet the stakeholders' needs—based on our surveys, observations, and interviews—proved important, as did early suggestions to use a more holistic wellness approach with Wesleyan theological underpinnings. Our anthropological approach allowed pastors to participate in the intervention design on an ongoing basis.

We identified an important generational shift in health awareness when, during a round of interviews with the District Superintendents, one noted in passing that it seemed like the younger clergy were more in tune with self-care than older clergy. This observation supported what had been anecdotal about generational differences. We subsequently incorporated a related question in all interviews. All District Superintendents responded that those clergy in their mid-thirties and younger took more personal time to dedicate to self-care than those in their mid-thirties and older. It was beyond our purview to pursue this in depth, but it was the kind of information that could have a profound effect on health programming. These data were reported and became part of a CHI and church activity resource for programming.

What Were the Key Strategies That Accounted for the Changes?

The messages we received in our research were clear that the ultimate strategy of offering a holistic approach to wellness, encompassing mind, body, and spirit, resonated well for clergy and for the Church. As faith leaders, they voiced the need to address spiritual well-being as well as mental and emotional health in addition to physical health.

Effective communication at different levels was integral to creating an enabling environment or sanctioned space to change the health culture, from clergy and congregants up, from the CHI out, and top down from United Methodist Church leadership. Having an open and multipoint communication strategy (website, blog, emails, meeting presentations, and professional journals) also helped communicate health messages to a broad audience.

As we had posited during the evaluation design, informing and encouraging support from different stakeholders revolving around the pastor, particularly spouses, family members, and CHI wellness advocates, proved critical to clergy wellness, including motivation for self-care and accountability.

The Anthropological Difference

As early as the initial oral interviews for selecting the evaluation team, the anthropological difference in approach was noted by the representatives of The Duke Endowment, the senior United Methodist Church leaders, and the CHI team. We did not simply take their proposed approach at face value and move forward with a design. They commented on our early use of Church language, our focused interest in learning from across the stakeholders, our use of straightforward language, and our suggested initial focus on understanding the causes and cultural means to address pastor health issues within the Church and within the pastor's family, congregations, and community circles.

The anthropological difference was woven through the evaluation activities. By using holistic and engaged approaches, which view persons, organizations, and events through a cultural lens, our work was to learn, understand, respect, and reflect back the cultures that comprised the Church body. It was to be the professional stranger (see Agar 2008) in the universe of this church in this place and to create a safe and welcoming place for all stakeholders to reflect and faithfully report their perceptions of the role of clergy and holistic health—and how to best integrate the two.[2]

On an ongoing basis, our reported findings led to earlier and more focused attention to shaping the CHI into a holistic intervention that brought increasing kinds of stakeholders into actively and positively addressing pastor wellness. The final focus of our work was on how the Church would become central to addressing pastor wellness, supplanting the role of the CHI—that is, how holistic wellness would become a core cultural concern.

Cathleen E. Crain and **Nathaniel Tashima** are the managing partners of LTG Associates, the oldest anthropologically based consulting group in North America, founded in 1982. Nathaniel holds a PhD from Northwestern University with a concentration in psychological anthropology. Cathleen holds an MA from McMaster University with a specialization in medical anthropology. For four decades, they have been pathbreakers, influencing the discipline of anthropology by promoting, valuing, and modeling examples of innovative anthropologically based research, policy, and practice to address health disparities in populations and ethnic/cultural groups in numerous communities in the United States and across the globe.

Terry M. Redding is currently a strategic communications specialist with a maternal and child health project funded by the US Agency for International Development (USAID). He received an MA in anthropology from the University of South Florida in 1998. In 1999, he contributed to and edited *Applied Anthropology and the Internet*, the first-ever fully online publication of the American Anthropological Association. He joined LTG Associates, Inc. in 2000 on a USAID-funded population project and was then involved in a variety of research and evaluation projects before working for several years as an independent editorial and evaluation consultant. He has served as president of the Washington Association of Professional Anthropologists, communications chair for the National Association for the Practice of Anthropology, and chair of the Praxis Award competitions of 2013, 2015, and 2017.

Notes

1. United Methodist pastors are expected to relocate regularly, as itinerancy is part of the Church's missionary strategy. Relocation not only affects the pastor but also the family members. In several cases that we encountered, families were living apart because parents wanted to keep their children in the same schools, or spouses could not easily relocate due to their jobs. In addition, we spoke with "clergy couples" (i.e., both spouses are pastors) who had been assigned to different churches at a distance from one another.
2. In addition to the authors, the LTG team included: Michelle Wilson, MAA, Kristen Hudgins, PhD, Reiko Ishihara-Brito, PhD, Jillian Brems, MAA, and Pamela Rao, PhD.

References

Agar, M. H. 2008. *The Professional Stranger*. 2nd ed. Bingley: Emerald Group Publishing Limited.

Bernard, H. R. 1995. *Research Methods in Anthropology: Qualitative and Quantitative Approaches*. 2nd ed. Walnut Creek, CA: AltaMira Press.

Coalter, M. J., J. M. Mulder, and L. Weeks, eds. 1990. *The Mainstream Protestant "Decline": The Presbyterian Pattern*. Louisville, KY: Westminster/John Knox Press.

O'Toole, R., D. F. Campbell, J. A. Hannigan, P. Beyer, and J. H. Simpson. 1991. "The United Church in Crisis: A Sociological Perspective on the Dilemmas of a Mainstream Denomination." *Studies in Religion/Sciences Religieuses* 20(2): 151–63. https://doi.org/10.1177/000842989102000203.

Patton, M. Q. 2002. *Qualitative Research & Evaluation Methods*. 3rd ed. Thousand Oaks, CA: Sage Publications.

Proeschold-Bell, R. J., and J. Byassee. 2018. *Faithful and Fractured: Responding to the Clergy Health Crisis*. Minneapolis: Baker Publishing Group.

Proeschold-Bell, R. J., and S. LeGrand. 2012. "Physical Health Functioning among United Methodist Clergy." *Journal of Religious Health*, 51: 734–42. https://doi.org/10.1007/s10943-010-9372-5.

Proeschold-Bell, R. J., and P. J. McDevitt. 2012. "An Overview of the History and Current Status of Clergy Health." *Journal of Prevention and Intervention in the Community* 40: 177–79.

Proeschold-Bell, R. J., A. Miles, M. Toth, C. Adams, B. Smith, and D. Toole. 2013. "Using Effort-Reward Imbalance Theory to Understand High Rates of Depression and Anxiety among Clergy." *Journal of Primary Prevention* 34(6): 439–53.

United Methodist Church. 2000. *The Book of Discipline of the United Methodist Church*. Nashville, TN: United Methodist Publishing House.

CHAPTER 11

~:~

Anthropology in an Epidemic
Ebola in West Africa

OLIVE MINOR

Project Background

In late October 2014, Oxfam humanitarian staff responding to the Ebola epidemic in Liberia and Sierra Leone realized that they had hit a wall. Despite Oxfam's previous experience responding to cholera, hepatitis E, and smaller Ebola virus disease (EVD) outbreaks, the scale of the 2014 epidemic in West Africa overwhelmed the templates humanitarian teams had developed in other contexts to deal with these types of epidemics. By the end of that October, the World Health Organization had reported over thirteen thousand infections in the region, and almost five thousand persons had died.

The problem no longer seemed to be a lack of messaging about the Ebola virus. By late October, Oxfam staff in Liberia and Sierra Leone observed that most residents in their areas of operation had moderate to high awareness of Ebola prevention and treatment information. The majority could list EVD symptoms, modes of transmission, and methods to prevent infection. Early symptoms of EVD include headache, muscle pain, and high fever, followed by vomiting, diarrhea, rash, and in some cases internal and external bleeding. Once symptoms begin, the virus passes to others through contact with the sick person's bodily fluids. Reducing the risk of transmission requires regular handwashing, avoiding direct contact with those exhibiting symptoms, and using gloves and other personal protective equipment when caring for the sick and the dead.

Despite knowledge of Ebola prevention and treatment information, affected families and communities did not always follow this advice, and infections continued to ignite "hot spots" across the region. Oxfam staff realized that, in order to save lives, one-way messaging was not enough. Their response needed deeper inquiry into the factors preventing people from taking the necessary precautions to avoid infection.

Project Description

In early November 2014, as the epidemic hit its peak, I joined Oxfam as response and resilience team anthropologist. Oxfam's humanitarian team had just launched a new three-pronged approach to the outbreak. This approach focused on (1) treatment, (2) containment, and (3) prevention. Treatment meant partnering with medical actors to provide water, sanitation, and health (WASH) services and materials for Ebola treatment units (ETUs), triage centers, and health clinics. Containment focused on community surveillance. In Sierra Leone, for example, health volunteers carried out house-to-house messaging and surveillance in the communities in which they lived. In Liberia, similar teams of volunteers engaged in contact tracing and active case searches, in addition to house-to-house messaging. In active case searches, volunteers walked door-to-door, identifying neighbors exhibiting symptoms of possible Ebola infection and encouraging them to seek treatment. Finally, prevention involved forming neighborhood public health promotion teams who worked to increase community access to Ebola prevention information, services, and materials while encouraging active community participation in local responses to the outbreak.

My assignment was to help the humanitarian team get a deeper understanding of local perceptions of what individuals could do to effectively protect themselves from Ebola. Anecdotal evidence suggested that strongly held cultural beliefs and practices, misinformation, and lack of trust in both national authorities and international agencies prevented people from seeking help early enough to maximize their chances of survival and minimize the likelihood of passing on infections. How significant were these barriers, and how might we address them?

The context of the Ebola epidemic presented significant challenges to carrying out ethnographic work. First, we needed to generate in-depth ethnographic insights on an emergency timeline. In a rapidly progressing epidemic, every hour mattered; processes on which anthropologists might normally spend months had to be condensed into days.

Second, the risk of infection put constraints on gathering ethnographic insights. The governments of Liberia and Sierra Leone tried to contain outbreaks by mandating nationwide curfews and shutdowns, banning public gatherings, closing schools, and imposing quarantines on entire neighborhoods or villages. In some areas, these restrictions, coupled with distrust of those involved in outbreak response, led to sporadic violence targeting healthcare workers, contact tracers, ambulance teams, and surveillance teams.

Oxfam's security protocols sought to limit our exposure to Ebola by preventing staff from entering others' homes, using public taxis, visiting crowded places like markets or bars, or attending gatherings (such as religious services). As nonmedical staff, our teams did not have personal protective equipment (PPE) like masks or gloves. We wore long sleeves, trousers, and boots to limit

Figure 11.1. Volunteers talk with a family under quarantine in northern Sierra Leone. © Olive Minor.

contact with human waste in areas that lacked sanitation. Offices, shops, and clinics set up mandatory handwashing stations for patrons to use before entering. Some Oxfam offices also constructed shallow boxes of chlorinated water to disinfect our shoes. We washed our hands until the chlorinated water dried and cracked our skin. We carried hand sanitizer everywhere.

We also operated under a "No Touching" rule: as much as possible, we had to maintain distance from others. For months on end, we could not hug a friend, or even shake hands—normally an important part of greeting and acknowledging other people in West Africa. If I organized a focus group, participants had to sit several feet apart. In other words, as an anthropologist, I could not access the most important spaces in which people normally interact and share information, and I had to maintain several feet of distance from anyone I encountered.

Third, our teams faced the everyday logistical challenges of carrying out programs in a resource-poor setting. In Monrovia's West Point neighborhood, we navigated narrow, crowded alleyways between homes built of scavenged, corrugated tin. Active case searches identified sick family members in what seemed like every home—whether from EVD or other infectious diseases, we did not know. Only one road wide enough for cars led into and out of the neighbor-hood. On one occasion, our exit was blocked after a man died in the road; neighbors covered him with a sheet and waited several hours for an ambulance team with PPE to safely recover his body.

In northern Sierra Leone, our teams drove for hours along potholed dirt tracks to reach adjacent villages, traversing fallen trees and tire-deep mud. On the outskirts of one village, a wood-plank bridge gave out under our truck; we spent hours digging and pushing it out of a shallow ravine, with the help of several villagers. Where the dirt tracks petered out into a footpath, we left the truck and hiked for miles through dense forest. These challenges meant that, some days, my data collection and the team's community messaging and sur-veillance work progressed more slowly than we hoped.

The final challenge in my role was that it evolved over several months. The Ebola response did not involve one discrete research project but rather an on-going process: throughout the response and recovery phases, I had to identify ways to integrate meaningful input into Oxfam's strategies and activities.

Implementation and Anthropologist's Role

The humanitarian team and I developed a few interventions to overcome our operational constraints. First, we had to address the need to generate lots of ethnographic data without much time. I found that, by supplying colleagues with quick-and-scrappy anthropological training and basic tools, staff at every level—from WASH engineers to gender advisors to local volunteers—could apply anthropological approaches to their work: asking critical questions, en-gaging with community members, making rich field observations, and copro-ducing analyses of our environment. Our national staff and volunteers often already held critical ethnographic insights, but we had not created opportuni-ties for them to formally share their observations. We created daily debriefing sessions as a way for team members to share input, co-analyze field observa-tions, and adjust the next day's activities according to our findings.[1]

The second key intervention involved embedding me as a participant ob-server with our staff and volunteers as they carried out door-to-door messag-ing, contact tracing, and active case searches. Each day, I paired with a volunteer as she canvassed her neighborhood or village. Early on, we learned that volun-teers working locally boosted our messaging and community engagement strat-egies; residents told us they placed more trust in someone from their own area. I was able to have face-to-face conversations about Ebola with demographically diverse households in Liberia and Sierra Leone, and they shared their perspec-tives with me. When our volunteers located symptomatic persons and had to encourage them to seek assistance at an ETU, I was able to record firsthand the individual, family, and community concerns that influenced treatment-seeking behavior.

In the Liberian neighborhood of Clara Town, Monrovia, for example, a young man reported to our volunteers that his sister had symptoms of possible EVD. He shared this information because he wanted to call an ambulance, but the rest of the family refused. The parents knew neighbors who had died in ETUs, and they feared that their daughter would disappear into the treatment facility where they could not monitor her care; if she went to an ETU, they believed they might never see her again. We had a long conversation with the family, in which Oxfam volunteers listened and responded to the family's concerns. Volunteers detailed exactly what would happen in the ETU, described the care that their daughter would receive, discussed how they might communicate with her in the ETU, and reiterated the serious risks if the family kept her at home. The family agreed to let our volunteers call an ambulance team.

In addition to the door-to-door conversations, other qualitative methods included:

+ key informant interviews with community leaders (such as local/regional chiefs, Mami Queens [female community leaders in Sierra Leone], religious leaders, and women's and youth leaders);
+ interviews with healthcare providers (including nurses, midwives, doctors, traditional healers, and pharmacists);
+ focus group discussions with Ebola survivors, affected families, women's and youth groups, and agricultural and business groups;
+ site visits to ETUs, triage centers, and health clinics.

In many cases, I found that noncompliance with Ebola prevention and treatment advice rested squarely on the lack of "staff, stuff, space, and systems" that Paul Farmer (2014) had noted months before rather than on cultural practices or beliefs. Nonetheless, significant cultural and social barriers remained. Ethnographic approaches helped to identify other points of friction between Ebola-affected communities and response activities and offered suggestions for improving Oxfam's strategies. Oxfam's humanitarian response teams used these assessments to adjust operations on a daily basis, incorporate recommendations into longer-term strategies, and capture lessons learned for future epidemic response.

Outcomes

Adjusting Daily Tactics

Much has been written about rumors and misinformation fueling the 2014 Ebola epidemic. These commentaries often characterized affected communi-

ties as irrationally "resistant" to public health advice and dismissed their concerns as ignorance. In this view, government and humanitarian actors simply
needed to provide more and better messaging to overcome ignorance and correct false beliefs.

Fortunately, Oxfam's humanitarian teams understood that one-way messaging had not been enough, and that we needed to have two-way conversations in which we listened to community members' concerns. My training as
an anthropologist also prompted me to listen to Ebola rumors as expressions
of legitimate fears and concerns. This approach led to surprising discoveries
that changed the course of our work. In one of my first days embedded with
our humanitarian teams in Monrovia, a volunteer and I came across an elderly
man in front of his house. When he saw me—a white American in an Oxfam
shirt—he shouted that white people had gone door-to-door giving poison to
his neighbors in New Kru Town. I believe he feared that I was one of them. A
crowd gathered, and we left the area, following Oxfam protocols, but we continued our canvassing in another section of the neighborhood.

It would have been easy to dismiss the old man as misinformed, but I remained curious about what led to his perception of events. In talking with
neighbors about the man's reaction, we learned that many area residents had
felt nauseated and fatigued in the preceding days. It emerged that a partner
organization had distributed malaria prophylaxes door-to-door that week,
which would drive down malaria infections that might be mistaken for Ebola.
Pamphlets instructed recipients to take the drug with food and explained the
potential side effects (which included nausea and fatigue). However, many recipients could not read the pamphlets, and when they experienced negative
side effects, a rumor circulated that the drug contained a poison. The volunteer
and I reported what we had learned to the volunteer coordinator, who worked
with our partner organization to coordinate messaging about the malaria drug
starting the following day.

Influencing Short- and Long-Term Strategies

In that first week with Oxfam, I also learned that our humanitarian team was
operating without much insight into Liberia's and Sierra Leone's health systems. The rapid pace of the epidemic had not allowed our team the time or
capacity to deepen their inquiry into local health-seeking behaviors. In organizing focus groups with Ebola survivors and families who had lost relatives, I
learned that health clinics often charge more than most Liberians can afford.
As a result, most patients first seek care from women in the home and then
from informal healthcare providers, including home-based nurses and pharmacists, midwives, traditional healers, or small-scale traders who supply basic
medicines to villages. If symptoms worsen, they might finally seek care from a

formal health clinic or hospital. For someone sick with EVD, this delay meant that survival was unlikely while infection passing to family members was almost certain. Ebola ripped through families like wildfire; I met survivors who had lost twenty relatives over the course of a few weeks.

Informal healthcare providers clearly formed a critical piece of the two countries' health systems, but we had yet to include them in our messaging, active case search, and referral strategies. Focus group participants emphasized to me that, if we wanted to strengthen community-based epidemic response and reduce distrust of ambulance teams and ETUs, we needed better outreach to women and informal healthcare providers. In response to these recommendations, Oxfam's teams immediately began to identify networks of informal healthcare providers by neighborhood or village and enlisted their help in creating community-based outbreak preparedness plans, addressing residents' fears of Ebola response providers, and referring potential Ebola patients to ETUs—with the assurance that care would be free of charge.

Ongoing qualitative research also influenced longer-term Ebola recovery strategies. In Sierra Leone, my key finding was that stigma and blame played central roles in perpetuating outbreaks. Stigma and blame operated at multiple levels of the Ebola response—from government quarantine policies to community bylaws to everyday social interactions—and were directed at affected individuals, families, and communities. These attitudes put pressure on families in ways that actually hindered epidemic control and ultimately protracted Sierra Leone's Ebola epidemic.

Interviews with families under quarantine, for example, highlighted the need to address the ways in which fear and stigma drove avoidance of testing and treatment. In Koinadugu District, Sierra Leone, we talked with families placed under quarantine without adequate access to water, food, or latrines. Since each new EVD case reset the clock on the twenty-one-day quarantine, families might spend months unable to leave their homes to tend crops, which would die without harvest at the cost of an entire year's food and income. A few neighbors were willing to bring water and food to the quarantine line, but most kept their distance, fearing infection if they passed near the homes of those under quarantine. One quarantined family included a pregnant woman, for whom local health officials had no plan if she went into labor.

For some families, fear of these social and economic repercussions outweighed fear of Ebola, leading them to avoid testing or treatment when they fell ill. Interviews and focus groups conducted in affected communities revealed ongoing fears of ambulances and ETUs, negative perceptions of burial teams, and resistance to government-led quarantine measures. Some individuals and families thus risked further spread of the virus by concealing illnesses, delaying biomedical treatment, moving across districts in search of alternative treatments, avoiding quarantine by evading testing for Ebola, creating false copies of the certificates given to patients who test negative for Ebola, and burying those who died of Ebola without protective equipment.

In response, Oxfam Sierra Leone designed activities to reduce the stigma and blame leveled at survivors and affected families. We held discussions with affected communities on how to reintegrate Ebola survivors, who continued to face stigma even after recovery. Because of their caregiving roles, women in particular described accusations that they were "wicked" or "careless" in the wake of their own and others' illnesses. While male survivors reported negative attitudes specifically related to fears that they might transmit EVD through sex, female survivors reported deeper issues: eviction, family rejection, loss of livelihoods, and loss of former leadership roles due to stigma. Oxfam began to develop plans to assist affected individuals and families through their participation in existing community groups (such as agricultural associations and women's groups).

Oxfam Sierra Leone also drew lessons from post–civil war ex-combatant reintegration programs. In Koinadugu District, for example, we worked with a drama club that specialized in postconflict reconciliation. The club traveled to hard-to-reach villages and trained local drama groups to write and perform skits aimed at reducing the stigmatization of Ebola survivors and affected families. We also facilitated face-to-face dialogues among public health officials, ambulance and burial teams, healthcare providers, survivors, and community members. During these "Community Information Days," community members could inspect ambulances and ask questions of those involved in the Ebola response. These events provided opportunities to reduce stigma and distrust through dialogue.

Capturing Lessons Learned

In the wake of the epidemic, Oxfam held discussions to capture the lessons learned over the course of the response. They invited me to offer reflections on our fieldwork, highlighting ways humanitarian organizations could improve community-based epidemic response in the future. For example, a survey of Oxfam staff found that we had missed opportunities to mainstream gender in the Ebola response. We had missed these opportunities, in part, because we initially overlooked the relationships between gender and vulnerability to infection. Cumulative national data in Sierra Leone, for example, showed that infection rates among women only slightly outpaced those of men. Subsequent data also showed that, once infected, men faced a higher mortality rate than women. Program managers took the relative parity of male and female infection rates to mean that gender did not play a meaningful role in infections and deaths.

Yet qualitative interviews with survivors, affected families, and healthcare providers revealed that the gendered division of labor in Sierra Leone put men and women at risk of Ebola infection in very different ways. Women faced high risks as household caregivers, whereas men faced risks of infection due to their roles in transporting the sick. Women's caregiving roles placed them in regular contact with the bodily fluids of sick household members, leaving them no option to follow the "avoid body contact" advice. In survivor focus groups, one female survivor after another described having fallen sick—not because of denial, resistance, or hostility to Ebola prevention advice but because of their critical role in caring for the sick and the dead.

Male motorcycle taxi drivers who had transported sick persons created new chains of Ebola transmission in previously unexposed villages. In postresponse discussions, culminating in an article for the journal *Gender & Development*, Oxfam's gender advisor, our team epidemiologist, and I argued that an analysis that only considered women's vulnerability, or one that did not consider gender at all, risked overlooking these critical causal pathways, resulting in a response incapable of preventing further transmission of the virus. Here we captured two lessons learned from the Ebola outbreak: (1) social roles (such as gender) do matter in an epidemic, and (2) understanding those social roles, and how they contribute to disease transmission, requires looking beyond the numbers with qualitative research.

The Anthropological Difference

Oxfam's proactive efforts to integrate anthropology into humanitarian aid, and their responsiveness to ethnographic data, demonstrates the key role anthropology can play in humanitarian contexts. It showed that anthropologists can offer emergency response teams a deeper understanding of community perceptions, beliefs, and practices—and that these insights can change humanitarian response strategies in meaningful ways.

In Sierra Leone, for example, asking respondents about the local terms they used to describe Ebola revealed information about how affected communities perceived and experienced the disease. Terms such as *boda wuteh* (in Mende, a "monster that kills the whole family") and *sweh* (in Krio, a "fever that kills the whole family") pointed to local conceptions of Ebola as an illness that affects the family rather than merely the individual body. These resonate with terms reported from Liberia such as *Ju'pa* (Kpelle), which means "to kill the whole family," and the darkly witty term "family visa" to the other side (Modarres et al. 2015). Rather than focusing on individuals as vectors of disease, this view recognizes Ebola as a crisis that devastates entire families.

In contrast, the international community grounded its response in public health approaches that tend to focus on individuals exposed to Ebola but do not address family or collective action. Yet families provide the most reliable source of assistance and care in a crisis, those to whom a sick person will turn for help. This suggested the need to understand Ebola risks from the perspective of families, with their expectations of mutual assistance. Our teams also needed to be thoughtful about how we supported selected individuals (such as survivors or orphans) in a context in which almost everyone experienced economic distress. Offering material support to survivors could create resentment and exacerbate existing tensions. On the other hand, sharing material support could help survivors and orphans reintegrate into families and communities. This perspective led Oxfam to more sensitive consideration and support for the needs of families whose members fell sick.

Yet anthropologists do not study just "the community" or "the other." Reflexivity is a central tenet of anthropology, requiring an awareness of how the anthropologist's own cultural background and social position affect the research process and the analysis of data. I found that a key contribution of anthropology to humanitarian aid was not merely to study affected communities but rather to focus on *the relationship between* humanitarian response and communities in which we work. Humanitarian organizations not only need to understand the perceptions and beliefs of communities in crisis, but they also need to remain reflexive and self-critical about the assumptions and beliefs that inform their own perceptions of an emergency, what kinds of support communities need, and how assistance should be delivered.

I encouraged colleagues to examine how Ebola response actors and activities themselves might lead affected families or communities to defy Ebola prevention and treatment advice. Affected families I interviewed in Liberia recounted terrifying early experiences with ambulance teams and ETUs: family members were taken away and never heard from again, with their medical records lost in the chaos and their bodies cremated and disposed of without the family's knowledge. Resistance to Ebola prevention and treatment was not merely due to ignorance or "traditional culture." Instead, I heard rational, human reactions to the prospect of isolation, suffering, and possible death.

I also advocated for colleagues to recognize the ways in which structural violence affected participation in the Ebola response. In every single interview and focus group I conducted in Liberia and Sierra Leone, participants pointed out the desperate lack of health clinics and schools. Many also discussed the need for water, transportation, and communication networks. They called attention to the dearth of first aid and hygiene equipment, such as soap, disinfectant, protective clothing, and oral rehydration salts. While most participants readily answered questions about social and cultural norms that might affect the transmission of Ebola, their final message was clear: communities only have meaningful ways to participate in epidemic response where they have functioning systems: of schools, healthcare, water, roads, and communication.

The final "anthropological difference" of my role, then, contained some irony: I actually urged Oxfam to move away from a focus on "culture" as the source of friction between communities and Ebola response activities. "Cultural" explanations for vulnerability can harm the vulnerable when they drive responses that overlook the lack of material resources. For example, unpaid labor emerged as a basic but key barrier to local participation in the Ebola response: in the transition from emergency response to recovery, government and NGO programs reduced or phased out cash incentives for volunteers. Instead, they began to rely on the donated labor of already impoverished volunteers to carry out recovery programs, which required ongoing community organizing work. Yet women already shouldered the double burden of domestic and farm labor, while men faced pressure to provide their families with cash and commodities. Nonparticipation in epidemic response may have reflected both men's and women's need to triage labor in a context of poverty and volunteer burnout. In the words of a female volunteer in Rokel, Sierra Leone, "An empty bag cannot stand."

Epilogue

I write these reflections from Seattle,[2] about ten miles from the nursing home where, in February 2020, the coronavirus sparked its first outbreak in the United States. Now, almost two years later, we mark several grim milestones: over eight hundred thousand dead of COVID-19 in the United States, and an estimated 5.5 million deaths worldwide. At the beginning of the pandemic, projected numbers like these provoked horror and disbelief. Now we seem to greet them with numb acceptance. As of this writing in January 2022, we once again face a wave of infections due to the omicron variant, and the number of deaths continues to climb, particularly among unvaccinated individuals.

Over the course of this pandemic, I watched history repeat itself. As in West Africa in 2014, the federal government mounted a belated and messy response to an outbreak of an infectious disease. The US Centers for Disease Control and Prevention (CDC) initially issued confusing and contradictory guidance under political pressure from the White House. In a shocking abdication of responsibility, the US coronavirus response suffered from the same shortage of "staff, stuff, space, and systems" that Farmer noted in West Africa, reflecting a similar disinvestment in public health and healthcare infrastructure. Impoverished communities in the United States have long suffered health outcomes on par with much less developed countries. However, we cannot blame extractive industries or low national GDP for these failures, only the absence of political will.

Two years into the coronavirus pandemic, we see misinformation, lack of trust in federal and local authorities, and strongly held cultural beliefs leading to (sometimes violent) resistance to COVID-19 prevention and treatment efforts. A fraction of the US population believes that the coronavirus pandemic is a hoax—perhaps based on early statements from President Donald Trump—as some did regarding the Ebola outbreak in West Africa. Fully a quarter of Americans believe that powerful people may have intentionally planned the pandemic, a rumor that also circulated in Liberia regarding Ebola: in Clara Town, Monrovia, a group of young men had told me that the WHO intentionally unleashed Ebola in West Africa to reduce the population and later rake in money by introducing a vaccine or antidote. African countries have hosted large-scale pharmaceutical trials in the recent past that raised serious ethical concerns, which may fuel such fears (see Schaeffer 2020). As Oxfam observed in Liberia and Sierra Leone, even those in the United States with reasonably good information do not always follow precautions to avoid spreading the virus. For some individuals, social and economic repercussions outweigh the fear of COVID-19, leading them to ignore public health advice and accept a certain amount of risk.

The absence of a coordinated national response, clear guidelines, and a sense of collective action has led Americans to direct stigma and blame at individuals whose risk assessments and behaviors differ from their own. As in 2014, however, focusing only on individual-level responses to the pandemic misses the mark. As my research participants in West Africa emphasized to me in 2014, individuals only have meaningful choices for participation in epidemic response in the context of functioning systems. "In the absence of structural security," author Rebecca Traister (2020) wrote, "it is far easier to home in on individuals . . . than it is to reckon with the enormity of what's wrong and what needs to be righted. These past months could not have made this dynamic any clearer: the reflexive turn to blame individuals for how they choose to behave when left adrift in the sucking, soulless chasm created by large-scale institutional infirmity."

None of this was inevitable. We had decision points when we would not have had to accept hundreds of thousands of deaths, and when we could have taken in lessons learned from the 2014 Ebola outbreak. We know that pandemic response demands both a strong, coordinated response at the national level and collective community action from the ground up. Although it can be difficult to find our sense of agency in this crisis, anthropologists still have a role to play in crafting culturally appropriate messaging, building community-led epidemic response, and keeping the pressure on those in power to address our political failures rather than focusing blame on each other.

Olive Minor is an applied anthropologist and user experience (UX) researcher working at the intersection of global health and technology. She earned her PhD in anthropology and master's in public health from Northwestern University in 2014. Her dissertation followed the everyday lives of transgender people in Kampala, Uganda, noting how they balanced visibility and risk under the 2008 Anti-Homosexuality Bill. Her MPH thesis examined access to HIV prevention and treatment services for transgender Ugandans. In 2014–15, she carried out fieldwork as part of Oxfam's humanitarian response to the Ebola epidemic in Liberia and Sierra Leone, followed by the Burundi refugee crisis in Tanzania. In 2016, she was awarded an American Council of Learned Societies (ACLS) Public Fellowship to conduct research and evaluation with the International Rescue Committee in New York. In 2019, she pivoted to design anthropology in global tech, and she has carried out research with companies such as Google and Facebook. Since 2011, she has provided pro bono expert witness testimony for queer asylum seekers from Uganda.

Notes

1. I believe this approach is replicable. In a later role as public health promotion team leader in Nyarugusu Refugee Camp in Tanzania, I took the same approach with team members and volunteers. I encouraged all team members to apply anthropological tools and approaches to investigate the underlying factors leading to problems in the camp. Team members found that soap shortages—which we initially thought of as a distribution problem—turned out to be due to the trade value of soap as a commodity. Households sold their soap in exchange for much-needed cash to augment inadequate food supplies. Oxfam staff thus began to engage with partners to improve nutrition in the camp.
2. Politically classified at the time by some federal leaders as an "anarchist jurisdiction."

References

Farmer, P. 2014. "Diary." *London Review of Books* 36(20) (October): 38–39. http://www.lrb.co.uk/v36/n20/paul-farmer/diary.

Modarres, N., S. Babalola, M. E. Figueroa, L. Wohlgemuth, A. Berman, S. Tsang, G. Awantang, S. Konneh, and S. Kpanbayeazee Duworko. 2015. "Community Perspectives about Ebola in Bong, Lofa, and Montserrado Counties of Liberia: Results of a Qualitative Study." Unpublished article, Health Communication Capacity Collaborative, Johns Hopkins Center for Communication Programs, Resource Center for Community Empowerment and Integrated Development.

Schaeffer, L. 2020. "A Look at the Americans Who Believe There Is Some Truth to the Conspiracy Theory That COVID-19 Was Planned." Pew Research Center, 24 July. Retrieved 30 September 2020 from https://www.pewresearch.org/fact-tank/2020/07/24/a-look-at-the-americans-who-believe-there-is-some-truth-to-the-conspiracy-theory-that-covid-19-was-planned/.

Traister, R. 2020. "It Shouldn't Have Come Down to Her." *The Cut*, 19 September. Retrieved 30 September 2020 from https://www.thecut.com/2020/09/ruth-bader-ginsburg-anger.html.

CHAPTER 12

⌣: ⌣

Caring Together, Living Better

Anthropologists' Contributions to
a Caregiver Support Program in
the South Suburbs of Cook County, Illinois

REBECCA L. H. BERMAN AND MADELYN IRIS

Project Background

In 2009, AgeOptions, the Area Agency on Aging for Cook County in Illinois, received a three-year grant to develop a regional caregiver resource network in south suburban Cook County. The fastest growing segment of the older population are those eighty-five and older, according to the US Administration on Aging. To cope with projected costs of caring for these older adults, publicly funded health and social support programs aim to keep chronically ill older adults in their homes and bolster family members who are challenged to provide skilled care to meet the needs of older persons unable to live independently. Despite a wealth of research on caregiving, caregiver support services, and evidence-based interventions, many family caregivers remain relatively invisible in their communities and do not know where to turn for support.

AgeOptions staff recognized that low-income communities of color were unable and/or unwilling to access supportive services for caregivers. One barrier was a lack of tailored services that both acknowledge and leverage community assets such as faith-based organizations. They were familiar with research on how African American faith communities can facilitate the ability of those who are developing interventions to reach marginalized caregivers and enhance understandings of the role of faith and church in caregivers' lives. Through the Caring Together, Living Better (CTLB) project, AgeOptions aimed to support the capacity of faith-based organizations to build awareness of caregiving and mobilize a regional support network in twelve predominantly African American, economically stressed suburbs south of Chicago that were experiencing high crime, high unemployment, and limited access to resources for meeting basic needs. The project utilized participatory and strength-based approaches to community development as promising strategies for mobilizing connections between churches and other community-based organizations to support caregivers.

AgeOptions engaged my colleague Madelyn Iris and me as evaluators because of our expertise in using multiple research and evaluation methodologies, both qualitative and quantitative, as well as our extensive experience in mentoring organizations engaged in community-based participatory research. As practicing anthropologists specializing in aging research, we had worked with AgeOptions on multiple projects over several decades and had demonstrated sensitivity to the cultural differences, mores, norms, and traditions of elder care. Our role was to conduct a process evaluation of the faith-based partnership and regional caregiver support network and to support AgeOptions in collecting outcomes data for the funder, the Harry and Jeannette Weinberg Foundation, as part of a national evaluation of all projects funded through their Caregiver Initiative.

Project Description

The goal of CTLB was to build a partnership among project stakeholders that could develop and sustain a regional resource and support network for caregivers living in the targeted communities. CTLB's objectives were to: (1) work with communities to mobilize local assets for addressing caregiver-identified needs, (2) improve access to caregiver services through innovative outreach via culturally appropriate materials and formats, (3) guide churches in the development of sustainable volunteer services and the regional network, (4) increase the availability of stress-relieving respite services that meet caregivers' needs, and (5) provide culturally competent training to relieve stress and increase the expertise of caregivers.

AgeOptions implemented the project over three years by providing small grants to churches for developing volunteer caregiver support projects (hereafter "caregiver ministries") and by facilitating connections between churches and social service providers. Project stakeholders included AgeOptions staff, two social service organizations, and seven churches. Collectively, these faith communities already provided much-needed support through their existing ministries, including but not limited to youth programming, meeting basic needs, transportation, and visiting ill or older adults. Many of their clergy participated in the Southland Ministerial Health Network, led by a prominent religious leader whose church also participated in CTLB.

We designed the project evaluation to capture the development of the partnership and network by using a participatory approach for data collection and process observations for the purpose of project improvement. Our evaluation objectives were to: (1) monitor the evolution of the grassroots network of organizations engaged in CTLB, (2) capture narratives that documented the project's impact on caregivers, volunteers, and community stakeholders, (3) document the perceived benefits of faith-sensitive training for informal caregivers such as family members, friends, or neighbors, (4) track service delivery by CTLB partners (as an indicator of developing connections between individual churches), and (5) document the overall development and maturation of the project. Evaluation and data collection methods included site visits, interviews with CTLB partners, focus groups with caregivers, observations of CTLB meetings and events, stakeholder brainstorming workshops, stakeholder stories of change, procedures for churches to document services provided to caregivers, and debriefings with staff to document project processes and challenges.

Implementation and Anthropologists' Roles

In the first year of the project, AgeOptions launched a call for proposals to churches throughout Chicago's south suburban area with the assistance of the Southland Ministerial Alliance and awarded small grants to seven churches. AgeOptions also funded Catholic Charities South Suburban Senior Services and Metropolitan Family Services, which then subcontracted with the Blue Island Commission on Aging, to expand caregivers' access to respite services. In the initial months of Year 1, volunteers at each church conducted an assets-based community development survey to determine existing community resources that could be leveraged to benefit caregivers and AgeOptions-conducted focus groups with caregivers to identify their needs.

AgeOptions also convened a leadership council, which met monthly, to increase stakeholder investment in CTLB, foster collaboration across churches, and seek input on the development of region-wide activities. Leadership council participants included volunteer project leaders (hereafter "ministry leaders") from the partnering churches, two caregiver specialists from Catholic Charities, the director of the Blue Island Commission on Aging, a program manager from Metropolitan Family Services, and staff from AgeOptions. The leadership council played a critical role in crafting culturally relevant language and images to define "caregiving," "caregivers," and "family" in outreach materials.

During the second year, the churches focused on outreach to caregivers within their congregations and communities, designing their volunteer services, and recruiting volunteers to provide those services. As churches encountered caregivers with significant needs, a pastoral counselor from one church also volunteered to offer spiritual support to highly stressed caregivers across all churches. The leadership council developed procedures for referring such individuals for additional support from service providers.

In years two and three of the project, we facilitated a series of Appreciative Inquiry workshops, hosted by AgeOptions. Appreciative Inquiry (see Cooperrider and Whitney 2013; Coghlan, Preskill, and Catsambas 2003) emphasizes a participatory, strengths-based approach to strategic planning in which narrative inquiry and theme identification lead to visioning, action planning, and prioritizing next steps for implementation. A first, day-long workshop was held with over fifty caregivers and volunteers to set priorities for developing a regional support network; a second round of Appreciative Inquiry was held a few months later with fifteen service providers. The leadership council then participated in a half-day follow-up workshop to complete the Appreciative Inquiry planning process.

The leadership council then established three subcommittees to address long-term goals identified in the Appreciative Inquiry workshops, including improving awareness of and access to caregiver resources, developing faith-sensitive self-care training for caregivers, and exploring strategies for sustaining the partnership and caregiver ministries at the churches. The leadership council worked with AgeOptions to initiate a Facebook page to serve as a communication hub and resource center.

Over the three years, the project encountered challenges related to: (1) the development of collaborative relationships, (2) volunteer capacity, (3) data collection for the national evaluation, and (4) sustainability. All of these were part of the job, but they had to be navigated using anthropology's holistic approach combined with our prior experiences and understandings.

First, evaluation interviews and observations revealed that individual churches did not have a history of working together to address shared community problems, as they typically developed their own ministries. In addition, ministry leaders and/or their clergy were reluctant to refer congregants to other churches for caregiver support for fear of losing them to that church. A history of demographic change also made it difficult for some churches to effectively reach out to white caregivers living nearby, as African Americans had established churches in previously white neighborhoods and sometimes experienced discrimination. Churches also had congregants from other communities, which made it challenging to serve caregivers located an hour or more away.

Second, as each church's caregiver ministry grew in scope, demands on ministry leaders' energy and time increased. Developing a caregiver ministry encompassed recruiting and training volunteers, reaching out to caregivers, educating church leadership about caregiving issues, promoting their services in the community, networking with other organizations, coordinating services with other churches, and collecting service delivery and evaluation data. Several ministry leaders and/or volunteers who worked with them also faced their own health problems and caregiving responsibilities during the project, which may have hindered the coordination of multichurch activities and likely slowed the growth of the network in the project's third year. When their capacities were stretched, ministry leaders prioritized supporting their own caregivers over partnering with other churches or networking in the community. Service delivery data in the last year of the project did not increase as it did in the second year, suggesting that churches may have reached a maximum level of volunteer service at which they could operate efficiently and effectively.

Third, churches were required to collect data as part of the national-level evaluation via initial and follow-up assessments of caregiver outcomes, but ministry leaders felt uncomfortable asking caregivers to complete lengthy surveys that included questions about health and mental health issues. They had legitimate concerns about caregivers' perceptions of privacy and confidentiality since many were fellow congregants. Pressure from the funder's program officer and national evaluator to improve survey completion rates led to tension and reluctance to collect data, which affected our role as project evaluators, particularly during the first eighteen months.

Finally, ministry leaders did not take active roles on the leadership council until subcommittees began to plan for the future of their caregiving ministries and the council itself. Prior to that, ministry leaders looked to AgeOptions for leadership, as their primary connector to service agencies and resources, and primarily focused on growing their caregiver ministries.

Throughout the project, and particularly with the above challenges, we used our anthropological skills to shape an evaluation that would balance the perspectives of AgeOptions and project partners, affirm community and cultural assets, and facilitate stakeholder dialogue about challenges being encountered. This began with designing an evaluation that would meet the priorities and expectations of AgeOptions. We participated in the development of CTLB objectives as part of the grant application process and wrote the project evaluation plan in collaboration with AgeOptions. During the application process, we utilized our ethnographic and interviewing skills to elicit ideas and assumptions from AgeOptions staff, which then fostered mutual understanding of CTLB activities, expectations for project partnerships, anticipated outcomes, and potential challenges. Our approach was informed by an underlying community ecology perspective that recognized and framed the project in the context of the cultural, social, historical, and economic environment of the south suburban area.

To achieve our evaluation goals, we tracked network relationships, observed leadership council meetings, and facilitated the Appreciative Inquiry process as part of monitoring the evolution of a grassroots network (Goal 1); documented stories of change from stakeholders as evidence of CTLB's impact (Goal 2); evaluated the pilot test of the faith-sensitive training for caregivers (Goal 3);

summarized service data collected by ministry leaders or AgeOptions (Goal 4); and synthesized findings across data sources to document the development and maturation of the project (Goal 5). We also worked with ministry leaders to meet requirements for the national evaluation of caregiver outcomes. We shared interim results from all data sources with AgeOptions and the leadership council encouraging them to use those findings to develop strategies for collaboration, make adjustments to accommodate the cultural context, address stakeholder concerns, and overcome challenges.

To monitor the evolution of the regional support network, we conducted site visits and interviews with ministry leaders and the Blue Island Office on Aging, following up every six months by phone or in person. During the first interview, ministry leaders named organizations with which they had developed a relationship due to CTLB, described the purpose of those relationships, and characterized the strength of each relationship by degree of formality (i.e., networking, alliance, coalition, partnership, and collaboration). During each subsequent interview, they amended the list of organizations, noting changes in the formality of the relationships. We used networking software to generate maps of relationships between churches, service providers, and community organizations that pertained to supporting caregivers; weighted links indicated the formality of the connections. As the project progressed, interchurch collaboration waxed and waned, and network maps provided AgeOptions and the leadership council with evidence of this pattern. Our interviews with ministry leaders also gave voice to partners' concerns about collaboration across churches, which we summarized and shared with AgeOptions, Weinberg Foundation staff, and the national evaluator as potential challenges.

One of our most important contributions was engaging with the leadership council. When the leadership council was first convened, we attended as observing evaluators and were also responsible for training ministry leaders in national evaluation data collection procedures. As relationships developed, partners engaged us in dialogue or asked for our observations on particular issues, which placed us in the role of participant observer. These discussions were critical for fostering a shared understanding of contextual factors that could impede network building and for identifying strategies for how to overcome challenges.

In facilitating the Appreciative Inquiry workshops for strategic planning, our skills in ethnographic interviewing and thematic analysis helped participants frame their narratives and identify shared themes. This was particularly important for moving participants up the ladder of abstraction, from the details of their own experiences to those of the group as a whole, and then toward a vision of a regional resource network and its component parts. Until they participated in Appreciative Inquiry workshops, ministry leaders did not fully recognize how they could be actively engaged in building a caregiver support network through CTLB and take ownership of the project. As part of an effort to foster ownership and sustainability of the project, AgeOptions also contracted with us to develop a user-friendly replication toolkit for ministry leaders to mentor other churches initiating a caregiver ministry.

To capture stakeholder perceptions of project impact, we adapted the Most Significant Change Story technique (Davies and Dart 2005) to make it more culturally relevant. The technique requires individuals to document stories told by others, after which groups review and select stories that were most significant. Leadership council members, caregivers, and volunteers, however, were uncomfortable with writing down stories. Caregivers and other stakeholders were most comfortable sharing "testimonials" about how CTLB made a difference at project events. To accommodate these cultural preferences, we prompted leadership council members with simple open-ended questions during meetings, over the telephone, or by email and then shared the written versions with the individual storytellers to validate the narratives. We also recorded testimonials in field notes and at CTLB events. The leadership council found it hard to select particular stories as being more significant than others. Therefore, we developed a topical and thematic coding scheme to analyze stories and testimonials, using Atlas.ti for coding, and then we used those themes to select examples of stories for their review.

To address the African American community's cultural values, we worked hand in hand with the CTLB curriculum subcommittee and AgeOptions to identify a tested educational intervention for caregivers that addressed self-care topics that stakeholders felt were important, and then we collaborated with them to create exercises that incorporated spiritual issues. Subcommittee members provided meditations, hymns, and other faith-based resources for use with the training. When AgeOptions pilot-tested the faith-sensitive training, we sought participant feedback via satisfaction surveys and informal discussions after each session and convened a focus group on the perceived impact of the faith-based components of the training.

We developed a spreadsheet template and data collection form to help ministry leaders track the number of caregivers as well as the types of support and amount of service provided by each ministry. Results were summarized for the leadership council, AgeOptions, and the national evaluator. We also supported data collection activities that AgeOptions and ministry leaders needed for other aspects of the project, such as developing questions guides, preparing summaries of caregiver focus groups, designing a database for the assets-based community development survey, and preparing assets data reports for each ministry and a project-wide assets report for AgeOptions.

As the project evaluators, we were also responsible for overseeing compliance with the national evaluation requirements. Throughout the implementation of the national and local project evaluations, we provided ministry leaders with group and one-on-one training and technical support in data collection procedures. We translated the national evaluation goals and data collection protocols into a set of understandable procedures and processes that addressed concerns for caregiver privacy, along with a clear rationale for collecting that data. This also gave ministry leaders the capacity to implement data collection for the national evaluation.

Outcomes

The ecological approach we used as the foundation for our evaluation efforts, combined with network analysis, was extremely valuable for empirically documenting growth in the regional resource network. Using the methods and strategies described above, we found evidence of project maturation in the following areas: (1) expansion of the leadership council, (2) achievements of caregiver ministries, and (3) growth of a regional network to support caregivers.

Expansion of Leadership Council

When the project was initiated, the leadership council was composed solely of representatives from the partner churches and social service organizations. Early meetings focused on building rapport, establishing trust among partners, encouraging stakeholder investment in CTLB, sharing information about caregiver ministries, and brainstorming solutions to challenges the ministry leaders encountered. In the second year, the focus of the meetings shifted to encompass the "bigger picture" of regional resource development and inviting representatives from other community-based organizations and businesses to join the leadership council. After subcommittees were formed, the leadership council worked on long-term goals identified during the Appreciative Inquiry process. Subcommittee activities fostered closer working relationships among subcommittee members. A small group of natural leaders emerged who could assume larger roles as the project shifted to a focus on sustainability during the third year.

Achievements of Caregiver Ministries

In all, CTLB served approximately 241 caregivers over 3 years, most of whom were reached in the first 2 years of the project. Services included information and referral, transportation, respite, meals, support groups, prayer groups, and social activities for caregivers. Twenty-three stories and 20 testimonials from CTLB stakeholders revealed themes of increased awareness of caregiving, improved quality of life for caregivers, and spiritual support.

Volunteers emphasized how much they had learned about caregiving and their newfound sensitivity to caregivers' needs. One volunteer described how supporting caregivers affected her:

> [CTLB] has opened my eyes so much as to what caregivers go through. When we have the caregiver support meetings, I am gleaning as much information as the caregivers. . . . It has made me have more compassion for caregivers and what they go through.

Many stories told of increased familiarity with available resources and how to connect caregivers to those resources. Several stories focused on the importance of meeting caregivers "where they are at." One pastor spoke to how he was able to successfully connect a caregiver who "was not letting anyone know of her situation" with volunteer respite services from the church.

Stories provided compelling observations of improvements in caregivers' quality of life related to peer support, interpersonal relationships, social life, ability to cope, dealing with difficult transitions, and attending to one's own needs. Some highlighted the importance of spiritual support, such as the following story about a stressed caregiver:

> Part of her frustration was not being able to do her annual trip to visit her grandchildren in Atlanta. She had no family here to help her. We . . . guided her in getting respite care . . . so that she could visit her grandchildren. She has many other emotional problems, including resentment towards her mother for the restrictions her care has put on her lifestyle. She was given spiritual counseling and support; she now also receives respite care weekly. She says the support and guidance we provided saved her.

Other stories pointed to how CTLB volunteer services "reconnected" caregivers to their faith, their inner strength and/or their "church family."

Growth of a Regional Network

Before churches began to form relationships among themselves, the baseline network map had a "hub and spoke" pattern because AgeOptions was playing a critical role in connecting them to each other. After several months, the number of links among CTLB partners increased, some relationships became more formal, and other community organizations appeared in the networking maps. After this initial growth period, the network remained relatively stable, with minor changes in the number and formality of relationships across subsequent data collection time points, but a variety of types of relationships had been sustained. Stories of change also provided evidence that stakeholders valued the grassroots approach to network building and the resulting collaborative relationships.

The Anthropological Difference

Our ecological approach, coupled with evaluation approaches that gave voice to the concerns of volunteer ministry leaders, helped AgeOptions overcome challenges, adjust strategies for engaging partners, and build relationships between churches and the community, and it affirmed the role of churches in these African American communities. We believe our most significant contributions to CTLB and to the larger Weinberg initiative was our role as culture brokers. We dedicated considerable effort to interpreting and negotiating differences in goals, perspectives, and practices across all project levels. For instance, AgeOptions aimed to build "service projects" and a "regional network of support" for caregivers, while church volunteers believed their role was to develop "caregiver ministries" that included prayer and companionship. Partnering social service organizations sought referrals from churches to increase the number of caregivers who receive the respite services. The national evaluation prioritized "caregiver outcomes" and hoped for evidence of a delay in nursing home placements. As anthropologists, we saw the cultural dissonance between the academic model used by the national evaluator, the social service model, and local community values and behavioral norms expressed by the volunteers.

To facilitate communication and enhance a shared understanding of project goals across multiple actors and levels of the project, we drew upon our ethnographic skill set, including participant observation and pursuit of an emic perspective. Because we are not African American (nor members of a Christian church), this was a challenging activity that required us to draw upon our previous field experiences in anthropology and recreate the sense of "other" that guides insights into particular systems of cultural practices, values, and beliefs. We both enhanced our own understanding and interpreted for others.

Our evaluation approach situated CTLB as a community-based intervention and the individual church caregiver ministries as "actors" within the larger, more complex ecological system of the south suburban region. This entailed consideration of historical factors, such as demographic shifts and racial relationships within some of the communities, as well as the impact of the 2008 recession, including significant foreclosure rates across the area, increasing crime, and lack of governmental supports. By drawing upon an ecologically based, multilevel collaborative approach, we were able to balance evaluation goals informed by scientific or academic assumptions with the values and goals of the local actors and communities involved in CTLB, resulting in more culturally appropriate priorities, processes, and outcomes.

Our evaluation approach was unique among the thirteen other projects funded by the Weinberg Caregiver Initiative in that CTLB relied heavily on volunteers as ministry leaders, direct service providers, and data collectors.

However, several other Weinberg-funded programs that were situated in their communities expressed similar types of challenges. By sharing our approach and experience with the national evaluator and other projects and advocating on behalf of CTLB stakeholders for more relevant, feasible evaluation procedures, these other projects likely benefitted. Repeatedly translating between different goals and concerns across different levels of the project eventually gave room for shared learning regarding the value of culturally relevant, context-specific, participant-sensitive evaluation data.

Finally, we could not have had a meaningful impact on the development of CTLB without fostering trusting relationships with AgeOptions, CTLB staff, service providers, and ministry leaders. Ultimately, those relationships allowed us to gain deeper knowledge of how AgeOptions and faith communities saw their roles in meeting the needs of the older adults and caregivers and presented us with opportunities for partnering. Over the course of the project, multiple levels of mutual trust between church volunteers, caregivers, ministry leaders, regional caregiver specialists, and us, as evaluators embedded in the project, enhanced the developing partnership.

Epilogue

Caring Together, Living Better successfully developed and expanded an inter-organizational network to support caregivers, which was sustained beyond the three years of the project. The partner churches maintained their volunteer services, tailoring their programs or ministries to match their volunteer capacity while still meeting the expressed needs of the caregivers in their communities. The success of CTLB in the south suburbs demonstrated that with adequate social capital and infrastructure support, sufficient financial resources, and strong commitments from grassroots organizations, such partnerships can mobilize community-based networks to provide accessible, meaningful support for caregivers in order to affect their lives in positive ways. By including non-project-funded organizations and resources, the project was not totally reliant on continuation funding for sustainability.

Acknowledgments by Rebecca L. H. Berman

I dedicate this chapter to the memory of the late Madelyn "Micki" Iris, who was the lead evaluator for Caring Together, Living Better. I am forever grateful for being able to share our thoughts together, inspire and be inspired by each other, and collaboratively innovate and write together. I thank AgeOptions for the opportunity to engage with them as an evaluator throughout the evolution of Caring Together, Living Better. I have great respect for the volunteer ministry leaders who devoted their hearts and souls to supporting caregivers in their communities and who were willing to work together, overcome the challenges of collecting meaningful outcomes data, and share stories about the project's impact.

Rebecca L. H. Berman received a PhD in anthropology from Northwestern University in 1988. Her doctoral research focused on the cultural meaning of interdepartmental meetings in a city government. She is currently a research scientist at the Leonard Schanfield Research Institute at CJE SeniorLife. After completing her PhD, she worked as a project-based researcher and then joined the Buehler Center on Aging in the Feinberg School of Medicine at Northwestern University. While there, she and Madelyn Iris codirected a project to build the evaluation research capacity of social service organizations. She also taught in the MA in Gerontology Program at Northeastern Illinois University. Her career has emphasized program evaluation, needs assessments, and research that informs service delivery. A primary area of interest is engaging older adults and community members as advisors or collaborators in research. She served as secretary and elections chair for the Association of Anthropology and Gerontology.

Madelyn A. Iris was director of the Leonard Schanfield Research Institute at CJE SeniorLife. She completed her dissertation on language acquisition among Navajo children in 1981, receiving a PhD in anthropology from Northwestern University, after an MA from the University of Toronto in 1970. After conducting research for several community-based organizations, she joined the Buehler Center on Aging at Northwestern University, where she held several leadership positions. She taught at the Feinberg School of Medicine and Department of Anthropology and served as director of Northwestern University Ethnographic Field School on the Navajo Nation. She had diverse research interests in aging, dementia, and caregiving with a particular expertise in protective services and elder abuse and neglect. She served on committees and commissions for the American Anthropological Association and Society for Applied Anthropology and was president of the National Association for the Practice of Anthropology and the Association of Anthropology and Gerontology.

Note

Madelyn (Micki) Iris passed away in January 2020. Rebecca Berman completed the revision of this chapter.

References

Coghlan, A. T., H. Preskill, and T. Catsambas. 2003. "An Overview of Appreciative Inquiry in Evaluation." Special issue, *New Directions for Evaluation* 100: 5–22. https://doi.org/10.1002/ev.96.

Cooperrider, D., and L. Whitney. 2013. "Appreciative Inquiry Commons." Champlain College and Case Western Reserve University. https://appreciativeinquiry.champlain.edu/.

Davies, R., and J. Dart. 2005. "The 'Most Significant Change' (MSC) Technique: A Guide to Its Use." Available at https://www.betterevaluation.org/en/resources/guides/most_significant_change (see the "View Resource" link).

CHAPTER 13

~:~

A Video Ethnographic Study
Raising Healthy Children in Poverty and Examples of Excellence in Addressing Childhood Wellness

CATHLEEN E. CRAIN, NATHANIEL TASHIMA,
REIKO ISHIHARA-BRITO, AND ERICK LEE CUMMINGS

Project Background

The California Department of Health Care Services (DHCS) has focused significant resources and effort on addressing the prevention of early childhood obesity. The DHCS conducted formative research, a multiyear effort undertaken with the National Opinion Research Center (NORC) at the University of Chicago, to understand the perspectives of professionals and individuals about areas of focus and how to best develop prevention approaches.

The final elements of the research were to be two video ethnographies; the first was to engage low-income individuals to discuss how they see issues of preventing early childhood obesity, and the second was intended to engage with those leading cutting-edge community wellness interventions around the state. Each video was to be fifteen to twenty minutes long and provide highlights of participant views, lives, and work. These videos were then intended to inform DHCS staff and policymakers, other policymakers in California and at the US Department of Agriculture, and California state legislators in shaping future health development policies and initiatives.

The NORC knew of our firm's (LTG Associates, Inc.) anthropological grounding, disciplinary focus, and ability to work effectively across levels and cultures, and as such they proposed LTG as the ethnographers. The DHCS was clear that approaching individuals directly as state policymakers would get them "canned" answers because of status and power differentials. They chose to engage anthropologists because of both their ability to gather and tell good stories and their ability to engage diverse populations. Because of the complexity of the cultural and community undertaking, LTG's managing partners, both anthropologists, co-led the project and tapped another senior-level staff anthropologist to provide support.

Project Description

The DHCS set out to explore early childhood obesity prevention particularly for Medi-Cal (California state health coverage for low-income individuals and families) and/or populations eligible for CalFresh (formerly "food stamps," now Supplemental Nutrition Assistance Program nationally). The DHCS was interested in focusing on early childhood, with special attention to mothers and young children. They were interested in understanding the opportunities for preventing early childhood obesity through the vision of those who serve communities and low-income families, as well as the barriers to achieving that goal.

The following were the core questions of the formative research:

+ What are perceptions among individuals receiving or eligible for Medi-Cal and CalFresh and those who serve them regarding the factors that support and prevent healthy eating and physical activity behaviors among low-income populations and communities in California?
+ What are possible evidence-based promising practices and partnerships for use in low-income communities and healthcare settings to prevent obesity for individuals receiving or eligible for Medi-Cal and CalFresh?
+ Which are the highest priority groups among Medi-Cal and CalFresh eligible or recipient populations to receive obesity prevention messages and interventions?
+ What are predominant issues and successes captured through stories and video narratives concerning factors that support and prevent healthy eating and physical activity behaviors among low-income populations and communities in California, and what are the most important audiences to receive selected video content on the issues identified?

The ethnographic videos were expected to provide an opportunity for the policy and program audiences to learn from providers and community members directly.

A critical element in the framing, conduct, and outcomes of this research was the highly engaged and collaborative nature of the relationship of the DHCS to us and the video project. That relationship and the highly supportive relationship with the NORC enabled the project to truly follow an ethnographic path and to learn from the participants.

In the planning stage, we worked to shape the project so that it had strong contextual and cultural sensitivity. We wanted to develop an emic perspective from each of the video participants so that their story became the focus rather than a clinical etic rendering of the narrative. Based on previous work and our views of most human behavior being highly culturally contextualized, we recommended and demonstrated three main changes to the original approach that we believed would make the project process and products valuable to all of the proximate and potential stakeholders.

A first shift in design was to move from focusing with community participants on preventing obesity to developing and nurturing early childhood wellness—that is, from inquiring about how to prevent children from being obese to inquiring about how parents and families work to raise healthy children in mind, body, and spirit in their cultural context. This triple focus was intended to move away from a Western, clinical approach and to encourage parents to place raising children in a wellness-supporting cultural context. This shift in no way obviated a discussion of nutrition and weight but rather framed it in the universe of concerns and priorities for parents and clearly explored and acknowledged the forces that shaped their living and health environments. This shift invited participants to not only provide a fully drawn picture of themselves and their families (nuclear and extended) and their efforts to build a healthy life but also describe the personal and environmental forces that were working both for and against that wellness. This anthropological approach provided opportunities for participants to shape the questions and their responses in language and stories that they believed were important to share with the DHCS and other stakeholders.

Second, we developed an approach to both the community leader and community participant videos that grounded us in working with each person to cocreate the process of telling their story. We had key issues that we wanted to learn about from each person, and we needed to be able to tell a visually engaging story. But beyond that, the ways the discussions and observations could be conducted was the result of building relationships and rapport with participants and shaping the discussions, observations, and video agenda together.

The result was a site and shooting agenda that participants largely controlled, populated with people important to them and their stories, and set in places that illustrated the backdrop of their lives and work. A central purpose of the video was to allow the viewer, an outsider with an etic viewpoint, to learn and experience the participant's emic views (insider viewpoint) and sense of their world. Information would be delivered in levels, starting with the video backgrounds, then focusing on the people, and finally narrowing the focus even further to the individual participants. Too often, the contextual information is left in the hands of the anthropologist rather than those of the participants to describe and highlight. We had to be mindful that even this unconscious shaping of emic knowledge begins to move the locus of storytelling from the participant to the anthropologist.

A third shift was to open up the opportunities for participants to bring others into the video process to help tell and illustrate the story. Over the course of the two days of filming with each participant, most participants populated the videos with family, and some chose to include friends and coworkers. Zumba classes, nutrition education sessions, parks, meals, work, and families at home all became backdrops for discussions. In the end, over one hundred persons appeared in the videos either as active participants or as part of an intentional depiction of community and contexts; the final videos show far fewer participants, as the editing process pared the 150 hours of video to the essential two hours. While this created a variety of logistical and administrative challenges, the result was richer and more contextually and culturally nuanced than it would have been without important others and events.

We actively planned for and enacted both ethnic and gender diversity in the outreach and recruitment of community participants. We particularly maintained that, in thinking about healthy families, men as well as women needed to be involved, and such diversity would take particular focus in recruitment. Also, the diversity of potential family makeup should be seen as an opportunity to educate. The final makeup of the participants reflected limited gender diversity due to DHCS recommendations for participants as well as the unwillingness of men who were eligible to participate.

All of the changes and enhancements to the original concept for the videos were grounded in our views of health and wellness being deeply cultural and contextual constructions. Also, truly understanding how to support individuals, families, and communities in being fully well requires an essential grounding in a strong and healthy culture—exemplified by some community participants and being built or enhanced by the community leaders. This fashioning of the context helped to illustrate the importance of accounting for cultural attention in considering wellness and in the development of interventions intended to support wellness. Too many health interventions have been focused on the individual in isolation and in attempting to shape her/him within a Western vision of (generally) physical health. Without reference to family, community, culture, and mind/body/spiritual health, these interventions have and will frequently fail, wasting time and resources, and leaving the participants and providers feeling frustrated and unhappy with the outcomes.

Implementation and Anthropologists' Roles

There were five major phases to the project as illustrated in figure 13.1. There were a variety of difficulties encountered along the way; all were actively ad-

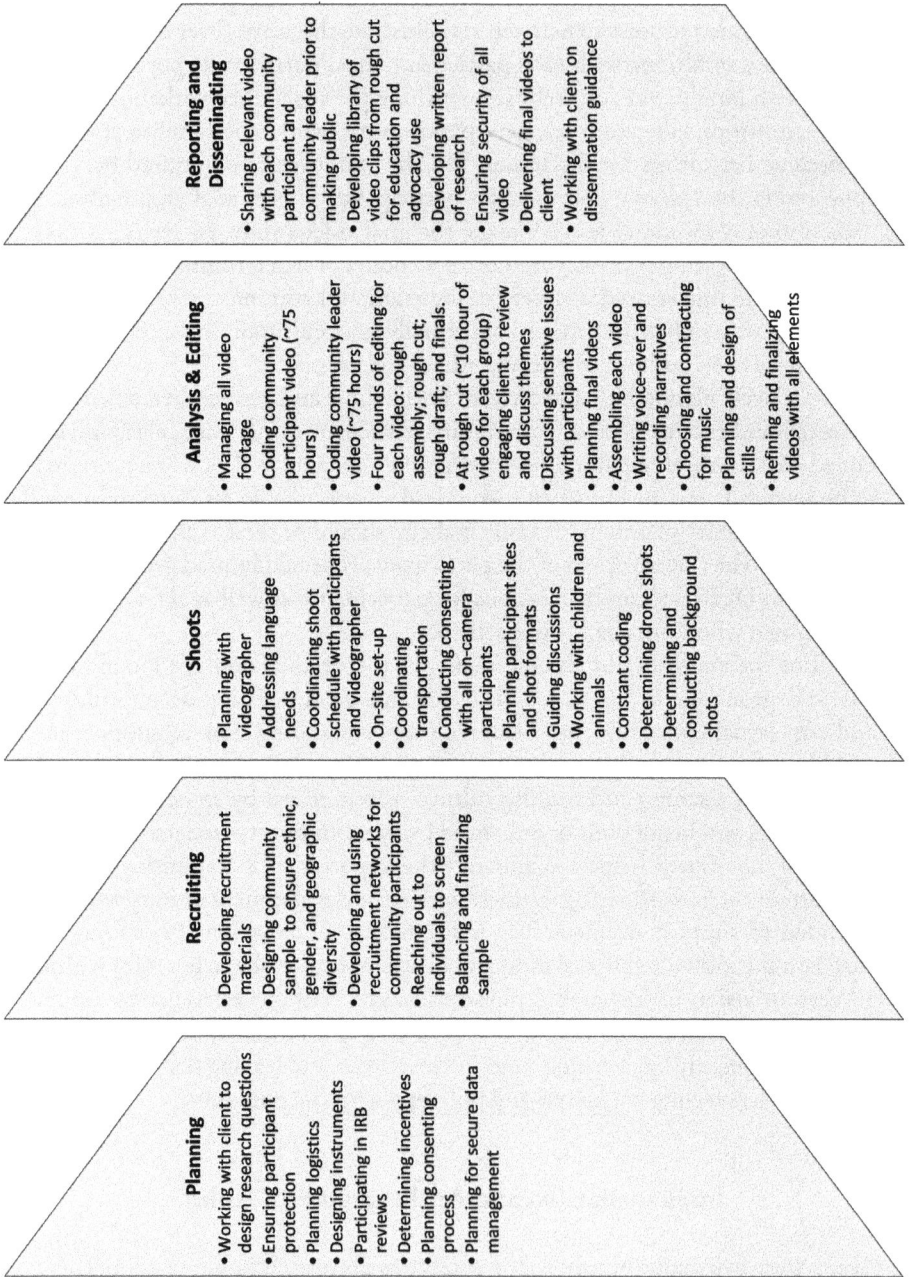

Figure 13.1. The five major phases of the video ethnographic study, including several components of each phase. © 2020 LTG Associates, Inc.

dressed and resolved. The first phase, planning, included developing a unified consent for the research and separate video consents. A critical element for the quality and utility of the project was the creation of continuous discussions with the client on progress, value of learnings, and issues affecting timing. The client was clear that quality was key, and so, for example, a timeline that would have challenged quality was revised.

Next came recruiting. We worked with the NORC and DHCS teams to conduct outreach and recruitment to providers doing creative work and parents with limited incomes raising healthy children. In recruiting parents, there were challenges in identifying both men and also Asian Americans interested in participating. We worked through professional networks to reach into communities. Men and Asian Americans were identified, and we were referenced in the networks as trusted partners, which lead to successful recruitment.

We also worked through our own statewide professional networks to reach into communities that were not generally included in state research. It is essential to highlight the importance of existing professional networks to successful participant recruitment. These networks were developed over a number of years and through a variety of our projects in California. The responsiveness of the networks was the result of demonstrating consistency in approach and in keeping commitments over prolonged periods and across a variety of issues.

The third and most challenging phase was shooting the videos. We worked with a professional videographer and traveled across California to film ethnographic interviews, events, and contexts. Planning for and managing these "shoots" was logistically complex. We also needed to be able to create safe spaces for each conversation and to be alert and respond to the reality of life for the participants without losing continuity of responses. The videographer had to respond technologically to inevitable noise and visual disruption issues. Kids, dogs, and life: every shoot included participants' realities; the team flexed with the participants' needs and challenges and incorporated them in the video as appropriate.

To ensure that we addressed all the key issues, we developed a constant coding process using a second offsite anthropologist; there were twice-daily debriefings, and we made on-the-fly adjustments to the shooting schedule as needed to ensure appropriate topical and environmental coverage.

Participants sometimes shared dangerous or very sensitive revelations. To deal with these issues, we developed signals with the videographer to suspend shooting. We also had to be mindful of participants' expenses. The video team paid for any associated participant costs, including meals, in addition to the honoraria participants received.

In a typical scenario, the shoot took place over two consecutive days in a participant's community. The first day was a time to talk and move through community spaces. By the end of the first day, we and the participant jointly finalized the schedule for the second day. We planned each day to be about six hours, but the timing was flexible to reflect the needs of the respondent. The videographer was present for both days, and, in general, all activities and discussions were recorded. The camera was turned off at the specific request of the respondent or the ethnographer. Generally, it was at the direction of the lead ethnographer to suspend filming in order to protect the privacy or safety of the respondent.

The fourth phase was the analysis and editing of the large volume of video. As noted, more than 150 hours of video were shot over a few months; the team then worked to edit the video while engaged with the participants and the DHCS. Ensuring fidelity of the vision and message was critical and ensuring the effectiveness of the products for their teaching and advocacy purposes was essential.

We created a multitiered video analysis scheme involving three anthropologists. In the final round, we engaged clients in reviewing themes and the chosen video clips; all the steps ensured a quality of process and product. Participants were also engaged in video review to identify any concerns about sensitive material and the appropriateness of their video representation.

It was also necessary to adapt the length of the available video. The videos were intended to be twenty minutes each, but the volume of quality video and important stories argued for longer products. In the end, each video was nearly an hour long as we worked with the client to focus on product quality and its utility for advocacy and education.

The final phase was reporting and dissemination. A significant topic that emerged here was the recording of highly sensitive issues that could not be used in a public video but were important for policymakers and program planners to understand, so we worked to include this material in reports. More on dissemination is included in the outcomes section.

Outcomes

Two approximately one-hour videos were the products of the work. The first, focused on service providers and developers, was called "Being the Change." The second, focused on parents and raising well children, was called "Raising UP the Children." Both were professionally narrated, and each featured a professional soundtrack. A companion product of the video ethnography was also produced: a library of thematically organized film clips that could be used by the DHCS to illustrate important issues for advocacy and education.

The videos have been widely disseminated by DHCS staff and the clips used for education and advocacy; the videos are archived on the DHCS website and freely available for viewing and downloading. Equally important, the individuals who were the subjects of each of the videos were pleased with their participation and excited in knowing that the results would be useful in shaping future policy and programs.

Ultimately, there were five major results from this project, although the process was as important as the outcomes.

It is important to remember that the client for the videos was the State of California Department of Health Care Services, Office of the Medical Director. California is a diverse state, with ethnicity being the most obvious element. However, California is also a state of great geographic diversity, stretching almost the equivalent distance from Bangor, Maine, to Richmond, Virginia. The population centers of the San Francisco Bay Area, Los Angeles/Orange County/Inland Empire, and San Diego contrast starkly with the agricultural Central and Sacramento Valleys and the "True North," comprising the northern tier of California's fifty-nine counties and representing an entirely different demographic, as do the Sierra Nevada counties. California is the most populous state in the United States and the fifth largest economy in the world; policies and programs developed here often influence the rest of the country. The videos, sited as they were, had the potential to become a ready representation of the key themes voiced by families and community leaders; these pointed to the challenges and opportunities of achieving wellness and the potential for policy and programs to respond.

Result 1: Enhanced Understanding

DHCS staff developed an enhanced understanding of the process of engaging communities through this project. They were thoughtful and engaged at each step and sought to understand the anthropological difference. We were also thoughtful about their culture and how that affected their expectations and understanding of our processes and products. The work with the DHCS and the NORC was as anthropological as the conduct of the videos. Ensuring that they understood our purpose and perspective and that our methods were well grounded in the discipline allowed them to respond flexibly to our requests. Providing them with stories from recruitment and from the field allowed them to continually experience the process vicariously as we discussed the implications and, in a limited way, the meanings.

At the end of the project, DHCS staff immediately began discussing the potential for using anthropological tools in a new project focused on the implementation of interventions in the field. There was also a very sensitive finding from the discussions with participants that we determined not to share in the videos but discussed with the DHCS. They decided that the finding was significant and would be immediately reflected in the planning for a large, statewide, community intervention project. The issue was discovered because of the trust and intimacy developed with the participants as we became partners in educating the DHCS and its stakeholders. An important aspect of educating was being able to clearly articulate emic perspectives to the clients.

Result 2: Videos

A total of thirteen individual ethnographies were conducted, and from those, two full-length videos were constructed and became the central result of the project. The videos told individual stories that, for community participants, illustrated the challenges to wellness as well as the strengths that they and their communities bring to creating wellness. Each segment had its own story arc, and each video as a whole told a story across diverse participants that in the end was thematically complete and sound. The narrative was distinctly anthropological, even as the events and views were uniquely those of the participants—both the community participants and the community leaders.

We invited the participants to be thoughtful and reflective; we respected their knowledge and expertise. They responded by sharing their views, their histories, and their friends, families, and colleagues with us, and by digging deeply into the context and meaning of health and wellness for them, their families, their communities, and those they serve.

As with most ethnographies, each was personal and often intimate; all were intense, with some including tears and all including laughter. Most concluded with an ongoing bond, even after only two days of being together in person. The design of the "fieldwork," the development of the relationships with the participants, the creation of the questions, and the cocreation of each encounter were fundamentally anthropological in their methods and disciplinary philosophy. Finally, the shaping of the videos honored the ethnographic tradition of clear and evocative storytelling complementing careful and methodologically sound analysis—in this case, married with videography. We wanted the viewer to be moved and informed through their encounters with the participants in the videos.

Before the penultimate version of each video was delivered to the DHCS, it was shared with each participant for their review to ensure that any concerns they had would be addressed. All responding participants were pleased with their segments. When the DHCS indicated it would share the videos generally, individual participants were informed and provided an opportunity to express concerns. Responding participants were all pleased that the videos would be available to the public and that their segments would be used for education, program and policy development, and advocacy.

The videos were disseminated to the DHCS and the US Department of Agriculture, Food and Nutrition Service, a cofunder of the work, and they have been used to inform these agencies' work. The DHCS also shared the videos with partners and stakeholders, including other state organizations, and planned to continue to use them with different audiences. When the videos became publicly available on the DHCS website, we ensured that participants were informed. Some held viewing events and shared them with family, friends, and colleagues.

The videos also highlighted the work of leading-edge programs and their staffs, which is creating new opportunities for programs on the front line. The program staffs were able to discuss their rationale for the construction of their interventions, relate their understanding of the important values and beliefs of their clients, reflect on their challenges, and honor their strengths and successes.

For each participant, our purpose was to tell a thoughtful story that respected and honored their lives, knowledge, and work, and which could be used to educate a larger public. The DHCS was committed to ensuring that the videos would be disseminated to those publics and that what was learned from the participants was woven into policy and programs.

Result 3: Final Report

The final report was not intended to be central to the project, but it turned out to be very important. It became a vehicle for telling fuller and more intimate stories of the participants in order to illustrate important issues that were not appropriate for the videos and the public. It also was an opportunity to discuss the methods and process that were used to develop the videos, which illustrated for the DHCS the benefit of using an anthropological approach. Finally, we used the report as an opportunity to discuss our analysis of the process and the data—150 hours of video and more of observations and discussions—and to suggest policy and programmatic ways to use the information. DHCS staff reported that, while the report would not be made public because of the sensitive nature of some of some of the information, they were actively using the results.

Result 4: Video Clip Library

In addition to the videos, DHCS staff requested that we create a library of video clips drawn from the ten hours of rough-cut video for each group. We utilized the analysis themes to select video clips. The clips were chosen to represent geography, gender, and ethnicity for community participants, and geography, topic, and clientele for community leaders. The DHCS has used the clips for presentations, briefings, educational events, and trainings. These expanded the opportunity for the videos to reach new audiences and to have a widening impact on policy and programs.

Result 5: Participant Experience

As discussed earlier, all participants engaged in cocreating their ethnographies and invited important others in their personal and work lives to participate. The process of cocreation was important not only as a feature of the creative ethnographic process but also because it gave the lead ethnographer an opportunity to interact with the participant multiple times prior to the onsite shoot. These interactions helped to enrich the creative engagement of the participants with the ethnographers prior to the filming and served to reduce anxiety about strangers entering their lives. Even with that preparation, all of the participants were somewhat nervous before the filming, and all admitted to being a bit intimidated by the prospect of being filmed. For the majority of participants, within an hour of being with the ethnographic team, they were fully engaged in the creation of their videos. When participants attempted to defer to the ethnographers, it engendered a conversation about what they and we wanted to be able to illustrate through the creation of their video; this generally encouraged them to provide direction for the video. Throughout the filming, we reminded the participants that they had an opportunity to talk about issues of importance and that policymakers among others would hear their voices.

Most of the participants commented that they found the entire process to be deeply respectful and felt honored by being asked to teach others through their reflections. For the community participants, they shared both the strengths and the challenges of their lives and communities with us. In some cases, they shared details of their lives that were raw and sensitive and, for a few, dangerous. We accepted their trust and ensured that they were safe in the process and honored in the outcomes while not hiding their challenges. For the community leaders, we offered an opportunity to share the difficulties and successes of working with communities struggling with extraordinary challenges and working to raise fully well children. In some cases, this allowed them to reflect on their own struggles to escape poverty in order to return and serve those communities.

In the end, the videos were the heart of the work and are the visual representation of the stories and lives we came to understand as a result of the ethnographic work.[1] They are intended to educate, persuade, and move audiences who have policy and program influence. They also allowed the participants to speak their truth to power and allowed policymakers and program professionals to hear and see the people they serve.

The Anthropological Difference

This project could have been completed without anthropologists. Had it been, it would not have truly achieved the client's purpose: to gain a different, deeper, more synthetic understanding of the issues that affect early childhood wellness for families with limited incomes and how leading-edge programs are working to affect wellness in communities. DHCS staff specifically sought to add to its formative learning through the use of video ethnography specifically practiced by anthropologists. And, while that is what they requested, they were open to learning and being surprised by both the process and the products. Working with DHCS and NORC staff created a nearly ideal environment to develop the videos in a manner that was completely consistent with the best of anthropological practice. When we discussed how we would approach the development of questions, they responded thoughtfully. When we recommended shifts in the approach or processes, they were interested in learning about our perspective and rationale. We in turn were transparent and collaborative, and always flexible unless or until we felt that a request would in some way degrade the process or product, at which time we shared our concerns.

The anthropological difference began with the reframing of the community participant-focused research questions so that they centered on families and their lived experience and context. It continued through the identification and recruitment of participants. In most cases, community participant selection worked through the ethnographers' social networks or social networks created by the ethnographers, which allowed the ethnographers to be passed from one contact to the next as a trusted source. Finally, the video interviews for both groups were a wholly anthropological process from the establishment of rapport through the filming; a traditional ethnographic process was the basis for all interactions. The editing process of the videos was an example of the constant comparative method. The creation of a presentation that depicted the lives of individuals and was validated by the participants closed the loop from interview to data to analysis to final video production.

Ethnography, a method of talking with individuals and communities, is generally used by anthropologists to understand how people see their world, understand their environment, and shape their lives. A video ethnography uses video to document the ethnography and is intended to present individuals and communities in natural settings conducting their daily lives, interacting with others, and responding to questions regarding the issues that affect their health and wellness. Each video was planned together so that it included time to discuss issues of importance and the time to see community scenes and events that affect wellness.

In the field, we were observers and participants; we were the students to be educated by the emic depictions of the participants' lives and environment. We were led by the participants more than we led, focusing conversations and events to ensure the full exploration of lives for the community participants and interventions for the community leaders. We asked them to explain the meaning, the culture, and the purpose at each step. For some, no one had asked them before to reflect in these ways; for others, their lives had already included reflection. All spoke to being touched and moved by the experience. Finally, the products have been used to inform, educate, and shape understanding of the needs and strengths of families, communities, and those who would serve them.

Cathleen E. Crain and **Nathaniel Tashima** are the managing partners of LTG Associates, the oldest anthropologically based consulting group in North America, founded in 1982. Nathaniel holds a PhD from Northwestern University with a concentration in psychological anthropology. Cathleen holds an MA from McMaster University with a specialization in medical anthropology. For nearly four decades, they have been pathbreakers, influencing the discipline of anthropology by promoting, valuing, and modeling examples of innovative anthropologically based research, policy, and practice to address health disparities in populations and ethnic/cultural groups in numerous communities in the United States and across the globe.

Reiko Ishihara-Brito, formerly senior research associate at LTG Associates, is currently at the compliance advisor ombudsman of the World Bank Group. Anthropologically trained, she is committed to understanding the needs of historically and socially underrepresented communities and raising their voices to relevant stakeholders and policymakers. Her work experience ranges from serving as a union organizer and bargaining team member for the University of California system to working with Indigenous communities in cultural heritage conservation and education in Central America, and it now addresses social and environmental concerns of communities affected by projects funded by the private-sector arm of the World Bank Group. She worked on a variety of projects for LTG, including a national exploratory project working with Asian American, Native Hawaiian, and Pacific Islander child wellness.

Erick Lee Cummings received his BS from the Art Institute of California, Sacramento, in 2015, with a specialization in digital film and video production. He has more than ten years of professional experience producing, shooting, editing, and directing video. He is currently a freelance digital filmmaker and video editor for various outlets, ranging from corporate media and promotional material to web video projects and commercial television. He also has an FAA certification in aerial videography. His skills include producing, directing, and editing; developing creative concepts; and effectively setting up lighting and audio.

Note

1. The videos are available at: https://www.dhcs.ca.gov/formsandpubs/publications/Pages/Obesity-Prevention-Project.aspx.

References

Backman, D., O. Stewart, and N. Kohatsu. 2017. "Formative Research to Guide an Obesity Prevention Program for Low-Income Californians." *Journal of the Academy of Nutrition and Dietetics* 117(10): A142. https://doi.org/10.1016/j.jand.2017.08.087.

Crain, C., and N. Tashima. 2015. "Family Matters: Exploring Cultural Values and Practices for Raising Healthy Children." Meeting presentation, Society for Applied Anthropology, Pittsburgh, PA, March.

Dao, L., N. Tashima, C. Crain, and R. Ishihara-Brito. 2014. "Over Two Million of the United States' 'Model Minority' Living in Poverty: Health Implications and Dispelling Myths." Meeting presentation, Society for Applied Anthropology, Albuquerque, NM, March.

Ishihara-Brito, R., C. Crain, N. Tashima, and L. Dao. 2014. "The Childhood Obesity Epidemic in the US—Says Who? Asian American and Pacific Islander Perceptions of and Attitudes toward Body Image and Relevant Factors." Meeting presentation, Society for Applied Anthropology, Albuquerque, NM, March.

Neuwirth, E. B., J. Bellows, A. H. Jackson, and P. M. Price. 2012. "How Kaiser Permanente Uses Video Ethnography of Patients for Quality Improvement, such as in Shaping Better Care Transitions." *Health Affairs* 31(6): 1244–50.

Tashima, N., C. Crain, and R. Ishihara-Brito. 2016. "Intersections of Cultural Values, Practices, and Public Health Policy: Understanding Cultural Assets in Context for Child Wellness Advocacy in Asian American, Native Hawaiian, and Pacific Islander Communities." Meeting presentation, Society for Applied Anthropology, Vancouver, BC, Canada, April.

Tashima, N., and C. Crain. 2015. "Culture(al) Matters: Results from a Multiethnic, Multicultural Assessment Exploring Values and Practices for Raising Healthy Children." Meeting presentation, American Evaluation Association, Chicago, IL, November.

PART V

❀

Sociocultural Change and Adaptation

CHAPTER 14

~:~

Dug-Well Revival
An Ethnographic Project for Drinking Water in North Bihar, India

LUISA CORTESI

Project Background

In the chronically flooded areas of North Bihar, India, a network of development organizations working on safe drinking water in a flood-affected region found themselves in a conundrum. Dug-well water, which is often contaminated bacteriologically, seemed far easier to clean than handpump water, which is often polluted with heavy metals. Yet the history of the dug-well is characterized by caste-based discrimination, and community members seemed to have definitively turned for their drinking water to the handpump, perceived as clean and modern. Ethnographic research, however, revealed residual value for the dug-well on several grounds—in addition to those that are religious and caste-based—as well as a variety of problems for the handpump. On the basis of these ethnographic data, a network of organizations called Megh Pyne Abhiyan (MPA)—literally "the clouds' water campaign"—decided to start working on dug-well revival, but they would do so only by stimulating conversations on the matter. Encouraged by positive responses, MPA started participating more actively in the revival process in order to ensure that dug-wells remain collective and open-access and to eschew the caste-based manipulation of drinking water.

MPA's five organizations, all of Gandhian inspiration, had been working separately on issues of development and poverty in their respective areas (the districts of Supaul, Saharsa, Khagaria, Madhubani, and West Champaran). Their leaders, however, all men in their early sixties, shared a common personal connection with the independence leader and political theorist Jayaprakash Narayan, who led a "total revolution" against Indira Gandhi in the mid-1970s. In accordance with such a history, and realizing the current difficulties related to drinking water in the area, MPA leaders chose to organize in the form of a campaign, which meant involving local people in conversations about the issue and possible coping mechanisms rather than following the typical development transfer of funds and technology.

During floods, as well as in their aftermath, finding clean drinking water is as challenging as it is vital for survival. The inhabitants of North Bihar access drinking water mostly from handpumps, although there are still dug-wells, which used to be the more common source of drinking water.

The dug-well in rural North Bihar is a man-made, brick-lined cavity in the ground that gives access to shallow groundwater. It is a communal technology, owned by several families together, unlike the single-owned handpump. A dug-well has to be cleaned of debris occasionally, and it takes several men to perform the maintenance together. The reason for the collective ownership of the dug-well, I was told, is precisely located in the practice of sharing the labor required to dig and maintain it, apart from the convenience of splitting the cost of the initial investment. Both digging and cleaning require shared labor and shared knowledge, the latter transmitted from one generation to the next.

Traditionally, dug-wells were owned collectively by members of a single caste, and the sharing of the water with members of other castes was restricted by rules of commensality. This practice translated not only into the inability to share water even when unevenly distributed but also into a climate of deep humiliation and violent discrimination connected to water and the technology of water access.[1]

The more modern handpump, on the other hand, is a hand-operated system of suctions and pipes inserted in the ground, a materiality aligned with the practice of individual ownership and usage. I found a high number of handpumps to be nonfunctional, however, a fact that locals most often explained as due to overuse. These frequent malfunctions are, I was told, the materiality that explains the individual ownership of the handpump. The other reasoning for the handpump to be owned by a single family is that, compared with the open dug-well, the handpump hides the extracted water from sight: the lack of visibility of the resource's quantity and quality means that accountability is unfeasible, as are collective adjustments in terms of demand. Nor is cooperation required for cleaning; although the handpump manuals prescribe regular cleaning, it is common practice to not do so.

Individual ownership does not ensure independence, however, although independence was also mentioned by some residents as the justification for preferring the handpump to the dug-well. Knowledge about the setup, function, and repair of the handpump, as well as the necessary maintenance instruments, are still mostly owned by technicians belonging to commercial entities (Cortesi, forthcoming). As a result, people rely on the handpump shop in the next big town instead of on each other.

The fact that handpump owners do not believe the handpumps need routine cleaning does not necessarily mean that they believe that the handpumps provide clean water. While handpump water is often cooler than ambient temperature, and thus feels refreshing to drink, it is often also foul smelling, and an opaque film settles on the surface of water that is left out overnight. In addition, handpump water stains buckets and the pump platform a rusty orange color. When used to wash white clothes, it often taints them a yellowish hue. It changes the taste of food that is cooked in it, in particular food cooked without spices, such as boiled rice. It is commonly said that certain animals, such as cattle, do not like to drink handpump water (Cortesi, forthcoming).

It was perhaps for these reasons that the handpump, introduced in the late 1970s by the Bihar government under UNICEF's advice, was at first refused by the rural population, although the official narrative attributes the refusal to a component of the pump mechanism that was, initially, made of leather, and hence rejected by upper-caste Hindus. The head of UNICEF India at the time, Rupert Talbot, the self-proclaimed man behind the introduction of handpumps, recalls in his memoirs that the handpump remained underutilized until the 1990s, when, mysteriously, the technology became increasingly accepted (Talbot and Black 2005). In today's North Bihar, residents have definitively turned to the handpump and thus turned their backs on the dug-well.

Program Description

In 2007 and 2008, I worked as state coordinator and applied anthropologist with MPA. As I experienced myself, North Bihar, the alluvial floodplain of the rivers that descend from the Himalayan range, is often a sea on land. A few months into my new job, when I had barely met all of my new colleagues, we were inundated by devastating floods that affected twenty-five million persons. The next year, one of the main rivers in the area completely changed its course and started running on a previous riverbed that had been dry for over a century, which had since become home to three million persons. While floods are nothing new in a river-dense landscape, the recent history of inundations in most of North Bihar shows that they are increasingly severe, frequent, and disastrous.

After the first few months of disaster management, I started redesigning my job in order to cater to the specifics of the organization and the contextual challenges. My previous year-long experience in ethnographic research in South India gave me the confidence to conduct new ethnographic research, through which, in line with my training in development studies and anthropology of development, I devised my inquiry to inform development interventions.

I also designed an extensive and comprehensive water quality testing exercise. After receiving opportune training by the Development Alternatives

Group, a New Delhi–based NGO, my colleagues and I tested fifty of the most-used water sources in each of the twenty-two *panchayat* (one of the smallest administrative units in the area). These were mostly centrally located handpumps, but there were also a few dug-wells that still had water. With color-coded reagents developed by the same organization that trained us, we tested for several parameters, including bacteriological contamination, iron, arsenic, fluoride, and residual chlorine. Each test result was associated with a synthetic sociological profile of the technology and the community accessing it.

Although our testing was eventually interrupted by a second major flood, we tested long enough to get remarkable results. We found several contaminants above permissible limits: in the handpumps, we found very high quantities of iron and arsenic, even in areas that were not officially declared as arsenic affected. In certain pockets we also found considerable amounts of fluoride. In dug-wells, we found biological contamination—detected through E. coli—rather than chemical contamination.

Our results were consistent with information obtained locally, as well as with the sensorial evidence of the water. Locals were very aware of the effects of the handpump on human health and its visible traces in the water, despite not identifying the contamination with iron at the time. In the dug-well, however, where water is visible—visibly available or scarce, visibly clean or dirty—people perceived the water as dirty and justified their perceptions with the fact that the well had not been cleaned.

Based on these results, we realized relatively quickly that MPA was facing the conundrum mentioned initially. While the campaign had focused on rainwater harvesting, we understood that rainwater—an excellent source of clean water locally, but the safe harvesting and storage of which requires some attention and resources—could not be the sole source of drinking water for the entire year. Despite its quality, groundwater is considered the primary source of drinking water. It is accessible, available, cooler than surface water, and socially advantageous, and we realized that not all rural residents possessing a handpump were likely to shift their consumption from groundwater to rainwater—thus the need to find an additional source of water.

We also realized that the dug-well, an open source that villagers had been cleaning regularly for generations, was, in this specific context of polluted groundwater, a more reliable source of clean drinking water than the handpump. Yet we had no intention, through the promotion of the dug-well, to offer opportunities of recrudescence to castism or to risk such a possibility. Adding to the intractability of the problem, the dug-well did not seem to have much credence among the generation of current family heads or the younger generation, who had chosen individual independence over collective management, regardless of the consequences.

Ethnographic research revealed, however, that those with gastric ailments who had begun drinking rainwater on a regular basis had started feeling some improvement, and they had thus begun to correlate some of their health concerns with handpump-sourced drinking water. This observation was aligned with the impressions of seasonal migrants, who found it difficult to return to the area due to the rusty taste of its handpump water. Others had started discussing the historical adoption of the handpump over the dug-well and their underlying political and commercial implications. The handpump, I found, was as riddled with power issues as the dug-well (Cortesi, forthcoming).

On the other hand, the dug-well continued to yield positive meanings of both self-help and community building. Even if dug-wells were a tradition from a religious perspective—several Hindu temples use dug-wells to secure water for rituals—the dug-well had emerged culturally as having residual value regardless of religious practices. Its utility was widely recognized, for example, in managing a disruptive fire emergency, which is a classic village-level disaster, given that the primary composition of housing material is organic fibers. During a fire, handpumps are unable to yield sufficient water and often break down under exertion, while dug-wells give people a chance to save their village.

Suresh Choudhary, a man in his fifties, was proudly maintaining the dug-well built by his great-great-grandfather and accessing water from it, although not for drinking purposes. Although he cleaned the dug-well regularly, he claimed not to know how to keep the water of drinkable quality, even though his father, who was around, seemed confident about its safety. Among the reasons to keep the dug-well clean, the family mentioned that (1) their rice remained white after cooking while others' rice turned yellow, (2) their lentils tasted better than anyone else's in the village, (3) their clothes remained white after washing them, while others were easily discolored, and (4) their cattle preferred to drink water sourced from the dug-well rather than that from the handpump. All the advantages of the dug-well over the handpump that were mentioned by this family are compatible with the effects of utilizing iron-free water instead of iron-contaminated water. These remarks also highlight a discourse of purity (purity of food and clothes are both of high symbolic value) that values dug-well water over handpump water (Cortesi 2022).

At MPA, we decided to explore the possibility of reviving dug-wells. How to do this was discussed intensely. In line with MPA's identity as a campaign and following the ethnographic research exercise that the partners experienced while accompanying me, we chose to eschew the typical NGO modality as a solution provider and instead set out to engage individuals in conversations about dug-wells and to encourage the transmission of local knowledge about how to clean them. This involved stimulating conversations about unutilized dug-wells in areas where water quality tests indicated their comparative benefits.

Figure 14.1. Suresh Choudhary's father, with his well in Bihar, India. © Luisa Cortesi.

This choice was difficult because the funding agency paying for the field-workers' salaries expected a one-size-fits-all solution that could be exported to other areas in India. Refusing to do as the agency expected was not easy, but after opportune discussion we all agreed that valuing local specificities was a safer, more respectful, and more progressive approach. Local knowledge, while never homogenous or endogenous (Agrawal 1995), was struggling amid multiple conflicting interventions by political and commercial entities (as discussed in Cortesi 2014). Further, a dug-well is not only a matter of water, but also a matter of soil. In the end, since dug-well revival entails the risky procedure of going down into a large and open hole in the ground, it seemed safer and more reasonable to trust locals in handling their water and soil (I have argued that these are "two faces of the same coin" in Cortesi 2021). The funding agency was flexible enough to continue to support our efforts, albeit modestly.

Implementation and the Anthropologist's Role

The floods of 2007 went mostly underreported because Bihar, just resurfacing from a period of political turmoil, was still considered too dangerous by international and even national development organizations. Media personnel refused to visit North Bihar, as infamous for its many kidnappings and lawlessness as it is for its floods (for example, see Ahmed 2007 on children kidnapped in the thousands in Bihar).

I faced the inundations mostly alone and with underdeveloped local language skills. I was caught in floodwater several times: stuck in the heavy rains that inundated all the roads and terrain around my forest shack in Saharsa; caught off guard by a surge of floodwater that obliterated the previously safe-looking road I was traveling on in Motihari; stranded in a flooded town in West Champaran; caught in a quick and dirty flash flood between Madhubani and Dharbanga; and trapped by a suddenly engorged river I was about to cross on foot in the north of Supaul. Walking through flooded areas to visit affected villages and self-made relief camps—sometimes among floating dead bodies and facing physical harm but also making uncomfortable decisions about relief operations and long-term planning—was demanding, but this experience was a watershed moment for me both personally and professionally.

When I joined MPA, I was not exactly welcomed by the NGO's leaders. While I was initially worried that my presence would echo colonial governance, perhaps of the interiorized type, I soon learned that my interlocutors did not identify or behave as victims. They had historical interpretations and antagonisms that were very different from what I had imagined. But they still had very good reasons to prefer not having me around: Why on earth would the heads of these five long-standing NGOs, all seasoned political and social leaders, accept a young, foreign woman who could barely take care of herself in that context? Why entrust her with coordinating all the teams, making programmatic decisions, and controlling members' finances? The fact that the network founder sought gender equity and wanted an outsider with no affiliations to leverage was, reasonably, not in their best interest. From the second visit, each team put me through tests of different kinds—patience, determination, but mostly physical endurance—devised to either give me the opportunity to prove myself or, even better, to exit and go back to where I came from.

But it was during the floods, my "baptism of water," that my relationship with the organizations and the team changed radically. Perhaps the awareness of what it means to live in rural Bihar during destructive floods changed my attitude toward my own colleagues. In part, they saw the amazement in the eyes of villagers at seeing a foreign young woman go through the floods with them, surprised that I had not simply taken the next flight home. It may also have been the way I handled the network and its involvement in relief operations that eventually proved my dedication to MPA and my alignment with their practical ideology.

Being accepted and trusted by fieldworkers and team leaders was essential to accomplishing the tasks my job entailed. Not only did I have to lead—and then co-lead, when the network founder returned from travels abroad—a complex network of NGOs through devastating floods a few months into my jobs, but I was also proposing to challenge long-term development frames. My plan was to rethink the typical cycle of social development intervention by introducing concomitant ethnographic research in the practice of development.

This was not the "design-intervention-evaluation" phased paradigm or the classic Participatory Rural Appraisal or Research Action (Chambers 1994), the limitations of which I had both studied in the literature and experienced firsthand in Tamil Nadu, but a form of research-cum-project that was based in a dialectic relation of mutual learning. Choosing to engage local stakeholders in extensive conversations about dug-wells and encourage knowledge transmission on how to clean them meant choosing the slow route, with less-than-immediate success stories and photographic evidence and without the relations of patronage that commonly involve both funding agencies and local NGOs at interconnected scales. Toward this goal, I reformed and trained the five teams of local residents for a total of fifty-two fieldworkers, men and women in equal parts.

After a few rounds of meetings in several villages, we were invited to visit a newly cleaned dug-well. The owner of the well, Ranvir Prasad, an eighty-eight-year-old man, welcomed us with all honors. While everyone's eyes were on the well's water, I noticed a sparkle in the old man's eyes. He was extremely proud of his century-old dug-well, not simply because he could source clean water from it, which he always knew was better in quality than the foul-smelling water sourced by his handpump, but because he descended himself inside the dug-well with his seventeen-year-old great-grandson.

When I heard the story of the old man *in* the dug-well, I was terrified—at least until I understood that being the source of information for his great-grandson, being able to teach him something worthwhile, and, on top of that, being *listened to* by him was, for this man at this point of his life, worth the risk. That meeting was a turning point. We recognized the safety precautions that we would need to warn others about. We also realized the emotions that this intergenerational knowledge transmission could stir up.

In the following months, several other villages started to revive dug-wells, cleaning and restoring them at their own expense. When invited, MPA provided some guidance. When extensive repairs were needed, MPA contributed materials such as bricks and cement. In poor villages inhabited by low castes, we contributed more bricks and cement, and in return we received plenty of enthusiasm and encouragement. Under my co-leadership with the MPA founder, MPA directly facilitated the revival of sixty-four dug-wells, of which forty-one were repaired. Many more were revived by locals on their own.

Our intervention had two conditions: first, the cleaning event must involve as many people as possible from all families present in the village; second, anyone and everyone should be able to access the well on their own, forever. This second condition was of course a pass for free riders, but we felt it was necessary to avoid the risk of castism. After my departure, discussed below, MPA's strategy slightly changed by only working with *Mahadalits*,[2] hence preventing, instead of fighting, discrimination by privileging the most discriminated.

As the news about the success of the dug-well was spreading on its own, the local governmental administration of the Khagaria district, a heavily arsenic-affected area, decided to financially sustain the program by reimbursing part of the expenses to the families who revived their dug-well or dug a new one and by digging new wells in *Mahadalit* villages. When my colleague and MPA founder excitedly related the news of the government's interest in the project to the organizations' heads, they laughed it off. "There isn't enough grease in it to make the machine work," they said. As we evaluated the hypothesis that the local government could be serious about collaborating, we all shared the same mixed feelings; we were enthusiastic that our initiative had the important partnership of the government but also wary that such a people-led initiative could be instrumentalized and misappropriated, or could then be perceived as yet another relief operation.

I went to meet the district magistrate of Khagaria (a representative of the state and the highest state authority of the district) at the time, Abhay Singh, and found him very approachable and sensitive to our concerns. He said he completely understood my preoccupations and was willing to set up a process with which we were also comfortable. We decided to work through the National Rural Development Employment Guarantee Act (NREGA)[3] so that the people themselves would continue to clean the wells but their work would be paid as wage labor. Despite the NREGA being relatively new at the time, cases of misappropriation already abounded. It was helpful that SAMTA, the local NGO operating in Khagaria, had a strong reputation for honesty.

On the other hand, as we weighed the alternatives, we realized that, given the circumstances, the NREGA was the best we could hope for in terms of government support. Mr. Singh rightly argued that while the dug-well was for the locals' benefit, it was also a public good for which the state was paying elsewhere, as with roads and bridges. In this case, however, public ownership did not mean government ownership, and we could still clarify that regular maintenance was the villagers', not the state's, responsibility. Shortly after our meeting and the revival of just a few dug-wells, Abhay Singh was transferred, and the initiative slowed down. Perhaps there was not enough grease in it after all.

After the first years of MPA's active engagement (2007–10), we had no budget for the dug-well intervention for the next two years. During that time, the project mostly ran itself, with MPA continuing to provide support, although that support was more reactive than proactive. Financial support for the next five years (2012–17) only included a very limited budget for dug-well revival.

At that time, my own involvement with MPA changed. During the second major flood we endured, I was severely hit by several major diseases in the span of a month. While I weathered them alone, there came a point when I was so weak that my ability to work was impaired, and I could not remain in Bihar without being a burden. Once recovered, I managed to return to India as a fellow in the United Nations Development Programme, and then as a water expert for the World Food Programme. During that time, I supported MPA from afar and visited whenever possible.

While I intended to eventually return to work for MPA, things took a different turn when I was offered the opportunity to continue my education with a double PhD in anthropology and environmental studies as Yale University. Although I was always writing, talking, and thinking about Bihar and its waters and people, and I spent all my summer holidays there, I was not able to be as involved in MPA's daily routine as I would have liked. However, having finished my third year in the program early and acquired research funds, I moved back to India for three more years, mostly in North Bihar. The events described next happened during a period when I was no longer involved in the daily management of MPA but rather participated as an advisor, a member of the board of trustees, a close friend to most of those involved, a frequent visitor, and also, at times, an enthusiastic host for MPA's members.

As our teams were spreading themselves thin under conditions of financial distress, several villages in the Khagaria district took matters into their own hands. In 2015, MPA detected arsenic pollution ranging from 50 to 400 parts per billion (ppb), with a seasonal average of 250–300 ppb, well above the permissible limit of 10 ppb. As a result, the management committee of the nearby temple, which had been set up to renovate the building, decided to divert part of their funds toward reviving the dug-well in front of the temple. They also pledged to maintain the water of the dug-well as a service to the community. Prioritizing the dug-well over temple repairs or embellishments is far from commonsensical, but the temple management committee clearly stated that the dug-well not only served as a source of clean water but also represented hope for a village suffering from high mortality rates (in all probability due to arsenicosis and consequent cancer) and that, as a collective resource, it would be the symbol of a cohesive community. The temple revival had therefore opened the possibility of collectively prioritizing and managing water.

Several more villages joined the movement on their own. In West Champaran, in one village that was—and remains—recurrently flooded, the inhabitants had been asking the government and the NGOs working in the area to financially help them to set up a dug-well, which was not, unfortunately, considered a priority by these institutions. Then a villager donated a piece of land for the purpose, an important step toward dug-well construction. In another area, I saw one specific revived dug-well being visited daily by persons from different villages and different castes, including *Dalits*.

Distance to a water source is no longer a deterrent: several women told me that getting a handpump from their guardians (i.e., husbands) had not been easy. Yet, now that they were aware of its problems, they preferred to fetch drinking water from the village's revived dug-well and only used handpump water for bathing, cleaning vessels, and similar domestic uses. I also heard of a Rajput woman, whose husband had recently died of cancer, who renovated a dug-well at her own expense as an offering to her village, inviting everyone to use it, including the Muslims of the nearby settlement.

Outcomes and Challenges

Practically, the dug-well fetches cleaner water, which leads to substantial improvement in the local living conditions, not only by decreasing the negative health impacts of dirty water but also by reducing the impact of related ailments on the family budget through medical expenses, lost time, and depauperated energy.

The dug-well renewal has not always been easy. Despite its successes, the program reached its objective only partially. In several villages, residents cleaned the dug-wells a few times, only to stop doing so once MPA began visiting less frequently. Of course, the project would have benefitted from a renewed commitment of funds. On the other hand, MPA has been proud of the self-supporting ability of its work, which proves the sustainability of its signature self-management formula. When I visited Ranvir Prasad's village a few years later, the great-grandson had taken over the management of the dug-well. Instead of hiring laborers, he cleaned it by himself, involving his peers from other families in the same village—although no low castes inhabit that particular village. He also reassured us that passersby could access the water of the dug-well, a fact that we confirmed with the inhabitants of nearby villages.

Other internal and external political forces have continued to push for the handpump, a sociopolitical dynamic that deserves a longer discussion (Cortesi, forthcoming). However, there was not a single case in which locals were unsatisfied with the quality of the water obtained from a well-maintained dug-well. In the villages that discontinued maintenance, the benefits of the dug-well are still recognized. Most often the reason for discontinued maintenance was lack of agreement on cost- and labor-sharing arrangements. "The water tastes sweet, they say," my field assistant and MPA colleague Pradeep commented ironically, "but cooperation does not."

Even in villages where the dug-well revival had been discontinued, however, it has become a more common practice to discuss water quality. These conversations now also involve women, which was not the case in the past and is not the case in other areas of North Bihar. While women are not supposed to bother about, understand, or talk about water quality, I have been privileged as the interlocutor of choice for those conversations.[4] This does not mean that women are to be charged with yet another task, to also manage water resources. Although women are assigned the hardest of tasks as laborers, cleaning the dug-well is not, for a variety of reasons, considered their prerogative, and I have not found women interested in doing so. As a result, dug-well maintenance was discontinued in particular in villages where male seasonal out-migration is very high. Women who are left to fend for themselves and the family often have to cut corners, their lives becoming even harder than usual in the patriarchal society of North Bihar.

One way in which MPA has been successful has been to intentionally oppose the reproduction of castism through the wells. When replastering and repainting the top of a well, the name Megh Pyne Abhiyan has often been written on the *chabutra*, the platform. I remember telling people that the wells were theirs, not MPA's, but then realizing that I was simply not reading the situation correctly. Typically, writing the name of an *Abhiyan* (a campaign, a social movement) is meant to be a sign that no individual owns the well, that the well itself is a social initiative. In a society where access to wells and their water has been discriminatory for as long as people can remember, naming the well after a social movement signals inclusion and gives implicit permission for anybody to access its water.

Caste-based discrimination is notoriously hard to overcome, but I have yet to encounter a case in which a dug-well renewed under the aegis of MPA was manipulated to reinforce caste-based or religion-based discrimination. Fortunately, MPA's principles against castism dovetail with contemporary trends in which refusing water is one of the types of *chuachut* (impurity as a basis for discrimination related to caste, religion, or gender) that is increasingly considered an old and cruel practice.

There are, however, many subtle ways in which caste discrimination continues to run through water. I have seen members of the Dalit castes asking for water to be poured on their palms or carrying their own glasses to avoid "contaminating" public vessels. I have heard of people cleaning vessels even though the person using it had not touched it with their lips, with the excuse of caste "contamination" affecting the water through some watery "connection." Since I myself look like I do not belong to the caste system, I have been served tea in plastic disposable glasses instead of glass or steel ones, an example I report not to divert attention to those whose daily life is violated by humiliating biases but instead to clarify how dispersed and diffuse those prejudices are. However, since 2015, I have not been able to visit the area as sufficiently as necessary to account for the recrudescence of religious intolerance that India is increasingly facing.

North Bihar is an area with recurrent disasters, where citizens have become accustomed to relying on government schemes and relief activities, which commonly operate through funds and technology transfers. In contrast, the MPA project has made evident that dug-wells—and water more generally—can be invested in and managed directly by its users, without the need for external forces or copious resources. This is not necessarily an argument against the state's involvement in water supply, nor does it undermine the right to water, but it demonstrates that people, in certain contexts, do not have to passively wait for the state to provide them with water.

As a result, however, the experience of dug-well renewal has not been without conflict. *Tikedars* ("fixers," middlemen), in particular, have not taken kindly to our refusal of their mediatory services. Nor have high-caste villages taken mildly our regrets to their offer to renew their well (or their pond), whose water they were not going to share. We received threats of different kinds, fortunately never fully acted upon. And yet, we have taken those instances as proof that our projects have succeeded in challenging local ideas about how social development interventions work, bypassing some, if not all, relationships of patronage.

In a context wherein both governmental and nongovernmental interventions are designed as packets of ready-made solutions, where only the experts are entitled to teach, MPA broke the mold by *not* presenting itself as an expert or a decision-maker on water management. Instead, the anthropological research methodology of participant observation and informal interviews, as well as the campaign's modality, placed MPA squarely in the position of the learner. The intervention was an occasion for provoking and facilitating informed conversations on water issues. Locals taught us about dug-wells, and MPA merely spread the information about their relevance. MPA tested the water and confirmed the results through authorized laboratories, yet the results were shared with caution and only in comparison to people's impressions about their health. No recipe for cleaning was provided, under the assumption that the best recipe was available locally through the village elders, which was confirmed by post-cleaning tests.

This method built confidence in local knowledge vis-à-vis official/government knowledge. In a few villages, this experience has promoted local knowledge beyond water, with residents openly discussing the disadvantages of modern agriculture vis-à-vis earlier methods and finding new arguments to antagonize genetically modified agriculture. Lastly, where dug-well revival has been successful, the confidence in local knowledge has, to a certain extent, countered the charismatic value of "modern" objects and technologies to the advantage of tried and tested local knowledge. The pride and value of the hand-pump as a status symbol declined in the villages where residents readopted the dug-well. This change was also partially felt by the younger generations, who were often more susceptible than their elders to the "gadget charisma" of the handpump.

The Anthropological Difference, Limitations, and Learnings

Reflecting back, there were important limitations to the way in which, as an anthropologist, I engaged with the project—I do have regrets. First, perhaps out of caution given the open prejudice against social scientists and anthropologists in particular in the field of water management in India, I did not explicitly market the dug-well revival initiative as an anthropology-based water and knowledge management project. This lack of an explicit "branding" discounted the relevance of the process in the media's wider representations of the project, which focused more on the water testing results and less on the process of reviving the well and the competence it takes to design and implement such a project. As a result, I feel that the project's social potential was diluted.

Similarly, I was not successful at involving other anthropologists. While MPA was—eventually—enthusiastic about having more applied anthropologists on board, we failed to recruit any, which may also have been due to the minimal salary offered. As noted above, I continued to help remotely and with annual visits of a few months at a time, but a stronger presence of applied anthropologists would help (1) renew the attention to the *process* of dug-well revival, without which the project would fail its potential; (2) enable MPA to reinforce its progressive stands against castism; and (3) expand the possibilities of MPA as an institution.

Most importantly, I regret the financial consequences of my modality of work for MPA. My full attention was dedicated to covering a large area, managing five organizations, training and supporting teams, testing the water, waving in new projects, and engaging in conversations with stakeholders across the social spectrum and ecological habitats in an area as large as Maryland and as populous as California. But I did not realize that such a simple project, with its implicit anthropological critique of mainstream development, and ironically even its small budget, would not, and did not, result in the enhanced popularity with funding agencies that MPA deserved. I regret not attending to the financial health of the organization, whose lack of funds eventually resulted in its untapped institutional development.

We were doing something innovative, simple, effective, commonsensical: I assumed that funding agencies would understand the value of this and would support the project and the organization. While I remain convinced that MPA is the hidden treasure that every funding agency wishes to find, I was proven naive: projects do not sell themselves, at least to funding agencies. The project's success was guaranteed by its so-called beneficiaries, who spread the news, and by those who took up the initiative on their own. MPA's popularity spread in rural Bihar as floods do. Its popularity grew in India, too. Media proclaimed MPA and even the dug-well revival project the success story of Bihar, as did the Government of Bihar and the Government of India on more than one occasion. MPA's founder won nominations and recognitions. Organizations wanted to visit and learn from our work. But MPA and its members remained on a shoestring budget that was unsustainable for our families and often forced us to take personal risks. After I left, there were long months when MPA's members had no salary to live on. As such, they become prey to the sector's vultures: organizations, research institutes, even a doctoral student(!) that promised funds only to extract ideas and research that they then portrayed as their own.

Theoretically, the dug-well project yielded at least three or four interesting results. First, by unpacking the concept of tradition, this research has built confidence that a development project, when informed by in-depth ethnography, can reinterpret traditional practices as an arena of sociopolitical action in order to avoid tradition's undesired effects, for example the reproduction of caste-based discrimination.[5] Because of the loopholes in the traditionalist discourse—a discourse that, particularly in relation to water management in India, overplays the importance of tradition and underplays its perils—we have risked "throwing away the baby with the bathwater" (Cortesi 2014). One of the findings of this project has been realizing that the way out of the loopholes of the traditionalist discourse lies precisely in engaging with the concept of tradition at the level of program design and implementation while countering its explicit use to avoid discursively hiding covert interests. At MPA, we worked out practices that valued "the old" if and when it is reinterpreted along progressive local values. Gauging the future prospects of a project, after all, takes awareness of both the historical and the contemporary—contexts that applied anthropologists are equipped to obtain and to juxtapose.

Second, while development is often accused of being "the anti-politics machine," strengthening traditional powers and even depoliticizing political issues, this project has been designed in antithesis to the handpump as a politically oriented gift (Ferguson 1990; the handpump gift is discussed in Cortesi, forthcoming). Doing so also required confronting the political stakes of the project, hence refusing the standard modality of development interventions and avoiding the facilitation of other mediators. Even when we agreed to partner with the local administration, the lack of opportunities drastically reduced the lifespan of such collaboration. In general, it was the anthropological rationale to put words to MPA's instinctual reluctance to become the instrument of power disputes.

Third, while this may have occurred elsewhere, this applied anthropology project has set a local precedent in terms of the feasibility of reinterpreting the development cycle as a continuum. While conceptually it makes sense to distinguish activities of research (including feasibility), project design, project implementation, and evaluation, these phases do not have to be temporally distinguished, at least not, as narrated above, after a robust initial research phase. Instead, uninterrupted research conducted by the same practitioners can inform the various phases of design and implementation in real time through continual readjustment and fine-tuning. MPA demonstrated that anthropological involvement should not be restricted to the pre-project feasibility study and the post facto evaluation report, as is often the case. Such restrictions, when applied, undermine the ability of anthropologists to lead development organizations and their human resources and to deploy ethnographic data in social development projects. This project stands to demonstrate that applied anthropologists do not simply have expertise in data collection but can also best serve development interventions when involved in all phases of the process.

Finally, the ethnographic research influenced the NGO's practices in honing their members' competence to work across multiple disciplinary fields, between the natural and the social sciences, thereby revealing the role that applied anthropology can play in managing an inherently interdisciplinary matter such as water. Involving the NGO's local fieldworkers in all phases of research convinced them that the way in which the project was implemented was key to the success of the project *even more than the technology itself.* This awareness increased the fieldworkers' ability to adjust their work to locally meaningful values instead of simply serving donors' priorities.

In MPA's dug-well revival project, anthropology, both in its research methodologies and its applied interdisciplinary experience, has proven critical to unpacking the complex dynamics of water management in disaster-prone areas, upsetting problematic modalities of development interventions that were well established in the area, dovetailing with progressive trends toward equality, and building confidence in local knowledge. Over the course of ten years, and even more so in the years after the end of the active project, the utility of anthropological engagement has been proven *by its inconspicuousness*. By being absorbed into the everyday and no longer sticking out, this applied anthropological commitment has proven its ability not only to understand society but also to become part of its commitment to improve it.

Luisa Cortesi is an environmental anthropologist who studies water disasters and climate change, environmental knowledge and technologies, environmental justice, and sustainable development. She founded and leads the Water Justice and Adaptation LAB, a platform for collaborative work between scientists and communities on water-related environmental justice. Holding a dual PhD in anthropology and environmental studies from Yale University (2018), she is assistant professor of water, disasters, and environmental justice at the International Institute of Social Sciences, Erasmus University; visiting assistant professor of environment and sustainability, Cornell University; and Marie S. Curie Fellow at the Freiburg Institute of Advanced Studies, Freiburg University. Recently, she was the Stanford Taylor Fellow at Cornell University in STS and anthropology, fellow at the Atkinson Centre of Sustainability, and the Josephine de Karman Fellow. In addition to the Praxis Award, her work has received several accolades, including the Field Prize, the Eric Wolf Prize, and the Curl Prize.

Notes

1. For an example, see the well-known short story by Munshi Premchand, "Thakur ka kuan," which narrates the deadly violence imposed through dug-wells on lower castes in many parts of India.
2. At the time of writing, *Mahadalits* are a political category of extremely discriminated *Dalits* initiated by the State Government of Bihar that affords special status to twenty-four *Dalit* castes.
3. The National Rural Development Employment Guarantee Act is a governmental scheme for guaranteeing one hundred days of salaried work by the public utility.
4. In fact, my gender was perhaps a reason for the job offer in the first place, given that the founder of MPA had taken several measures to ensure gender equality despite the deeply patriarchal context.
5. With the exception of the next paragraph (starting with "Second" and ending with "power disputes") that makes reference to party politics, I use the adjective "political" to describe that which is affecting the distribution of social power toward a more just

society. Neither MPA nor my anthropological work has any interest in any sort of politics.

References

Agrawal, A. 1995. "Dismantling the Divide between Indigenous and Scientific Knowledge." *Development and Change* 26: 413–39.

Ahmed, F. 2007. "The Missing Kids." *India Today*, 10 September 2007. https://www.indi atoday.in/magazine/states/story/20070917-the-missing-kids-733945-2007-09-10.

Chambers, R. 1994. "The Origins and Practice of Participatory Rural Appraisal." *World Development* 22(7): 953–69.

Cortesi, L. (forthcoming). "In Unquiet Waters: Knowledge and Technologies of Floods, Toxic Drinking Waters and Other Wet Disasters."

———. 2022. "Hydrotopias and Waterland." Geoforum. https://www.sciencedirect.com/science/article/pii/S001671852100302X.

———. 2021. "The Ontology of Water and Land in Flood-Affected North Bihar, India." *Journal of the Royal Anthropological Institute* 27(4): 870-889.

———. 2014. "Filtering Dirty Water and Finding Fresh One: Engaging with Tradition in the Dug-Well Intervention in North Bihar." In *Informing Water Policies: Case Studies from South Asia*, edited by A. Prakash, C. G. Goodrich, and S. Singh. Pp. 314–333, New Delhi: Routledge.

Ferguson, K. 1990. *The Anti-politics Machine: Development and Bureaucratic Power in Lesotho.* Cambridge: Cambridge University Press.

Talbot, R., and M. Black, 2005. *Water, a Matter of Life and Health: Water Supply and Sanitation in Village India.* Oxford: Oxford University Press.

CHAPTER 15

~:~

A New Model for News
Studying the Deep Structure
of Young-Adult News Consumption

ROBBIE BLINKOFF

Project Background

The Associated Press (AP) is the world's largest news organization, with three thousand journalists worldwide covering news in every media format from text to photos to audio and video. Every day, more than a billion people worldwide see news from the AP.

However, over the course of the first decade of the 2000s, the AP recognized that a significant shift in news consumption behavior was taking place among younger generations. Research conducted by the AP and its partner organizations had clearly documented that younger consumers, ages eighteen to thirty-four, have adopted ways of getting their news that are much different from those of past generations. Younger consumers not only rely less on newspapers to get their news but also consume news across a multitude of platforms and sources, all day, constantly. The result of this shift has been triggering adjustments, even revolutions, at media companies in every part of the world. Amid its own revolution from predominantly print-based services, the AP sought help in gaining a deeper and more holistic understanding of young consumers. How is news read, viewed, and used by this generation throughout a typical day?

Project Description

Our Baltimore-based firm, Context-Based Research Group, was commissioned by the AP to conduct a cultural ethnography focused on the news consumption habits of young digital consumers in six cities around the world. The project sought to put a human face on twenty-first-century news consumption, answering the question: What is the "new face of news"?

During the summer of 2007, we embarked upon an ethnography of news consumption, producing a model for digital news consumption that the AP integrated into its strategic planning process. In 2008, AP reengaged with us in another effort, again relying on anthropological theory and ethnographic methods to analyze the field data further and extract findings and recommendations that could be shared with all those interested in pursuing new approaches to news gathering and delivery.

We designed a project to look at consumers from a holistic perspective, delving into their lifestyles and how their current attitudes and beliefs tie into larger cultural news consumption constructs in the United States and abroad. The ultimate goal of the research was to assist the Associated Press in understanding how and why younger consumers search for news in a rapidly changing technological landscape, and in revealing opportunities for traditional media sources to become a part of this population's daily news agenda. To achieve this goal, the project was organized around the following objectives: develop a better understanding of the news consumption behaviors and habits of young consumers throughout a typical day; document the frequency with which study participants are searching for or consuming news; identify the news sources consumed, including preferred or primary and supplementary sources, the range and number of sources, and the reasoning behind each source's use; distinguish among the various means that young consumers use to access these news sources; examine young consumers' platforms for news consumption, especially new and/or nontraditional channels and devices; and expand common understandings of what constitutes "news" to include participant-generated definitions.

Implementation and Anthropologists' Roles

The first phase of the project ran for approximately two months, and included several members of the firm, most of whom hold PhDs or MAs in anthropology, as well as six outside field researchers who hold degrees in anthropology, journalism, and sociology.

To gather as broad a group of participants as possible, eighteen participants were recruited between the ages of eighteen and thirty-four (with an emphasis on the eighteen-to-twenty-four age group), representing a mix of ethnicities and genders. Each participant had to have access to the internet, and, in addition to checking the news at least once a day, participants had to report how they accessed news through means other than print, television, and radio. This bias was assumed to capture young people who were digital consumers of news.

The participants were recruited in three countries—the United States, the United Kingdom, and India—and six metropolitan areas. Houston, Silicon Valley, Philadelphia, and Kansas City were chosen in the United States to provide a broad geographical sweep while staying away from cities where the influence of major media might be more prominent. Brighton, England, was selected because the city is quickly attracting a new young population with its universities and established cultural life. In India, Hyderabad was a natural choice, as the influx of technology companies has brought extensive urbanization.

After an initial phase, the AP contracted us to refine the findings of the initial stage of the project and perfect the new model for news consumption we developed. The refined findings and model were then presented to the World Editors Forum (a gathering of the international press) in June of 2008. This phase of the project involved further analysis and writing for three key staffers.

It was clear to us that we would need to conduct ethnographic fieldwork by going into the natural settings of news consumers as opposed to studying them in a controlled environment. But ethnography alone is just a technique, a process by which thick and rich descriptions are provided that illustrate people's lives, emotions, social relationships, decision-making processes, and more. The secret to ethnography lies in anthropological analysis. Anthropologists conducting ethnographic research and analysis get to what we call people's "Deep Structure"—the place beneath the surface of easily observed behaviors where cultural values and individual motivations are produced and supported.

The ethnographic approach is deductive and iterative. As the patterns from the research start to take shape and suggest a certain structure, then anthropological theory guides the explanatory models that emerge. Simply put, the models resulting from anthropological studies suggest: (1) the underlying deep structure for why people do what they do and (2) what in people's lives—be it products, services, institutions (e.g., education, government, religion, economies)—are working or not working. Most important, anthropological investigations provide a platform to create change, grounded in a truly deep understanding of human behavior.

Using this foundation as a starting point, our firm's research director, with assistance from the lead analyst, designed several methods for the fielding of this project with the AP. To gather a foundation of information about the participants' lives, particularly their behaviors, values, news sources and news consumption habits, all the participants in the study received a Send-Ahead Behavioral Journaling Exercise titled "My News." To complete the journal, participants received a Polaroid camera and a set of instructions on taking pictures of their daily lives over the course of three to five days. Participants then completed the behavioral journal by addressing a series of questions, both visually and textually.

To capture behaviors and motivations while consumers were away from home and in the varied and different environments they visit in their daily lives, we designed a second method for participants to complete: a mobile blog and news diary. For this structured assignment, participants were asked to capture moments of news consumption behavior, in real time, over the course of one weekday and one weekend day, from start to finish.

Day-in-the-life immersions were also conducted to obtain firsthand information about news consumption, as it actually happened, and to put in perspective the information gathered in each participant's self-reported journal and diary. In these sessions, an anthropologist spent part of the day shadowing and observing participants through their activities. To gain a deeper understanding of participants' lives and how they interface with news, the immersion encompassed a broad sampling of their daily activities, including work, school, leisure or entertainment activities, interactions with family and/or friends, and more.

After participants completed their journal and diary exercises, the lead analyst and the contracted field researchers went to their homes, debriefed these exercises, and conducted in-depth interviews. Debriefing the journals and diaries provided a launching pad to conduct a conversational interview designed to uncover further details about how participants consumed or otherwise received news. The interview was structured using an observation guide that followed the same themes as those directing the immersion observation, although questions were introduced as open-ended to assist participants in providing vivid and self-directed descriptions of their life experiences. The interview also provided the participants with a chance to explain in greater depth the behavior observed by the anthropologist during the immersion period and to discuss the relationship between real-time behaviors and what participants recorded in their journals and through their blogs and news diaries.

Outcomes

We relied on the critical lens of anthropology to turn the stated goals of the project on their head. For example, the stated goals included uncovering the "face of news today." Anthropologically, we uncovered that the "face of news today" did not exist. At best, the "face of news today," we found, is the consumers themselves. By accepting this insight, the AP was forced to rethink most of its assumptions about the delivery of news.

In addition to going beyond stated goals, the project also turned on its head certain assumptions about eighteen-to-thirty-four-year-old news consumers and news consumers in general. Specifically, the news industry was under the impression that the frequency of news consumption measured by the extraordinary high volume of clicks on headlines showed that people were satisfied with the type of news content they were getting via this method of delivery. By conducting an ethnography, we were able to show the AP that in fact people's behavior did not match the underlying beliefs at the root of people's feelings. From an anthropological point of view, news consumers were showing what we termed "news fatigue." They were "clicking" along with the barrage of headlines, but mostly out of habit rather than true desire. In reality, they were tired of the news they were getting in the form of headlines and looking for more—more depth and easier ways to find the depth that fit the way they lived their lives.

Finally, from the anthropological study, the AP received an ethnographic/ experience/behavioral model that illustrated the current state of news consumption along with a recommendation about where consumers would like the model to go. With the "model," the AP then had the vehicle to influence their decisions and, more importantly, influence the future of news—two extremely high-level goals for the AP which were not written into the stated goals of the project.

The AP emerged from this research with a renewed commitment to new content development and digital technology. The new model we developed from the research split the news into its fundamental "atomic" parts and provided a conceptual framework for that work, much as the old "inverted pyramid" model once did for news writing.

As our study confirmed for the AP, the increasing movement of the audience online is rapidly changing the overall news environment. Consumers, like those in the study group, have grown up using digital tools and view the old, packaged news products as much less efficient. The ability to search for news and information makes it even easier for consumers to eschew a scheduled date with packaged media. Add the capability of viral sharing to the mix, facilitating electronic word-of-mouth interactions among consumers, and the utility of packaged media appears increasingly limited. Newspaper stories, packaged as a snapshot in time, struggle to connect with an audience that is being conditioned to aggregate and manipulate unpackaged information on their own.

For the AP, these trends delivered a clear directive to adjust the newspaper "story first" mentality. A shift to "fastest formats first" had already been made at the agency well before the consumer study. As a result of the study, that shift was accelerated with key new initiatives to enhance the differentiation of services to match platform and market needs.

Chief among the initiatives affected by the ethnography is a fundamental new process for newsgathering in the field called "1-2-3 Filing." The name describes a new editorial workflow that requires the first words of a text story to be delivered in a structured alert (headline format), to be followed by a short, present-tense story delivering the vital details in a second step. Then, in a final step, a story takes whatever form is appropriate for different platforms and audiences—a longer form story or analysis for print, for example. Other media types are coordinated along the way in similar fashion.

That subtle but powerful change to the present tense is all-important to the digital audience, as our study confirmed. Those consumers said they wanted to see real updates, not duplicative stories presented as updates, and they wanted some coverage to go much deeper. Present-tense alerts and updates, followed by deeper dives for print as well as online, are designed to answer those calls.

A second major initiative involves the biggest stories of the day and the need for them to get even more attention from a new "Top Stories Desk" at AP headquarters in New York. The editors on that desk are urged to consider the big-picture significance of a select number of stories each day and to provide the perspective and forward-looking thinking that can enhance their development across all media platforms. This attention to key stories also plays out on a slightly smaller scale at regional news desks situated in three locations outside the United States and, by the end of 2009, in four US cities.

Taken together, these changes in workflow directly address the needs to both tighten and deepen the news report that consumers, like those documented in our study, can find as they surf and search for information.

The results of this ongoing engagement produced substantive changes across how the AP gathers and delivers the news and, after the presentation of findings at the World Editors Forum in the summer of 2008, has had continuing impact on the news industry worldwide.

The Anthropological Difference

When we were contacted by the AP, they believed the ethnographic research would at best provide anecdotal support for an upcoming biannual strategy summit for the organization. However, in the epilogue to the published report, our main client at the AP said this about the recommendation to do an "ethnography":

> An analyst on the planning staff suggested doing an "ethnography" of young adult consumers, and after a quick Google search to understand exactly what that meant, we decided to give it a try. To be frank, our expectations were modest. We sought some real people to put a human face on the accelerating shift to online and mobile consumption of news around the world. We knew young people were at the leading edge of that movement and a cultural science study of their media habits sounded like fun. In the end, it proved to be as transformative as it was fun.

At the final presentation of the research to the AP, the main client stood in front of the ethnographic model for contemporary news consumption and saw the reasons for the grim future for news in general—if the trajectory remained the same. What he also saw was the strategic opportunity and business model for the future of news and the AP. Without the anthropological perspective, without getting to the deep structure behind contemporary news consumption, the AP may not have landed on the clear direction, the path, for moving forward and the rationale—grounded in the ethnographic approach and anthropological perspective—for doing so.

One ethnographic story from the research sums up the importance and impact of taking the anthropological approach for the AP project. One of the study participants was a young man living in Hyderabad. He was moving up the social ladder in India, and knowing the news was an integral part of his plan of upward mobility. Each day, this young man would literally take the top news stories and, using a whiteboard in his apartment, sketch out the story and the overall narrative. In this way, he was able to study and retell the top stories in a smart and memorable way to those he was trying to impress or sway. The anthropological or cultural insights from this ethnographic interview were so powerful that the president and CEO of the AP continues to frame his remarks about the future of news in terms of this young man:

> Madi Reddy is a twenty-two-year-old resident of Hyderabad, India, with ambitions to rise above his hereditary caste. He's a newshound, investing time every day turning the news into diagrams on a whiteboard in his small apartment. He then breaks the news into conversational chunks he can use to win friends and influence people, online or in person. Madi's story was captured by anthropologists hired by AP to study news consumption patterns of young adults. Madi was by far the biggest news junkie of the bunch, but he was not unique.

This ethnographic moment made it possible for the AP's president and CEO to argue a compelling case for (1) the continued importance of news in our world, (2) the desire for more depth from news rather than continuing to deliver shallow headlines as news, (3) the importance of delivering news in contemporary formats/technologies, and (4) the value of news as "social currency"—content that people can share in our digital world that helps them move through their day and "up" in society, as in the young man's case in India.

Each of these findings is a direct result of our anthropological work for the AP, which made the insights possible. And the last finding, the importance of news as "social currency," was also used by the president and CEO in closing remarks he gave about the future of news and the AP's mission heading into the future:

> You can bet that if they [the founders of the AP] saw a Google, a Yahoo, or a Facebook, they would have figured out what to do about them. You can bet that if they found a newshound like our friend Madi Reddy in India, collecting news and tidbits to share with friends, they would have found a way to feed his obsession . . .

Ironically, what was initially seen as a limitation to the ethnographic study was in fact its most important and critical piece. The AP, like so many other institutions, had a difficult time reconciling the small sample size of the ethnographic study with their traditional quantitative as well as qualitative approaches. However, it became clear that their traditional approaches to understanding news consumption were leading them to incorrect assumptions about news today, especially among the critical eighteen-to-thirty-four-year-old demographic.

Another irony in this whole story goes back to the simple but profound insight that the AP president and CEO mentioned above. What the AP's anthropological investigation helped them to see was actually some very good news: that there are plenty of persons in the world who are hungry for solid news and that there is plenty of content for them to find. The bad news is that the content is not reaching them in the best way possible. In the business world, and to business strategists in particular, bad news is typically good news too; it becomes an opportunity for the business to find a way to properly deliver a product to people, given contemporary contexts. Since the AP arguably owns the distribution network for news, the current opportunity is even better.

Robbie Blinkoff has been actively engaged in marketing, communications, advertising, branding, and website design in the Washington, DC–Baltimore area for more than twenty years. For most of that time he was managing director of the Context-Based Research Group, a global ethnographic research and consulting firm. He oversaw research design, analysis ideation, and go-to-market recommendations, and his approaches employed ethnography, observational research, in-depth interviews, and focus groups. His firm's clientele included a spectrum of governmental and private-sector entities. He received a PhD in anthropology from Rutgers University in 2000.

References

Denny, R. M., and P. Sunderland, eds. 2014. *Handbook of Anthropology in Business.* Walnut Creek, CA: Left Coast Press.

Ferraro, G. P., and E. K. Briody. 2013. *The Cultural Dimension of Global Business.* 7th ed. Boston: Pearson.

Jordan, A. T. 2013. *Business Anthropology.* 2nd ed. Long Grove, IL: Waveland Press Inc.

Sunderland, P., and R. M. Denny. 2006. *Doing Anthropology in Consumer Research.* Walnut Creek, CA: Left Coast Press.

CHAPTER 16

~:~

Learning to Live with Difference
How CEDAR Takes Anthropology
Out of the Classroom and Into the World

DAVID W. MONTGOMERY, ADAM B. SELIGMAN,
AND RAHEL R. WASSERFALL

Project Background

A radical Muslim activist from the United Kingdom, organizer of anti-Israel demonstrations and Relief for Gaza convoys, calls home in dismay when she finds herself participating in a program with Zionists—and then sums up her two week experience saying, "I learned I could be friends with people I hate."

A conservative Catholic priest from Africa feels deep personal and theological chagrin when he has to confront intensely pious transgendered Muslims in Indonesia—and then returns home to organize just such encounters with difference in his home country.

An Italian teacher spends two weeks with Muslims, Orthodox Christians, Protestants, and Jews in Bulgaria—and on her return to Rome begins a campaign to reform the multicultural education in her school: to stop sweeping difference under the carpet and allow the school's many families to encounter the varied and different communities they actually are.

The above characterizations capture the essence of what our work aims to do: facilitate experiences that allow participants to envision a world in which the significant differences between peoples are no longer a source of conflict (see Seligman, Wasserfall, and Montgomery 2015). It is only through engaging with others who are different from ourselves—a tenet of anthropology—that we can appreciate the challenge and potential of community. While academic training prioritizes processes of understanding, without further engagement we are left with a sense of difference as a problem in need of a solution. Cognizant of the need to engage the world's problems beyond description, we have oriented our sociocultural training toward shaping group experiences to address the challenge of living with difference.

In 2003, operating as the International Summer School on Religion and Public Life (ISSRPL), CEDAR—Communities Engaging with Difference and Religion—launched its first school in Bosnia and Herzegovina and Croatia, creating a unique model for persons with divergent religious identities to live with, recognize, and learn about "the other" together. It has since met annually in countries ranging from Bulgaria to Britain, Israel to Indonesia—drawing more than five hundred students, professionals, and religious and civic leaders from over fifty countries.

Unlike other interfaith and intercommunal programs, which play down fundamental dissimilarities between people in favor of emphasizing what they have in common, CEDAR places difference squarely at the top of the agenda. In fact, the key to CEDAR's approach is the requirement that participants confront one another's differences—and then learn how to live with them. In two intensive weeks of combined lectures, site visits, and hands-on learning, participants experience unfamiliar religious customs, grapple with beliefs that contradict their own, reexamine lifelong assumptions, and figure out how to share time and space.

CEDAR's programs create new social and interpersonal spaces, broadening the range of possibilities to present a new way of "living together differently." We seek not to build a community in which everyone agrees and shares the same assumptions but rather to teach people how to live with different understandings of home, life, faith, worlds of meaning, and belonging. In short, we model the reality of how to live in our existing communities with people who are not like us—whether these differences are religious, national, tribal, linguistic, or sexual.

Engaging with the "other" in practical and constructive ways prepares CEDAR fellows to apply their experiences in their home communities around the world when the school is over. Throughout the years, a number of alumni have been inspired to develop affiliates using CEDAR's model in East Africa, Central Asia, and Southeast Asia, as well as in the Balkans and North America. As a result, CEDAR is fast becoming a pioneering global educational network that enables members of disparate communities to recognize and accept their differences as they work toward a civil society.

Project Description

Our organization was conceived during a multireligious discussion around a restaurant table in the central market of Sarajevo in December 2001, when a conversation among a group of Jews, Christians, and Muslims—against a background of wartime destruction—sparked the idea for an experimental program using religion as a tool for understanding, not a weapon for intolerance. In 2003, it launched its first two-week program in Bosnia and Herzegovina and Croatia as the ISSRPL, creating a unique model for those with divergent religious identities to live with, recognize, and learn about "the other" together. Since then, the school has been held in a different country or countries each year, meeting in over a dozen locations on four continents.

In 2013, the ISSRPL changed its name to CEDAR and transformed itself as an organization. Instead of running one school a year under the direction of an international team and local hosts, CEDAR is now an international network of programs—in East Africa, the Balkans, Southeast Asia, Central Asia, and East Asia. The first affiliate program—the Equator Peace Academy—was launched in December 2012 in Uganda and Rwanda, and it continues as a biennial program. Additional continuing and emergent affiliate programs are taking place in Bulgaria, Indonesia, Japan, and Kyrgyzstan, and others are being organized in Kenya, the Democratic Republic of the Congo, and Ukraine at the time of publication. All programs have been initiated by former fellows and hosts of CEDAR programs together with the international team.

The twenty-five different programs that we have run between 2003 and 2021 have taught us a good deal about difference and how to get people to live with difference—not just with the cognitive dissonance it produces but also with the challenges to building trusting relations across different communities of belonging that result. We learned early that while religion may be a prime marker of difference, it is far from the only one. As we expanded our programs beyond the first schools in Bosnia, Croatia, and Israel, we gradually realized that the issues we were addressing were not limited to differences between religions, or even those between religious and secular individuals. We came to recognize as well the importance of ethnic, tribal, and sexual orientation as sites of conflict, intolerance, and distrust among many individuals and groups. Consequently, we integrated these themes into our programming.

We learned too that shared experience, as opposed to academic learning, is critical to providing a safe space in which people can explore their differences, even in the face of challenges to their own taken-for-granted categories and expectations. Shared experiences provide the frame within which fellows process and make sense of intellectual analysis. Consequently, as the program developed over the years, the time spent on more academic study was decreased and replaced with greater emphasis on shared experience, joint projects, and other forms of noncognitive learning.

In addition, we came to realize just how important the group itself was to the work we wished to accomplish. In the first years of programming, we believed that the "other" whom the fellows would encounter, interact with, and come to understand was someone in the selected environment: Palestinian refugee camps, gay and lesbian churches, Alevi communities in Istanbul, Pomak villages in Bulgaria, and so on. What we discovered, however, was that these site visits and meetings were just the backdrop for the real encounter—of the fellows with one another. We realized then how critical it was to bring fellows from all over the world with as much diversity as possible in race, nationality, ethnicity, religion, age, gender, sexual orientation, profession, and so on. The "other" we came to recognize was not outside the group, but inside—and it was in that internal encounter, and the act of building a group despite these multiple differences, that the key learning took place.

After nearly two decades of programming, we have produced a body of knowledge, a methodology, and a comprehensive pedagogy that is universally applicable and that, with training, can be adopted by others. While we strongly believed that deep learning comes from the experience of going through the program, there was also a need to share our pedagogic insights more broadly. Thus, in 2015, *Living with Difference: How to Build Community in a Divided World* was published as both a description of the problem and a tool for community organizers interested in implementing the CEDAR pedagogy. Elsewhere, we have engaged with core problems underlying social division that the pedagogy can help to address, and in 2019 we began piloting a workbook for those trained in the CEDAR programs to use in integrating the pedagogy across longer periods of engagement into their home communities.[1] The goal has always been to create an environment where a productive experience of living with difference inspires community leaders to adapt the CEDAR pedagogy to their local contexts, integrating it to help mitigate local division, with the tools we have produced being targeted to more applied local needs.

While a growing number of nongovernmental organization (NGO) and university-based programs focus on conflict and peacebuilding, none focus on the problem of difference per se and the value to be achieved in encountering difference directly rather than shying away from or denying it. Not surprisingly, academic programs mostly comprise traditional learning in which students theorize about the issues relating to conflicts. To supplement the classroom environment, students often try to visit an area of conflict, either to carry out research or to perform an internship with an organization. The strength of such programs is also, to some extent, a limitation, in that they are almost always geared to those who can take the requisite time to pursue a degree. Moreover, while these programs provide strong and useful training in individual problem-solving and leadership, they devote little time to the challenge of building group ties and mutuality among people who have fundamentally different identities, share different moral codes, and construct their social, moral, and political worlds of meaning in different terms. While recognizing the importance of the work done by these and other organizations, CEDAR addresses a different demographic, in a different way, with different results.

First, the typical CEDAR participant or "fellow" is much older than the typical student. CEDAR fellows range in age from their late twenties to early sixties. They are usually religious and civic leaders, academics, or other professionals who are well embedded in their societies. They are generally unable or unwilling to take time off to pursue a further degree; rather, they are looking for tools to deal with problems and the sources of conflict in *their* community. Second, CEDAR gathers together fellows from all over the world and brings them to a site relevant to that year's topical theme: Plovdiv, Bulgaria, to work on religious syncretism; Uganda and Rwanda to work on history and memory; Nicosia, Cyprus, and Tel Aviv–Jaffa, Israel, to work on divided cities; and so on. Third, while other programs focus on the individual, CEDAR programs center on the group experience as it evolves over the school's two weeks. Each CEDAR program location is carefully chosen to facilitate an understanding of the challenges and possibilities of living with difference. Fourth, many programs, especially in the area of interfaith dialogue, stress either shared values or the importance of realizing a common purpose. CEDAR, however, does not aim to have its participants recognize the importance of any particular set of value commitments, such as a commitment to pluralism. Its goal is simply for people to learn to live with difference as a fact of life, a necessary aspect of the world in which we all live.

Additional Program Details

Each year, a CEDAR program will accept on average twenty-four to thirty fellows to participate in the two-week program. The ideal model (not always realizable due to financial and other constraints) is that one-third of the fellows come from the host country (Bulgaria, Turkey, Uganda, Indonesia, United Kingdom, etc.), one-third come from the broader geographical area (Balkans, East Africa, Southeast Asia, Western Europe, etc.), and one-third from anywhere else. The broad age range from the late twenties to early sixties affords diversity across periods of life. The program is rigorous, so it can be a bit strenuous for older participants and a bit too demanding in terms of maturity for younger ones. Critically, however, the fellows selected are usually what might be called "secondary elites," typically including schoolteachers and school principals, NGO leaders, clergy, social workers, United Nations relief workers, government administrators (in areas of culture, education, communal relations), municipal workers, and youth leaders.

Selection among applicants (done by committee) is according to the above criteria (age and social role) with an eye to forming the most diverse group possible (by age, gender, religion, and ethnic—and where relevant, tribal—affiliation) and our assessment of who has the most to contribute and to gain from participation. All applicants complete an application and submit an original essay framed as a response to a question that appears on the application (different programs have different questions), generally asking them to think through how the theme of the program relates to their home environment. The reasoning here is to encourage participants to begin the program aware of how it is relevant to where they will return.

Programs combine three different modes of learning: cognitive, experiential, and affective. All are organized around set themes that change annually and are relevant to current challenges in not only the host country but other areas of the world as well. Thus, for example, in 2010, the program met in Nicosia, Cyprus, and Tel Aviv–Jaffa, Israel, on the theme of *Divided Cities: Apart Together*, both municipalities being divided in very different ways: one with an international border running within it, the other putatively one city but actually divided along religio-ethnic lines. In 2011, the program met in Plovdiv, Bulgaria, around the theme of *A Mosaic of Margins* and focused on non-Orthodox Bulgarian communities: Armenians, Catholics, Uniates, Jews, Roma, and ethnic Bulgarian Muslims, known as Pomaks. Other programs have looked at the impact of the past on the present through rethinking colonial history (e.g., Indonesia 2017; Japan 2019), the challenge of refugees and strangers as neighbors (e.g., Uganda 2017), and the changing role of families and tradition (e.g., Kyrgyzstan 2022). As can be seen, all are themes that are both country specific as well as relevant to much broader areas of the world.

The typical program day runs from 7:30 A.M. to 9:30 P.M., with fellows and staff together the whole time. All attendees are expected to participate in all events. Shared meals—and providing for the dietary restrictions of all, be it vegetarian, halal, or kosher needs—are a critical component in the program.

There are on average two lectures per day. In addition, every day the group travels to program-relevant sites—these may be abandoned Palestinian villages in Israel, transgendered madrassas in Indonesia, Roma ghettos in Bulgaria, transformed neighborhoods (ethnically or economically) in England, refugee encampments in Uganda, and so on. In addition, schools make time for religious services (Friday, Saturday, and Sunday) and—as a group—attend different services. This too is a critical learning component as fellows begin to realize that where they are comfortable and feel at home—with the liturgy, smells, foods, and so on—their new friends may feel extremely uncomfortable, and vice versa. Learning that one's comfort is not the sole criterion of what is right or moral or desirable is an important part of program learning.

Program fellows also participate in iterated group-work exercises in which a more personal (if not intimate) aspect of the day's theme is discussed in small groups (four to five individuals) that remain together for the length of the program. What is shared in the small group is not brought to any plenum but remains solely in the group. Here too, an important learning process develops as fellows must negotiate memberships in different groups—their small group, the group of fellows as a whole, and of course the larger group, which includes staff, lecturers, and others.

Programs also include some daily physical activity—most often yoga—as part of the program philosophy is focused on joint "doing" as opposed to simply "knowing" or "learning" (which are mostly individualized activities). Movies are also used to great effect.

Finally, in some programs, fellows spend some nights and days in the homes of the local populace to gain a very brief taste of anthropological fieldwork and participant observation: yet another form of experiencing the "other" and seeing the world through the eyes of the other. Fellows are fully briefed by on-staff anthropologists before their stays with local hosts and are provided with opportunities to discuss any problems arising from this experience, as are the local hosts.

There are, it should be noted, only two "rules" to the program: (1) everyone must participate in all events, and (2) no one individual or social group—be they Jews, or Palestinians, or women, or members of the LGBT community, or Africans, or Muslims, etc.—has a "monopoly on suffering." Admittedly, this is easier said than done. Yet establishing it as a sort of subjunctive boundary marker for behavior and interaction is important to keeping the program on course and the shared space a safe one.[2]

Implementation and Anthropologist's Role

The anthropologist works on many levels both during and after each program.

The small groups of organizers, locals, and internationals are not always mindful of their pedagogical tools. The anthropologist helps to bring these tools to the full awareness of the organizers, which in turn results in the conscious incorporation of them in following years. Thus, the anthropologist plays a crucial role in creating structures that are reproduced and become part of the school's methodology. Part of this process sees the anthropologist collecting stories that emerged as symbolizing the group experience and presenting them to the organizers. This then becomes the prism through which the experience of the school is viewed by its different members.

The staff anthropologist, however, plays a role far beyond advising staff or the introduction of fieldwork to fellows. Critically, through both her or his formal as well as informal interventions, the anthropologist makes clear to the fellows that individuals are part of cultures and carry with them shared models, ideals, and ideas that are important factors in their behaviors. Furthermore, the anthropologist makes explicit to the fellows one of the most important insights of the schools: that individuals bring to their individual interactions their social, taken-for-granted assumptions. Becoming aware of these is a process that the anthropologist—and so also, the fellow—can uncover.

This is accomplished by slowly sharing with the fellows some of the basic methodological assumptions of anthropology as a discipline, such as learning to occupy the space between insider and outsider; looking at social groups as small cultures; learning to be a keen observer of social interactions, including those that are created in the program; and, crucially, learning to minimize our own taken-for-granted assumptions or already formulated questions when entering new social spaces.

All these are the crucial tools of the anthropological approach to understanding human society and interaction. The successful CEDAR anthropologists bring them to the conscious attention of both organizers and fellows through her/his many interventions—written and oral, in staff meetings and sessions of developmental evaluation, in informal meetings as well as in formal presentations, consultations, and interviews.

Outcomes

Institutional

Outcomes of CEDAR programs are neither linear nor uniform across countries or years of implementation. In some cases, tellingly, we have seen the replication of CEDAR programs and pedagogy in the seeding of newly emergent organizations as a way to train persons in our approach. Thus, the following affiliate schools have been established: Equator Peace Academy (Uganda); Balkan Summer School on Religion and Public Life (Bulgaria); Nusantara School of Difference (Indonesia); and the Central Asian Program on Pedagogies of Solidarity (Kyrgyzstan). In their different contexts, the focus of all these schools is on training NGO leaders, social activists, teachers, clergy, United Nations workers, and others involved with tribal and communal conflicts. Further long-term projects are being developed in Japan (with workshops ongoing in Nagasaki and Hiroshima), Kenya, the Democratic Republic of the Congo, and Ukraine.

Raw data from a longitudinal survey carried out in 2014 by an external evaluation organization also showed that following the CEDAR experience, fellows went on to found journals; restructure multicultural education in their schools in Rome, Italy; develop new technologies and community activism for high school students from twenty-nine different places in Bosnia and Herzegovina; construct summer retreats for clergy on CEDAR principles in Zimbabwe; develop intercommunal educational programs in Israel; construct a research center within an existing NGO in Bosnia-Herzegovina; and develop conferences, research projects, and one-time workshops on themes of community difference and conflict.

Ideational

Quite apart from institutional multiplier effects, what is created at the end of all the two-week programs is an opening of possibilities. Individually, participants attest to a deep, personal transformation of their taken-for-granted ways of thinking; collectively, they achieve a new awareness of what can be done, evidenced by the emergence of what are effectively new spaces and modes of interaction.

Paradoxically, recognizing differences facilitates connections that denying them precludes. An ideology of sameness and relative homogeneity traps us into continually maintaining a false reality. On the other hand, the acceptance of difference frees us from investing vast amounts of time and energy in what is essentially a pretense. The first step in this process is the realization that knowledge must be understood as knowledge *for* (action) rather than knowledge *of* (content).

By the end of the program, fellows have assembled a working "toolkit" of guidelines to further such reflective thinking and openings to shared experience, including, for example, to:

+ hold all claims to absolute truth in abeyance;
+ recognize the partial nature of any and all understandings;
+ allow experience to precede judgment;
+ place knowledge *for* action above knowledge *of* others;
+ distance oneself, in approaching "the other," from commitments to one's own group.

These are the anthropologically informed tools, or building blocks, with which CEDAR equips fellows to use in new spaces for interaction and joint, shared action with those who are different. With these, CEDAR alumni are able to return to their home communities and, should they choose to do so, adapt the pedagogy to address the challenge of difference within their local contexts. As noted above, to facilitate the transmission of the pedagogic experience to these local contexts, we have developed a workbook that facilitates the application of the "toolkit" to projects ranging from three-day workshops in Japan on the role of memory in shaping prejudice to months-long youth soccer leagues in Uganda that use the pedagogy to explore ways of living across tribal differences.

The Anthropological Difference

In emphasizing the importance of local experience and long-term engagement, the anthropological way of considering people and events is an essential step toward understanding cultural differences and their social consequences. For our program, the anthropological difference has been one marked by epistemological humility and the demand to consider the context from which the other comes and frames his/her world. It has not been an approach of cultural relativism that assigns equal value to perspectives rooted in different experiences but rather an appreciation that, despite our tendencies to prioritize the needs and sufferings of one's own group over that of the other, to live together in an increasingly diverse world requires us to pay attention to the dynamics of quotidian engagement. Such engagements are the concern of anthropology and areas where the potential for shaping a more hospitable community emerge. Anthropology allows us to see others where they are rather than where we imagine they should be. And when we are able to see the other, to see the other see us, and to see ourselves seeing the other, we open a window of possibility for living with difference.

David W. Montgomery is research professor in the Department of Government and Politics and the Center for International Development and Conflict Management at the University of Maryland, College Park. He is also the director of program development for CEDAR—Communities Engaging with Difference and Religion. Montgomery received his PhD in religion and society from Boston University in 2007. He has conducted long-term anthropological research in Central Asia and the Balkans and has taught at the University of Pittsburgh, Emory University, and Boston University. He is a former policy fellow with the American Association for the Advancement of Science and served as a US Peace Corps Volunteer. His books include *Living with Difference: How to Build Community in a Divided World; Practicing Islam: Knowledge, Experience, and Social Navigation in Kyrgyzstan; Everyday Life in the Balkans*; and *Central Asia: Contexts for Understanding*.

Adam B. Seligman is professor of religion at Boston University and director of its Graduate Program in Religion. He is also founding director of CEDAR—Communities Engaging in Difference and Religion, which, since 2001, has developed a unique pedagogy and set of practices in the field of tolerance and has run yearly programs all over the world on the challenge of living with difference. Seligman received his PhD in sociology and social anthropology from the Hebrew University of Jerusalem in 1987. He was Fulbright Fellow in Hungary from 1990 to 1992 and has been visiting professor of sociology at Harvard University and visiting professor of management at the Massachusetts Institute of Technology's Sloan School of Management as well as in universities in Uganda, Japan, and Israel. He has written or edited close to two dozen books and in 2020 was the recipient of the Dr. Leopold Lucas Prize in Tubingen, Germany.

Rahel R. Wasserfall is a Certified Iyengar Yoga Teacher (CIYT, level 2). She is also director of evaluation and training for CEDAR—Communities Engaging with Difference and Religion, where she helped create and assess structures to fit the organization's mission. Wasserfall received her PhD in social anthropology from Hebrew University of Jerusalem in 1988. Over the past twenty years, she has worked in school settings, developing ethnographic studies to help reach and assess schools' goals. And as part of a group of researchers at Brandeis University, she has studied second language learners. Currently, she spends much of her time as a CIYT, teaching and researching the Yoga Sutras of Patanjali, and during 2020 she created a recurring program interviewing international yogis to learn about their experience with the COVID-19 pandemic and to create a global community of yogis. Her books include *Living with Difference: How to Build Community in a Divided World* and *Women and Water: Menstruation in Jewish Life and Law.*

Notes

1. The pedagogical aspects and value of the CEDAR approaches have been discussed at length in the documents cited in the bibliography. The CEDAR Workbook was first drafted by Adam Seligman, Chad Moore, Kendra Holt Moore, Rahel Wasserfall, and David Montgomery in 2019, with revisions, translations, and adaptations being done by CEDAR affiliate program staff and alumni trained in the CEDAR pedagogy.
2. For CEDAR's Pedagogic Principles, see http://www.cedarnetwork.org/about-us/pedagogic-principles/.

References

Montgomery, D. W. 2020. "A World without Human Rights? A Response." Reset Dialogues, 23 July. https://www.resetdoc.org/story/a-world-without-human-rights-a-response/.

Seligman, A. B. 2020. "The Tragedy of Human Rights: Liberalism and the Loss of Belonging—A Reply to Our Critics." Reset Dialogues, 23 June. https://www.resetdoc.org/story/the-tragedy-of-human-rights-liberalism-and-the-loss-of-belonging-a-reply-to-our-critics/.

Seligman, A. B., and D. W. Montgomery. 2019. "The Tragedy of Human Rights: Liberalism and the Loss of Belonging." *Society* 56(3): 203–9.

Seligman, A. B., R. R. Wasserfall, and D. W. Montgomery. 2015. *Living with Difference: How to Build Community in a Divided World.* Berkeley: University of California Press.

Wasserfall, R. 2012. "Eating Together: The Hidden Story of the International Summer School on Religion and Public Life." *Practical Matters* 5: 1–19.

———. 2017. "Le CEDAR, une methodologie pour un vecu dans la difference." *Plurielles* 20: 105–17.

~:~

CHAPTER 17

Birangona
Toward Ethical Testimonies of Sexual Violence During Conflict

NAYANIKA MOOKHERJEE

Project Background

Sexual violence during conflict is understood to be a cost of war, consigned to oblivion and silence. In response to the assumed silence about wartime rape, feminists and activists have found it imperative to testify, to witness, to speak out, to "recover," to give voice to raped women's narratives. Such activism has publicized the rapes of comfort women in Japan during World War II, the rapes in Bosnia and Rwanda in the 1990s, and sexual violence in Darfur and Congo.[1] However, in Bangladesh, wartime rape was part of a public conversation immediately after the Bangladesh war of 1971, then reemerged as part of the public discussion in the 1990s, but remained as a public memory throughout its near fifty years by means of literary and visual representations.

In the years after the East and West Pakistan partition from colonized British India in 1947, various West Pakistani administrative, military, linguistic, civil, and economic controls over East Pakistan resulted in a nine-month war in 1971 and ultimately the formation of a wholly independent Bangladesh. Bangladesh was faced with a staggering three million dead, and with two hundred thousand women (official numbers) raped by the Pakistani army and *Razakars* (local Bengali collaborators). The Bangladeshi government took the globally unprecedented step of referring to the raped women as *birangonas* (war heroines) to prevent them from being socially ostracized and attempted to rehabilitate them by enabling them to have abortions, facilitating the adoption of war babies to Western countries, and marrying the women off or providing them jobs.

Unfortunately, for various political reasons, the Bangladeshi press and government fell silent on the *birangonas* between 1975 and the 1990s. The issue of wartime rape, however, still remained on the public stage as a topic of literary and visual media (newspapers, films, plays, novels, poems, and photography), ensuring that the raped woman endures as an iconic figure. Since the 1990s, various direct testimonies of *birangonas* have been recorded, and many women have spoken out publicly about their wartime and postwar experiences (see Akhtar et al. 2001).

During my research in Bangladesh in 1997, I indeed found that sexual violence, instead of being hidden as elsewhere, was continually invoked, and not only in state speeches and policies eulogizing the *birangonas*. The figure of the *birangona* could be found in newspapers, museums, and in various literary (novels, poems, plays) and visual (photographs, films, street plays, advertisements, paintings) representations throughout the near fifty years of Bangladesh. I gathered in-depth ethnographic information and insights from eleven survivors (as well as their families and communities) who were publicly known and were speaking about their experiences on their own volition for various reasons. I also worked with activists and state officials and researched archival, press, literary, and visual sources. This public memory of wartime sexual violence is highlighted in my book *The Spectral Wound: Sexual Violence, Public Memories and the Bangladesh War of 1971* (Mookherjee 2015).

My research and activities address three main problems surrounding the *birangonas*. The first is that this public memory of the *birangona* contradicts the prevalent assumption that there is silence regarding wartime rape. My work highlights various socioeconomic dynamics within which the ideologies of gender, honor, and shame are practiced among the *birangonas*, showing that the public memory of wartime rape manifests in Bangladesh in three ways: first, the state category of raped women as *birangonas*; second, an extensive archive of visual and literary representations dating back to 1971; and third, human rights testimonies of poor and middle-class *birangonas* since the 1990s.

The second problem emerging during my research is that nongovernmental organization (NGO) activists, human rights lawyers, intellectuals, writers, journalists, academics, and feminists who knew about my research among poorer *birangonas* would invariably ask: "Are they married?" "Do they have a family, children, *kutumb* [in-laws]?" "Did their husband know of the incident of rape?" These questions revealed a class bias among the activists who assumed all poor *birangonas* were not absorbed by their families. My answers would amaze them: the poor, rural, landless, and illiterate women continue to be married to their landless husbands with whom they were married even before 1971, *in spite* of the rape. My research shows that identifying raped women only through their suffering not only creates a homogeneous understanding of victims but also suggests that wartime rape is experienced in the same way by all victims.

The third problem involves postconflict urgency to record survivors' testimonies to achieve justice. The Bangladeshi liberal left activist community in the 1990s started collecting these testimonies as evidence of the injustices and what many would consider to be genocide committed through the 1971 rapes and killings.[2] With this sole focus on documenting the "horrific" experiences of wartime rape, inadequate attention is paid to both the conditions (how they are interviewed) under which such testimonies are recorded and the way the war heroines themselves want to articulate their experiences, not only of 1971 but of the trajectories of their subsequent, postconflict lives.

As a result, ethical (relating to principles of informed consent, sensitivity, doing no harm, protection of survivors, anonymity and confidentiality, and risk assessment) practices of documentation before, during, and after the testimonial process can be flouted by journalists, human rights activists, government officials, nongovernmental organization personnel, and researchers in their pursuit of recording wartime rape. Hence, survivors can experience a double set of transgressions—first of sexual violence, and then being retraumatized through the recording of their testimonies through insensitive and unethical means. This can lead to a critical disconnect between survivors' needs and transitional justice processes.

Project Description

The project that emerged from my initial research involves the creation of interviewing guidelines, a graphic novel, an animated film, and a website (Mookherjee and Keya 2019) to assist those taking testimonies from survivors. One of the central findings of my book *Spectral Wound* was how survivors of sexual violence found the process of giving testimonies to be an equally transgressive process with negative consequences when ethical practices are not followed by those recording their experiences. The goal of this project was and is to contribute to the welfare of survivors by ensuring their process of giving testimonies does not prove to be another source of trauma along with the past experiences of sexual violence. This can be possible by making academic work more accessible to nonacademic individuals and organizations and applying the research findings of *Spectral Wound* among them.

After the publication of my book in 2015 and of its South Asian version in 2016, I was invited to have a book launch event at the Centre for Women, Peace and Security at the London School of Economics (LSE) in October 2016. The panelists for the book launch included academics as well as NGO leaders and government officials. I was also invited to speak at the Dhaka Literary Festival in November 2016 about the book and also launch the South Asian edition. I took this invitation as an opportunity to initiate the first collaborative workshop with my partners Research Initiatives Bangladesh (RIB) as well as invited participants, which included survivors who were in the public eye, academics, researchers, government officials, policymakers, NGO representatives, feminists and human rights activists, journalists, filmmakers, and photographers.

To be mindful of the survivors' concerns and not sensationalize their experiences for the purpose of testimonies, it is essential to have a set of guidelines to record their experiences. Guidelines that serve as a list of ethical practices were codeveloped through these workshops and are visualized through various illustrations in a graphic novel, making them more accessible. These guiding principles help to raise questions among those seeking to record testimonies. Before the first workshop, I had started developing storyboards and was collaborating with Najmunnahar Keya (a Bangladeshi visual artist) to develop the graphic novel. Before the November 2016 workshop, I predistributed a set of guidelines based on my monograph; we developed these further based on the workshop participant feedback. In the second half of the workshop, we developed the initial plans for the graphic novel.

After that first workshop, we further developed the guidelines via email, and the graphic novel came together through online exchanges across a six-hour time difference over a span of two and a half years, with support from the Economic and Social Research Council's Impact Acceleration Account and Durham University's Research Impact Fund. After five consultative workshops in Bangladesh (RIB) and the United Kingdom (UK) (Centre for Women, Peace and Security, LSE), we coproduced the guidelines, graphic novel, and animated film in collaboration with various stakeholders in Bangladesh and the UK, with support and participation by the Ministry of Liberation War Affairs of the Government of Bangladesh and the UK's Foreign and Commonwealth Office's Preventing Sexual Violence in Conflict Initiative (PSVI). The novel, film, and guidelines can be used by those who record testimonies of sexual violence in conflict (researchers, human rights activists, feminists, lawyers, filmmakers, photographers, journalists, writers) and future researchers and activists. It would also generate interest on sexual violence during conflict and enable sensitization of these issues among children (twelve years and above).

I have a long-term interest in ethics, and as the ethics officer of the Association of Social Anthropologists of UK and the Commonwealth (ASA) from 2007 to 2012, I completely updated the ethics code in 2011 through a long consultative process with ASA members. I have also been part of the ethics committee of the World Council of Anthropological Associations. These engagements with ethics were brought out in my monograph and in turn in the guidelines, graphic novel, and film. I was also inspired by the University of Toronto Graphic Ethnography series as well as various American Anthropological Association panels on this theme. The graphic novel was also made part of the Royal Anthropological Institute's *Illustrating Anthropology* series.[3] The

Figure 17.1. A page from the graphic novel *Birangona: Towards Ethical Testimonies of Sexual Violence During Conflict.* © 2019 Nayanika Mookherjee and Najmunnahar Keya.

graphic novel follows the debates involved in creating these anthropological ethics codes and applies them in the context of sexual violence during conflict. The graphic novel follows *Spectral Wound* in utilizing a political and historical analysis to highlight the varied experiences of wartime rape during 1971.

Through an intergenerational story, the graphic novel opens with Labonno/ Labony needing to do a school project on family memories of the 1971 Bangladesh War. When coming to ask her grandmother, she wakes the latter from one of her frequent nightmares. What follows is her grandmother's (Nanu/ Rehana) narration of the history of *birangona*. Her mother, Hena, also tells her of the oral history project through which they tried to collect testimonies. This leads them to talk about the various points that need to be covered and incorporated into ethical guidelines to record testimonies of sexual violence during conflict. Hidden in these discussions of the guidelines, Labonno discovers an intricate secret family history. The graphic novel highlights the ten guidelines through which anthropological concepts and ethnographic manifestations related to ethics, stigma, honor, and shame are visualized. The purpose is to suggest ways for activists and researchers to document accounts of wartime rape and avoid exacerbating conditions of survivors.

Through long-term ethnographic research, participant observation, and engagement with ethics, it was possible to explore what transitional justice meant for the survivors of sexual violence and their families. On reading the graphic novel/reviewing the film, a survivor said:

> We cried and laughed on reading this book and seeing this film. It should be read and seen by all children and their parents. By reading this book and seeing this film children will not question the war again. No one will question who fought, and no will ever give *khota*/scorn to *birangonas*. Along with children, their parents would read, their mothers would read, and they would get to know about the war. All our stories are here in this book, and I want this book to be in every school in Bangladesh so that all children know about us. (Rural *birangonas* and their children)

A sexual violence survivor from the Denis Mukwege Foundation said:

> The format of this approach is so inspiring, educative with a pinch of compassion in the telling of the shared experiences of the *Birangona*. As a "survivor" myself, I still cannot claim and own that word upon myself. During the Luxembourg retreat we had a session on what do we address ourselves. Globally in the network, the Colombian and Guatemalan women preferred to use and to be addressed as victims, while the majority of the women related to the word survivors. But for a government to decide to honour their victims by naming the *Birangona*, right there from the start stigma is addressed effectively and beautifully, even though there is still a lot to be done in our societies today after such recognition. (Email communication, May 2020)

Implementation and Anthropologist's Role

The guidelines, graphic novel, and website were launched by survivors, their families, and the Minister of Liberation War Affairs in August 2018 and April 2019 in Bangladesh, and at the Centre for Women, Peace and Security in May 2019. The survivors and various organizations reviewed earlier versions of the guideline and graphic novel and received hard copies and online versions of the graphic novel and film.

As an anthropologist, I approached this work by highlighting the reality on the ground rather than identifying established and assumed facts relating to silence, stigma, shame, and trauma—which are often deemed to be the effect of wartime sexual violence. As a result, counter to the prevalent assumption of silence relating to wartime rape, my ethnography highlighted the public memory of wartime rape. Use of the archival materials interspersed among the sketches of the graphic novel brought alive the relevance of documents from nearly fifty years ago. This also enabled me to counter the limited understanding of the impacts of wartime rape whereby the raped woman is only understood to be an "abnormal," horrific, dehumanized victim, abandoned by her kin. Instead, the graphic novel highlights the lives and experiences of various *birangonas* and how they have dealt with wartime sexual violence. As a result, the concepts of honor, silence, shame, and stigma are understood through idioms relevant to various survivors. The graphic novel also highlights the various socioeconomic and politico-historical dynamics within which the ideologies of gender, honor, and shame are practiced among the *birangonas* and which cannot be understood homogenously.

Viewed through another lens, the project shows that oral history accounts and interviews can be cross-referenced through secondary documents like land records. We find that the land of those who underwent sexual violence during the war was also appropriated by powerful local forces after the war. As a result, stigma and shame can often be used to keep the weak in their position and strengthen the strong (Mookherjee 2006).

A focus as well on the postconflict experiences highlights the continuum of violence, the various connotations of trauma, and the varied effects of sexual violence on the lives of the *birangonas* and their families. For example, sex worker Chaya Dutta feels she was raped because she was made vulnerable by the death of her mother; she feels that if her mother had been alive, she would have protected her. For Shireen, her trauma is that she cannot talk about her first husband to her second husband; she married the latter after being raped during the war and after her first husband was killed. Rural landless woman Moyna Karim was caught and raped when she was cutting fish during the war, and she has never cut fish since. The sculptor *birangona* Ferdousy Priyobhash-ini was the protagonist war heroine who was present in various national commemorations but was still called a collaborator after the war. This is because she could not flee the country as she had to sustain her young siblings and widowed mother. She went to work every day, which was also the site where she was regularly raped. Many assumed she was collaborating with the Pakistani army, not realizing she did not have an opportunity to escape.

Feedback about the project is still being collected and implemented on an ongoing basis. This feedback is gathered through public testimonials as well as social media posts, video recordings, and letters from stakeholders in both Bangladesh and the UK. Feedback also informs how the guidelines and graphic novel are being implemented by various stakeholders across the world.

There have been unanticipated challenges along the way. One concerned the time needed for government departments to approve the guidelines and graphic novel, even though officials had been quite positive about the two products. In addition, translating academic work into a visual form took significant time, and, honestly, it took me out of my comfort zone. Universities do not provide additional time for such work, and so disseminating this to nonacademic audiences had to be coordinated in conjunction with my existing commitments and duties.

Outcomes

This project has contributed directly to the welfare of survivors. For example, Drishtipat, an activist network seeking redress and compensation for thirteen war-affected women, used my research in a successful fundraising effort to collect $15,000, and this provided funds for daily sustenance for these *birangonas*. In addition, there are several instances of secondary impacts in which my work was used by others to improve the understanding of the survivors.

Along with the survivor-led guidelines and graphic novel, the project has changed policies, practices, and perceptions.

Changes to Policy

The research influenced the Government of Bangladesh's First National Action Plan (NAP) on Women Peace and Security (2019–22) as part of the Ministry of Foreign Affairs remit of adopting the landmark UN Security Council Resolution 1325 in 2000. Our research on how *birangonas* were addressed by the Bangladeshi government is foundational for the history of the country and the women, peace, and security narrative. Our research brought out archival documents and ethnographic accounts not available in any other documents before. In addition, the Bangladesh Ministry of Liberation War Affairs is reviewing formalization of the guidelines and graphic novel into ministry policy.

The Prevent Sexual Violence Initiative team with the Foreign and Commonwealth Office is using our guideline and graphic novel and hence directly linking to our research to inform the extensive consultation and formulation of the Murad Code (named after 2018 Nobel Peace Prize laureate Nadia Murad), which is a global code of conduct for the documentation and investigation of conflict-related sexual violence.

Changes in Practice

Various organizations working with survivors have confirmed that they are using the graphic novel and guideline to train their personnel regarding the process of recording testimonies of sexual violence. These include international NGOs such as the Dr. Denis Mukwege Foundation, Eyewitness to Atrocities, International Alert, Amnesty International, Survivors Speak Out Network, and Institute for Social Care Excellence, as well as Bangladeshi NGOs, museums, writers, artists, and the media (the *Dhaka Tribune*).

The Dr. Denis Mukwege Foundation (the key international organization on sexual violence in conflict; Mukwege was the 2018 Nobel Peace Prize co-winner with Nadia Murad) stated: "We have incorporated these in our own guidelines and have distributed it in our survivor networks; this contributes to the social welfare of survivors by ensuring the testimonial process doesn't harm them." Bangladeshi NGOs like Ain O Shalish Kendra (ASK) notes: "This graphic novel has not only raised consciousness about the ways in which birangonas are continuing their lives. It is also a fantastic medium of teaching us how to avoid retraumatizing the survivors and record their testimonies with caution." Research Initiatives Bangladesh has used the guidelines effectively to train their personnel and collected testimonies among Rohingya refugees, and it has also used them to train Asian human rights defenders.

Changes to Perception

Our research has changed the perception of survivors and their families, as well as the perception of those who represent them. As mentioned earlier, survivors (who feature in the graphic novel) and their families have been hugely appreciative of the graphic novel.

The research has been instrumental in changing two plays that address the ways in which survivors of sexual violence should be represented. It directly influenced and changed the script of a play on the women raped during the Bangladesh war, staged by the theater group Komola Collective in the UK (2013–14) and in Bangladesh. By engaging with my findings, they were able to reconceptualize ideas of trauma and stigma, as well as the historical and political context. The graphic novel and guidelines for testimony collection were also used by Research Initiatives Bangladesh in a project to prevent sexual and gender-based violence against Rohingya women refugees through interactive theater.

I have also been invited as a woman leader, speaker, and expert to various locations and events, such as Buckingham Palace, the British Broadcasting Company, the UK House of Lords, and the Global Summit to End Sexual Violence in Conflict. My research on gendered violence during wars was also shortlisted as a finalist for the Michelle Z. Rosaldo Book Prize from the Association of Feminist Anthropologists at the American Anthropological Association annual meeting. Above all, the feedback from the survivors makes this project worthwhile.

The Anthropological Difference

Ethnography revealed that as a result of unethical practices, survivors can experience a double set of transgressions when testifying about their violent experiences during wars. A focus on this by international relations, public health, or psychiatry would have tried to understand the context of sexual violence during conflict through sweeping terms like *silence, shame, stigma,* and *trauma,* thereby identifying women through their suffering only. The anthropological difference is rendered by anthropology's ability to unravel homogenous narratives to bring out a more holistic understanding. Hence, instead of using the oft-reified concepts of stigma, honor, and shame, the project identified, for example, the economic context of these concepts.

This project not only counters the claims of the prevalence of silence relating to sexual violence but also shows that sexual violence is intrinsically linked to political, racial, and historical contexts; additionally, enabling survivors to speak about their violent experiences contributes to a public memory of events. The research highlights the varied contexts and everyday experiences of rape among survivors and how they develop resilience based on their contexts—something that needs to be kept in mind by researchers.

Other disciplines have approached sexual violence in conflict through a focus on horrific testimonies of sexual violence. Instead, this project's focus on postconflict experiences highlights the continuum of violence, the various connotations of "trauma," and the varied effects of sexual violence on the lives of the survivors and their families. This allows us to ethnographically identify the various "socialities of violence"—the various ways the past violence erupts socially—and through which *birangonas* live with this experience. As a result, instead of focusing on voyeuristic testimonies of sexual violence, which leads to retraumatization, ethnography allows us to highlight the "fragments" through which survivors refer to their violent, embodied experiences. This not only interrogates the global term *trauma* but also allows us to use language as an analytical tool to comprehend the experience of the survivors.

Anthropological interpretations of honor, silence, shame, and stigma are understood through idioms relevant to various survivors as they emerge in the graphic novel. For example, many non-anthropologists often assume stigma and shame to be inherent in Muslim communities and are a natural response toward all survivors of sexual violence during conflict. In the graphic novel, we show the socioeconomic and politico-historical contexts of the invocation of stigma by communities and argue that shame cannot be understood homogenously in all instances of sexual violence. The novel shows an instance when a *birangona* is wondering why people scorn her, and she realizes that since all the neighbors are poor, they are assuming she is becoming rich. Also, she realizes that using *khota*/scorn of her rape against her is a way to belittle and humiliate her in the context of the land disputes that exist between families. These visualizations and various other illustrations show how the politico-historical and socioeconomic contexts of silence, honor, shame, and stigma are significant to understanding the postconflict context of survivors and to not assuming that these concepts are inherent in Muslim societies. Tracking these socioeconomic contexts enables researchers to address the well-being of survivors.

In short, through unethical practices, survivors can experience a double set of transgression when testifying to their violent experiences during wars. Those who document testimonies of wartime rape need to undertake this process ethically. Silence, stigma, honor, and shame among survivors needs to be understood through their historical, political, and economic contexts.

These guidelines and graphic novel, and now the film, have emerged from the experiences of violations of survivors. These outputs should also help us reflect on whether there is further need for recording of testimonies and if there are adequate secondary sources to provide the needed insight. While a longer time is advisable for those recording testimonies, those with less time should be able to provide a nuanced survivor perspective about the reasons for sexual violence, the varied contexts of testimonies, the use of language, and euphemisms and gestures by survivors to uphold their narrative. The development of the film has further enabled circulation; we have also been able to reach survivors in Colombia and the Democratic Republic of Congo.

Nayanika Mookherjee is a professor of political anthropology at Durham University, UK. As a Felix scholar, she did her PhD in social anthropology from the School of Oriental and African Studies (SOAS), London University. Her research concerns an ethnographic exploration of public memories of violent pasts, namely gendered violence in conflicts, memorialization, and transnational adoption. Based on her award-winning book (*The Spectral Wound: Sexual Violence, Public Memories and the Bangladesh War of 1971* [2015 Duke

University Press; 2016 Zubaan]), she has coauthored a survivor-led guideline, graphic novel, and animation film: *Birangona: Towards Ethical Testimonies of Sexual Violence During Conflict* (2019).

Notes

1. For further details, see the bibliography for Brownmiller (1975), Tanaka (1996), Stiglmayer (1994), Taylor (1999), Baaz and Stern (2013), and Prunier (2005). In the UN Beijing Declaration of 1995, rape during war was declared to be a war crime. The Japanese government has also apologized to the comfort women.
2. In Bangladesh, the events of 1971 are considered to be genocide, taking into account mass killings; impositions on culture, language, and religion; and national feelings during 1971.
3. Portions of this graphic novel became part of the Royal Anthropological Institute's "Illustrating Anthropology" ongoing series, which explores human lives through visual works of anthropological research. See https://illustratinganthropology.com/nayanika-mookherjee/.

References

Akhtar, S., S. Begum, H. Hossein, S. Kamal, and M. Guhathakurta, eds. 2001. *Narir Ekattor O Juddhoporoborti Koththo Kahini* [Oral history accounts of women's experiences during 1971 and after the war]. Dhaka: Ain-O-Shalish-Kendro.

Baaz, M. E., and M. Stern. 2013. *Sexual Violence as a Weapon of War? Perceptions, Prescriptions and Problems in the Congo and Beyond*. London: Zed Books.

Brownmiller, S. 1975. "Bangladesh." In *Against Our Will: Men, Women and Rape*, 78–86. London: Secker and Warburg.

Mookherjee, N. 2015. *The Spectral Wound: Sexual Violence, Public Memories and the Bangladesh War of 1971*. Durham, NC: Duke University Press.

———. 2006. "'Remembering to Forget': Public Secrecy and Memory of Sexual Violence in Bangladesh." *Journal of the Royal Anthropological Institute* 12(2): 433–50.

Mookherjee, N., and N. Keya. 2019. *Birangona: Towards Ethical Testimonies of Sexual Violence During Conflict*. Durham: University of Durham. Graphic novel and film, available in Bangla and English from https://www.ethical-testimonies-svc.org.uk/how-to-cite/.

Prunier, G. 2005. *Darfur: The Ambiguous Genocide*. Oxford: Hurst and Co.

Stiglmayer, A. 1994. *Mass Rape: The War against Women in Bosnia-Herzegovina*. Translated by Marion Faber. Lincoln: University of Nebraska Press.

Tanaka, Y. 1996. *Hidden Horror: Japanese War Crimes in World War II*. Boulder, CO: Westview Press.

Taylor, C. 1999. *Sacrifice as Terror: The Rwandan Genocide of 1994*. Oxford: Berg.

PART VI

~:~

Policy Change

CHAPTER 18

~:~

Anthropology in Action
An Anthropologist's Role in Restoring US Support to the United Nations Population Fund

BARBARA PILLSBURY

Project Background

In 2002, the George W. Bush administration rescinded US support for the United Nations Population Fund (UNFPA) based on allegations that the UNFPA was complicit in forced abortions and sterilizations in China. Barbara Pillsbury, an applied medical anthropologist with extensive knowledge of Chinese culture and healthcare, believed firmly that, to the contrary, the UNFPA was a major force in promoting reproductive choice and voluntarism in China's family planning program. She therefore participated in efforts to bring about restoration of US funding for the UNFPA. This chapter depicts the political milieu in which Pillsbury worked to effect policy change, describes how she carried out her project, and credits her anthropological knowledge and approach for its successful outcome.

The UNFPA is the principal UN agency dedicated to women's and reproductive health. As a sister agency to the World Health Organization (WHO) and UNICEF, the UNFPA supports countries in using population data for policies and programs to reduce poverty and is dedicated to supporting family planning and reproductive health services in more than 150 countries around the world. It has helped many countries to initiate and strengthen voluntary family planning programs and is an important force and advocate for improving the status of women. Its emphasis has always been on family planning that is safe and voluntary. As a UN organization, it is an important source of worldwide assistance, in both funds and advice, to less-developed countries. UNFPA funds come from voluntary contributions made by approximately 180 countries. The United States helped establish the UNFPA in 1969 and has played a leadership role in its management. Until 1985, the United States was the largest donor, providing nearly one-third of the UNFPA's total annual funding.

It is also useful to summarize an underlying problem explored by this project: population growth in China. The Chinese government has struggled since the 1950s with the challenge of lifting the country out of poverty. Slowing the rapid population growth was recognized early on as being essential for meeting the challenge. China began systematic efforts to control population growth in the early 1970s from concern over persistent poverty and rising birth rates. Whereas the country had taken 2,000 years to reach a population of 60 million, and then 200 years to reach 430 million, it gained 350 million between 1950 and 1973 alone, for a total of 890 million people. In the late 1960s, the average Chinese woman had six or more children, especially in rural areas where about 80 percent of the population lived.

The UNFPA began assisting population-related matters in China in 1979–80. With the US Census Bureau, it helped carry out China's first scientific census in 1982. The UNFPA supported training abroad for some two hundred Chinese demographers and public health officials and set up population science curricula in twenty-two Chinese research institutions, including bringing in visiting foreign professors.

In the early 1990s, the UNFPA worked with UNICEF in China to bring improved mother and child health services to three hundred poor and remote counties, markedly lowering mortality rates. This provided the basis for a World Bank loan and subsequent expansion nationwide. UNFPA also supported the production of modern, safe, and effective contraceptives.[1] In the 1990s UNFPA played a unique leadership role in introducing quality standards for a reproductive health approach based on voluntarism.

For the fiscal year 2002 budget, the US Congress earmarked a $34 million contribution for the UNFPA's global program. In July 2002, however, the Bush administration yielded to pressure from Christian conservatives and groups hostile to China, contraception, abortion, and women's rights, and rescinded the $34 million authorization. The Bush administration's decision was based on testimony and feeble allegations that the UNFPA was complicit in forced abortions and sterilizations in China; in 2001, a militantly anti-China and anti-family planning group had produced a report using data from the 1980s contrived to appear as if the UNFPA had been and was currently supporting coercive abortion and sterilization. (Contributing to the complexity was the reality that coercion *had* occurred in parts of China, where local officials were overzealous, especially in the 1980s, in carrying out China's "one-child" policy.) The antichoice groups and certain conservative members of Congress were pleased with the Bush administration's withholding of funding for the UNFPA.

Pro-choice Americans were incensed over US support being withheld when ample evidence showed that the UNFPA was a major force in denouncing coercion and promoting voluntarism in China.[2] Withholding US support was punitive not only to China but also to the UNFPA's work worldwide. US funding for UNFPA programs, they argued, was crucial to improving the health and lives of women and families globally and for addressing demographic trends and promoting sustainable development. The Bush administration continued each year thereafter to withhold the US contribution. (Congressionally approved funding for the UNFPA withheld by the Bush administration from 2002 to 2008 totaled $244 million.)

Due to Pillsbury's extensive knowledge of China, international healthcare, and population, the Rand Corporation provided funding for her to carry out a health study in China in 1978, the year the country opened its borders to outsiders. She produced a long narrative report, one of the first insights into healthcare dynamics in China (Pillsbury 1978). At about that time, she was also a founder of the International Women's Health Coalition, which helped to mobilize constituencies to broaden programs—from family planning to women's reproductive health—more comprehensively.

Project Description

An important goal of reproductive rights advocates and organizations was the restoration of US funding for the UNFPA. This would enable the UNFPA to more effectively support reproductive health needs globally, not just in China. Unlike a conventional administrative project, the restoration of US funding for the UNFPA was a multipronged effort, necessarily and unavoidably engaged in politics at the highest level in the United States. Thus, for the project described here, there was not the typical internal organization, staffing, schedule, total funding, or annual budget for the effort. Many organizations with reproductive rights agendas were engaged, each with their own budgets and activity structures.

From 1992 to 1994, and prior to the project activities described here (which took place from 2003 to 2009), Pillsbury was contracted by the WHO as consultant to the UNFPA, UNICEF, and the Chinese Ministry of Public Health for the project "Strengthening Maternal Child Health and Family Planning Services at the Grassroots Level." Her primary contribution was to design and conduct training workshops on evaluation and qualitative research, in Chinese and English, for project physicians and for the project's External Evaluation Unit at Shanghai Medical University. A highlight was mentoring young physicians as they applied participant observation and other anthropological methodologies; some even lived several weeks in villagers' homes to observe and understand family practices related to child health and family planning.

By 2002, she had made additional technical assistance visits to China and traveled widely in the country. This included sponsorship by a provincial women's federation and social science institute, with resulting publications in Chinese, evaluation of a project (Contraceptive Introduction in Rural China) implemented by the Rockefeller Foundation with China's State Family Planning Commission, design of a "Leadership Development Program for High-Level Officials of China's National Family Planning Program," and workshops with the Kunming Medical University in Yunnan. Most of these projects and activities involved collaboration with the faction of Chinese officials who sought to implement quality-of-care and voluntarism in family planning, which the UNFPA was promoting.

In September 2003, an interfaith delegation of prominent US religious leaders and ethicists undertook a mission to China to investigate the validity of the charges against the UNFPA and to assess the value of the UNFPA's work. A nongovernmental organization in Washington, DC, engaged Pillsbury to help put together and guide the delegation. As a delegation consultant, she played a crucial, lead role in coordinating all planning and implementation of the mission. The delegates were Christian, Jewish, Muslim, and ethicists: a very senior, credible, and representative group.

Implementation and Anthropologist's Role

Both prior to and during the delegation's travels, Pillsbury shared her anthropological knowledge of China, such as Chinese customs that the delegates would need to observe to function effectively in China, knowledge of the norms of working with translators, and dimensions of cultural relativity in addressing policies and their implementation.

A particularly thorny question for the delegation concerned coercion and what constitutes coercion. All agreed that physically forcing a woman to have an abortion or sterilization was unacceptable coercion. But what about the requirement to limit children to only one or two per couple? Was it coercive when the Chinese government was also deciding where citizens should work, live, and go to school? In this context, was it any more coercive for the government to decide who could have one, two, or more children? Did the goal of reducing poverty and abject poverty make acceptable the policy of limiting numbers of children? Such questions had no easy answers, but it was Pillsbury's responsibility to provide the cultural understandings that would allow the delegates to reach conclusions.

At the end of the delegation's inquiry and explorations, the delegates concluded that the role of the UNFPA in China was, beyond doubt, very positive. "The Chinese government is taking active steps to end the use of coercion in its family planning activities nationwide," stated their report. "UNFPA has been and remains a major force and a vital catalyst in achieving China's transition to a fully voluntary and non-coercive family planning program." The delegates advised: "It is reasonable to be concerned about China's family planning policies and practices, but it is even more important to actively assist and engage the Chinese on these matters.... The US policy toward China's family planning program should become one of constructive engagement.... US funding for UNFPA should be restored and if possible increased" (Catholics for a Free Choice 2003).

While the interfaith delegation report added yet more evidence as to the positive impact of the UNFPA in China, the anti-China sentiments in the Bush administration prevailed, and US support was again withheld. Indeed, the major challenge in the applicant's efforts was US presidential and congressional politics. The Bush administration was ideologically oriented against the UNFPA and its role in China, and it did not have a high interest in actual evidence. Many of the conservatives in Congress held similar views.

In early 2008, Pillsbury was asked to serve as the team leader for an intensive, nearly year-long review of the UNFPA's ongoing program in China. Her teammates were an eminent Chinese medical doctor (female), who had worked for many years with the WHO, and one of China's leading demographers (male). Once again, she drew on anthropological theory and knowledge to provide guidance to her teammates as they traveled to the provinces to observe, interview, and collect data. In hundreds of subtle decisions, her anthropological knowledge and trained intuition made it possible to weave the findings into a cogent and appropriately nuanced report of nearly 150 pages.

The significant achievement of the UNFPA, the team found, was that new approaches to reproductive rights and client-centered quality of care were being further developed and extended, with positive influences on law and policy. The team found that progressive colleagues in China's National Population and Family Planning Commission had fully embraced the program of action of the UNFPA-led 1994 International Conference on Population and Development (ICPD) in Cairo and were devoted to full implementation in China of its principles of reproductive rights. Birth quotas and targets were removed nationwide; the UNFPA-led, client-centered quality-of-care approach was extended to more than eight hundred of China's nearly three thousand counties; and the four-year birth spacing requirement was eliminated in many of the UNFPA's thirty pilot counties and entirely in nine provinces (United Nations Population Fund 2008). Without the UNFPA, it is fully possible that China's Communist Party, prioritizing economic growth, might have continued with bureaucratically imposed birth quotas and targets as a means to control population growth. Guided by the UNFPA and the ICPD, however, the team judged China to be on the path to full voluntarism in its population/family planning program.

Outcomes

Pillsbury and her team presented the report of their in-depth review of the UNFPA program to the Chinese government in December 2008. By that time, the United States had a new president, Barack Obama, who was calling for evidence-based decision-making. The team's report constituted important and very current evidence. In January 2009, before Obama's inauguration, Pillsbury met with concerned congressional staff and various advocacy organizations that would be contacting the White House on this issue, sharing with them the major findings on the positive role of the UNFPA.

On 11 March 2009, President Obama signed legislation to restore US funding for the UNFPA, fulfilling a pledge he made during his first days as president "to resume support for UNFPA and join 180 other donor nations in working towards slashing poverty, boosting the health of women and children, preventing HIV/AIDS, and providing family planning assistance to women in 154 countries" (United Nations Population Fund 2009). UNFPA's executive director, Thoraya Obaid, responded:

> This is a great day for women, girls, and their families around the world.... The US contribution will allow UNFPA to maintain its life-saving work, particularly improving maternal and reproductive health in the world's poorest communities, especially during this financial crisis. We are delighted that the United States will once again take a leading role in championing women's reproductive health and rights, alongside all other countries and partners that have supported us over the years.... UNFPA stands ready to work with President Obama, Secretary Clinton, and the American people to achieve our dream of helping women and girls in the poorest countries reach their fullest potential. We welcome the opportunity to work with the United States again as a full partner (United Nations Population Fund 2009).

On 24 March, the US State Department announced it would contribute $50 million to the UNFPA in 2009. The department's press release proclaimed, "This decision highlights the Administration's strong commitment to international family planning, women's health, and global development. The United States is a global leader in promoting voluntary family planning and the health of vulnerable women and children in the developing world" (US Department of State 2009).

The results of this project were immense: it effected a major policy change that should have innumerable and ongoing positive impacts on programs and people's lives. Were they directly attributable to the role of Pillsbury? Certainly, she made clear and very important inputs that contributed to the signing of legislation by President Obama (Pillsbury 2009). Given his campaign declarations that his decisions would be based on evidence rather than ideology, the two reports in which she had major roles—especially the report completed in December 2008—were influential in giving confidence to supporters in Congress and the Obama White House that the UNFPA should be trusted and supported.

The Anthropological Difference

This example of an anthropologist in action illustrates the potential for anthropologists to marshal anthropological knowledge and approaches to influence both policy at the highest level and matters of global importance. It cannot be said that, but for her efforts, the policy change by President Obama would not have occurred; however, her anthropological input doubtless helped precipitate the change.

In the process, many others benefited from her application of anthropological knowledge and methodology. These included the Christian, Jewish, Muslim, and ethicist delegates that Pillsbury guided through China. Influential leaders within their own communities, they gained and took back to others new and enhanced understandings of cultural relativity and its use in assessing cross-cultural challenges. Her Chinese teammates on the 2008 in-depth review gleaned and gained confidence in the use of anthropological methods of data collection and qualitative analysis for producing program and policy guidance. Other advocates and actors back in Washington, DC, also benefited from what was gained through anthropology in action.

Pillsbury's training in anthropology led her to respond to China's population challenges in a way that few others in similar roles would have done. She understood the policy control decisions and sought to "soften" those policies in the direction of human and women's rights. This was recognized early on in a 1984 *New York Times* article featuring her efforts (Wren 1984).

Other anthropologists knowledgeable in Chinese language, culture, society, and politics, and with a similar attraction to and sensitivity concerning policy dynamics, might also have achieved what she did. However, fewer are the persons from other disciplines who have the acuity to move effectively among cultures as diverse as those of Chinese peasants, Chinese officials of various factions and multiple levels, and American politicians. Anthropology remains unique in providing frameworks for effective human and cultural action.

Barbara Pillsbury was a pioneering cultural and medical anthropologist who was passionate about international development, women's health, and public health and who specialized in reproductive and sexual health rights. She received her PhD in 1973 from Columbia University, where she studied with Margaret Mead and wrote her thesis on Muslim women in China. She subsequently received tenure in cultural anthropology at San Diego State University, but realizing her passion was for applied anthropology, she left to join

USAID, where she continued to lead research and evaluation for Asia. She went on to steer international development governmental and NGO projects, guiding research in reproductive and sexual health, HIV/AIDS, child survival, and gender issues. She was an active member of the Washington Association of Professional Anthropologists (WAPA), served as a member of the board of directors of the American Anthropological Association (AAA), and was a founder and first president of the National Association for the Practice of Anthropology (NAPA). Barbara Pillsbury died in 2012.

Notes

Barbara Pillsbury passed away in 2012. With the assistance and approval of her family, the editors have reshaped her original Praxis Award application into this chapter.

1. This included establishment of four factories to produce the copper-T 22OC and 3804 intrauterine devices (IUDs) to replace the previous, inert stainless-steel ring, which was the cause of many unintended pregnancies and consequent abortions, as well as other important measures to improve the quality of condoms and hormonal contraceptives.

2. In rescinding the $34 million contribution, the Bush administration had ignored the recommendation from the US Department of State's own investigative team. This team, which had been sent to China in May 2002 to evaluate the UNFPA's role there, judged it positive and urged that the UNFPA be funded. (See US Department of State, *Report of the China UN Population Fund [UNFPA] Independent Assessment Team*, released by the Bureau of Population, Refugees and Migration, 29 May 2002.)

References

Catholics for a Free Choice. 2003. *The United Nations Population Fund in China: A Catalyst for Change*. Report of the Interfaith Delegation to China. Washington, DC: Catholics for a Free Choice.

Pillsbury, B. 1978. *Post "Gang of Four" China: Health, Development and Technology in the People's Republic*. Internal report, Social Science Department, the Rand Corporation, Santa Monica, CA, 16 June.

———. 2009. "The Politics of Family Planning: An Agenda for President Obama." *Anthropology Newsletter* (February): 30.

United Nations News Center. 2009. "$50 Million US Contribution Will Boost Women's Rights, Says UN." 12 March. https://news.un.org/en/story/2009/03/293762-50-million-us-contribution-will-boost-womens-rights-says-un.

United Nations Population Fund. 2008. *Government of China-UNFPA 6th China Country Programme (2006–2010): Mid-Term Review*. Beijing: United Nations Population Fund, December.

———. 2009. "UNFPA Welcomes Restoration of US Funding." Press release, 23 January. https://www.unfpa.org/press/unfpa-welcomes-restoration-us-funding.

US Department of State. 2009. "U.S. Government Support for the United Nations Population Fund (UNFPA)." Press release, 24 March.

Wren, C. S. 1984. "China Adds Compassion to Its Birth Control Drive." *New York Times*, 18 May, 2.

CHAPTER 19

༄༅

Decent Care
Shifting the Healthcare Paradigm

CATHLEEN E. CRAIN AND NATHANIEL TASHIMA

Project Background

The International Labor Organization developed the concept of "decent work" and, beginning in 2000, initiated an agenda to highlight "the role that good working conditions play in promoting development and poverty reduction" (International Labor Organization 2021). In 2006, staff at the World Health Organization (WHO) sought to explore an analogous concept of "Decent Care"[1] and how it could be implemented in healthcare policy and services worldwide. The WHO is the preeminent healthcare authority globally, and as such it must lead into new territory carefully, as the organization's decisions will affect WHO regions, country governments, faith-based organizations, global nongovernmental organizations (NGOs), and others. The challenge then, was to explore the concept of Decent Care through the respectful engagement of diverse stakeholders and to move through a process of concept development and refinement to a series of exploratory implementation steps. The introduction, development, and piloting of Decent Care by the WHO was an evolving global process that involved multiple distinct but interconnected activities.

The concept behind Decent Care is values based and orients all health prevention, care, and support activities to the needs of the affected individual as defined by the affected individual, inverting the traditional medical model, including, as a central theme, the affected person's family, community, tribe, and/or clan. Decent Care presents a dramatic restructuring of a healthcare system in which the patient/client (affected person) is presented with medical options by providers or told what is available based on a menu of services or the practical realities of existing services. The affected person may sometimes choose from available options, while in other cases he or she is directed to follow specific actions. The patient's role is to comply with medical directives and directions in order to gain or recover their health.

In Decent Care, the affected person is at the center of the health system, directing the available health or other service resources to achieve their desired outcomes. This may mirror the existing health service approach to care, but the affected person may select options not prioritized and/or controlled by the healthcare system, employ resources in a manner that is most comfortable to the individual, or even decline to utilize services. The health provider becomes a supporter and guide to the affected person and their decision-making process rather than a director. The values-based system of Decent Care also stresses the position of the affected individual in relation to the cultural and community context and assumes that is the starting point.

The perspectives of anthropology were highly supportive of defining, re-fining, and implementing processes that focus on the sensitive engagement of affected individuals, and in accounting for cultural, linguistic, class, and other differences that may affect the priorities and appropriate provision of care.

The six fundamental values of Decent Care are agency, dignity, interdepen-dence, solidarity, subsidiarity, and sustainability (Karpf et al. 2008). The values that would make care decent emerged organically from a WHO global con-sultation. Over the course of that consultation, participants converged around these values and identified them as the essential principles of Decent Care. In other words, it is these six values, taken together, that make care—the provi-sion of care—"decent."

The first two values, agency and dignity, are individual values and in many ways are the centerpiece of Decent Care. These are the values that focus on the inherent value that all humans share, the recognition of unique needs ev-ery individual has, and the direct control and decision-making every individual should have in the care he or she receives and how he or she receives it. At the root of the care process, every individual must be recognized as having the power—the agency—to construct, direct, and manage the care they receive (or elect not to receive. Similarly, recognizing the dignity of all persons in health-care and respecting and protecting the value of each individual means including the individual and her or his community in creating and sustaining her or his care processes.

The second set of values of Decent Care, interdependence and solidarity, are social values that focus on the unique relationship all individuals have to their particular social contexts and the communities around them. Interdependence and solidarity focus on the social nature of being cared for and caring for an-other—caring as a social process. The value of interdependence helps or ben-efits not only affected people and their families and communities but also the caregivers who serve them. Solidarity focuses on the specific communities each individual identifies with and how humans live together and advocate for each other. Despite the many differences that separate individuals and communities, the real challenge is to find ways for individuals to stand by and with each other.

The final two values of Decent Care, subsidiarity and sustainability, draw attention to the systemic nature of the provision of care and to issues such as need assessments, resource allocation, healthcare models, and the short- and long-term development of access to care. The fundamental concept of subsidiarity is relatively straightforward: the individuals or groups closest to problems "on the ground," who deal with the problems or issues directly and at the most fundamental level, should be the ones who help to resolve those issues or problems. For a community, this means that care processes are developed and implemented directly around those needing or receiving care and that those who receive care are central to the development of their own care processes. It also means that the community should have the resources and skills it needs to develop and manage the care processes for those who need it most. There is one overarching challenge to sustainability: it does not mean maintaining the *status quo*. Rather, it means being open to, and aware of, who has access to care and who does not—sustainability does not close the door on these issues: it should always be an open and reflective process that places the goal of human flourishing at its center.

Project Description

There were three connected projects conducted by the WHO for which we (the LTG anthropologists) provided significant support. The primary client for this work was the WHO Office of the Director-General's Representative for Partnerships and United Nations Reform based at WHO headquarters in Geneva, Switzerland. In addition, the World Council of Churches and the Ford Foundation were sponsors of ongoing project elements. There were three initial activities that were directed by the WHO and that we supported, as noted below. Additional projects related to the diffusion and uptake of Decent Care will be described later in the chapter. It is important to note that while this narrative focuses on our work, the projects were fundamentally collaborative and based in teams of highly skilled and experienced professionals. All of the teams were led by Reverend Ted Karpf, a senior WHO professional whose vision sparked the development of Decent Care. Table 19.1 provides a brief description of the projects, the activities conducted, and products developed by the team of anthropologists.

The first task was to convene a global conversation about how to define decent care and what it could mean in different settings to different stakeholders. The initial convening was held in Vevey, Switzerland, and focused on decent care in HIV/AIDS prevention and treatment. It was the first-ever global as-

Table 19.1. Summary of the many activities and products resulting from the Decent Care planning processes.

Initiative	Activities/Products*
Vevey, Switzerland **Global convening to define** **Decent Care values**	• White paper on Agency* • Planning of Vevey, Switzerland, convening (process, methods)* • Implementation of process* • Facilitation/rapporteur* • Analysis of data in process* • Idea-building for report • Writing contributions to report
Community Health Response **Program (CHRP)** **Design of a three-country** **Decent Care pilot project**	• Decent Care translation at Chateau Bossey, Switzerland* • Project development—London, England, and proposal development* • Project refinements—Nairobi, Kenya,* and Lusaka, Zambia* • Evaluation planning
Hammamet, Tunisia **Palliative care convening**	• Planning of Hammamet, Tunisia, convening* • Methods refinement* • Training development and provision • Facilitation* • Observation and documentation* • Methods/process adaptation* • Analysis and reporting • Methods codification and dissemination*

Note: * Significant anthropological content in activities.

sembly of a geographically, ethnically, and religiously diverse group of HIV/AIDS activists, ethicists, faith leaders, donors, and faith- and community-based providers of prevention, treatment, care, and support services to people living with HIV/AIDS. The task was to consider the notion of decent care—a new concept in the taxonomy and politics of HIV/AIDS care—and identify points of convergence between the values of decent care and both primary healthcare and palliative care services. Decent Care as it emerged from the initial convening had to be flexible enough to function in any culture and any language without being an etic imposition on emic categories. The activities around the convening spanned approximately nine months.

The Vevey convening was followed by a proposal development process and several planning activities. These activities were, first, intended to place Decent Care on the ground and test its practical application and, second, to move beyond primary care into a field anticipated to be hospitable to Decent Care palliative care.

The second activity was the development of a demonstration project in which Decent Care values would be applied in the revitalization of primary healthcare in three countries in Africa. This demonstration was titled "Community Health Response Programme" (CHRP). The CHRP was focused on the revitalization of primary healthcare in Malawi, Rwanda, and Zambia through the application of Decent Care values. CHRP concept development meetings were held in Bossey, Switzerland, and London, England, and followed by a planning meeting in Nairobi, Kenya. Finally, a site visit was conducted in Zambia with the stakeholders who would carry out the demonstration project.

Through a convening process that mirrored that in Vevey, the participants—two global health NGOs, the World Council of Churches, the WHO, representatives of the Norwegian Foreign Ministry, and the anthropologists—developed a plan and a proposal to demonstrate Decent Care. We provided documentation of the process, introduced concepts of evaluation and accountability into the planning, and edited and harmonized the proposal. The implementation of the demonstration was to have been funded by the Norwegian Foreign Ministry through a grant to the World Council of Churches and overseen by the WHO. We were to be the project evaluators and documentarians.

The third activity was the design and conduct of a global convening on the relationship of Decent Care values to the principles of palliative care. Palliative care in the WHO context is defined as engaging from the moment of diagnosis of a life-threatening or life-altering condition to improve the quality of life for affected persons. This convening focused on the relationship of the core values of Decent Care and the principles through which palliative care is practiced.

The convening was held in Tunisia in January 2009, with fifty participants from five global regions. The consultation was hosted by the WHO, funded by the Ford Foundation, and attended by persons affected with life-altering/threatening conditions, healthcare providers, policymakers, advocates, and donors. For five days, the participants discussed issues around palliation and Decent Care, culminating in regionally based conversations about ways the dialogue might be replicated at country, regional, or local levels.

Our participation included the planning and conduct of the consultation. In Tunisia, three anthropologists participated. One of us provided documentation for the convening, while the other two served as facilitators; the authors developed and provided training to facilitators new to the convening process, conducted the analysis of the convening, and developed the report for the WHO.[2] Regional activities were developed through the network of participants established at the Tunis convening. The timeline for the full process was approximately one year.

Implementation and Anthropologists' Roles

We engaged in the development of the concepts and piloting of Decent Care and played a number of different roles, including planners, designers, facilitators, rapporteurs, observers, evaluators, documenters, analysts, and reporters/ writers. However, perhaps our most significant role was to maintain the distinctions between emic and etic constructs as the values inherent to care being decent began to emerge. It is important to note that we were careful not to assume duties in which role conflicts could occur or in which we might have conflicts of interest.

Planning and Design

We worked in a small planning group that was disciplinarily diverse and led by a senior WHO official. For each of the projects, the planning group and the length of its engagement were tailored to the challenges of the undertaking. The CHRP project required the longest and most complex engagement, which included multiple in-person meetings in four countries. In the CHRP proposal and implementation planning process, our anthropologically informed inputs were critical to the synthesis of a variety of information, processes, and perspectives to develop an overarching understanding of the CHRP process and implementation. The nuances of three African countries, European NGOs, a global health agency, a global faith-based organization, a government funder, local dynamics, and the interplay among these perspectives and the bridging of Decent Care values was a complex and sometimes delicate cultural brokerage process. We served as partners in both the design and development of the CHRP.

In the design work, we brought in basic concepts about language and culture and considered how concepts might translate to various participants' experience and knowledge. By emphasizing the distinction between emic constructs (those of English language) in contrast to what might exist as parallel emic constructs in other languages, Decent Care began to emerge as an orientation that allowed for varying emic relations to the English-language emic concepts. Since the design for the originating convening on decent care was constructed in an American/Western European (English-language) context, our role as observers was critical to bringing the design to a place where it could respond to the myriad cultures and languages that would eventually participate.

Facilitation/Rapporteur

In the role of facilitators, we actively assisted working groups in the convening to move forward, remaining clear about the emerging etic constructs of Decent

Care, and reflecting on the etic construct of Decent Care to the various emic experiences of the participants. As rapporteurs, we reflected to the participants the content and possible meaning(s) of the conversations, and at the end we summarized and verified their understandings.

Observation/Evaluation

As observers and evaluators, we monitored the convening processes and reflected to the planning group the overall experience as well as the development of small-group experience. We assisted both the planners and the participants in reflecting on the process and outcomes and both utilized the lessons in the convening and recorded them for future work. This role also brought immediate improvement and accountability to each step of each process.

Documentation/Reporting

As documentarians and reporters, we created a means for recording the work of the participants, both in large and small groups, and a method for immediate verification of the process and outcomes of discussions. This method and its teaching to facilitators resulted in participants being assured that their work was faithfully rendered; additionally, we recorded meeting notes that provided a clear lineage from participant to report. Our reporting utilized the carefully developed meeting notes as the basis for reports and provided a transparent method for coming to conclusions and developing recommendations. It allowed those who did not attend the meetings to understand the substance of the discussions and to easily recognize the basis for the outcomes, resulting in a high degree of confidence in the process and its results even where people were skeptical of the concepts.

Ultimately, our contributions to the projects and processes were several, including creating "sanctioned space" for community and individual voices; focusing on the valuation and understanding of the emic perspective; acknowledging the importance of local language; supporting the importance of cultural beliefs about health, community, and the individual; and emphasizing cultural relativism in all processes. Perhaps the single most anthropological and critical contribution to the Decent Care development was defining "agency" as a critical, core value. Agency is a concept that firmly places the affected person at the center of all activity, where they are responsible for determining what services are needed to create or maintain health and how they are to be delivered. This concept is clear that resources are a function of the context, however; the control of those resources and how they should or should not be delivered is a function of the agency of the affected person. Agency as a concept does not demand the isolation of the affected person but rather ensures their primacy and interests in decision-making. It is a concept that, as adopted, creates an emic understanding and vision of health and care. This was a singularly anthropological contribution and resonated with all participants in the processes reported. It resonated, in part, because the process of the convenings drew participants from their professional personae into working from a vision as an affected person or as one who cares for an affected person. This challenged and changed the understanding of concerns and priorities for many participants. As one clinician stated at the end of the Tunisia convening, "These are the values of decency, as a doctor, as a parent, as a human being."

Understandably, over the course of the three projects, we were presented with many challenges that reflected the nature of the complex undertaking at hand.

The first challenge was immediate: how to define what decent care could mean. A series of white papers was commissioned for the Vevey convening, one of which we wrote. In that paper, we defined "agency" as meaning the right of the affected person to direct their own care, as a critical, central concept in defining what would constitute decent care. While that concept became a fundamental value of Decent Care, it also created controversy, as it framed a foundation that fundamentally changed the affected person and services/ provider dynamic.

A second challenge was collaborating with the WHO and others to develop meeting processes that could work for participants from around the globe and that would yield the outline of the concepts of decent care. The meeting was held with the imprimatur of the WHO, hosting diverse participants, while guiding work that radically departing from the status quo. The process was developed with a small team, including an applied philosopher, a health trainer, and a priest, and was necessarily complex. The meeting process was designed not to force participants to come to a single, unified vision but rather to allow participants to find common ground and common language to describe decent care while respecting difference. This process became known through the initial meeting as "convergence." The convening outcomes then were to be used as a starting point for conversations about the application of the concept of Decent Care to a variety of health concerns in different parts of the world. A central challenge for the Vevey convening was to find commonality among faith perspectives, the experiences of affected individuals, diverse cultural traditions, and those providing services.

A final challenge was to develop the Vevey results into a report that would allow diverse stakeholders to understand and utilize the concepts and values of Decent Care. To address this, we conducted an overnight analysis of each day's experiences and informed the process and approaches used for the conversations to be held during the next day. We then led the planning group through a full analysis and presented it to the full body of participants to support them in shaping the final day of the convening. This rapid review allowed participants to refine concepts and then develop them further during the convening. After the convening, we engaged in report development and in making the concepts broadly accessible.

Taking the concepts developed at Vevey and moving them beyond theory and into practice was the next challenge. Proposals were developed and funded that supported further exploration into particular areas of healthcare practice, into on-the-ground exploration of how decent care could be implemented, and into the effects on all participants and systems. Developing practical proposals, shaping practices, and establishing Decent Care as a central global concept were all challenges. Teaching the methods designed for convenings and supporting the development of practical projects in accordance with the values of Decent Care presented the next challenges. The final and most fundamental challenge was to develop the means and methods by which those who have vested interests in healthcare systems and delivery remaining as is could embrace and utilize Decent Care. All of those challenges were experienced in the design and development of the CHRP projects and the Tunisia palliative care convening.

The core challenge for the development of decent care as an organizing principle for healthcare began with its first assumption: that a values-based orientation to healthcare would change the relationship of patient and provider and the functioning of the health and related care systems. A second challenge existed in the origins in English and American/Western European cultural values as the starting point for the process. The English terms and the underlying constellation of concepts are fraught with specific cultural meanings and thick definitions. It was critical to focus attention on the fact that the terms themselves are culturally grounded. For the concept of decent care to be applicable beyond the American/Western European experience, the ideas and concepts would require local definitions and interpretations, without a loss of their central purpose and relationships. This translational process was a significant challenge for our engagement in the development of Decent Care as a values-based approach to healthcare.

The multiple challenges in each Decent Care activity required a full range of anthropological skills to work through. The first and most persistent difficulty was the need to help activity participants to move out of their professional roles in order to free them of the inherent limitations. This required that the convening process be respectful but deliberate about moving participants to common ground from which convergence on issues can be found. This required sensitivity to the ethnic/tribal/national cultures from which participants were drawn; gender and sex roles; socioeconomic and class roles; and professional roles and values. Without sensitivity to and a process that actively accounted for and managed these differences, the convenings would rapidly have become about roles rather than values. The second difficulty was in supporting the participants in not only understanding Decent Care and its values but also being able to incorporate and defend them in use once back in their context.

Outcomes

A cornerstone result was defining the values of decent care. The development and conduct of the decent care convening in Vevey and the final report were key subsidiary results. The report served as a deliverable to the WHO and a ratification for the participants of the work conducted and the outcomes they developed. The report also allowed those who had participated to begin discussion of Decent Care in their home countries and organizations. The Vevey report also provided the impetus for a follow-on Ford Foundation–funded project on the convergence of the values of decent care and the principles of palliative care. The Vevey report became the basis for the CHRP, a demonstration of the application of the values of decent care in the revitalization of primary healthcare in three African countries. The CHRP was to have been funded by the Norwegian Foreign Ministry through the World Council of Churches; however, for unknown reasons, that funding was not finally made available.

As noted earlier, in the development preceding the Vevey convening, a series of brief papers on decent care was commissioned by the WHO. Our paper, "From GIPA to CAP: A New Model to Health Entitlement," was chosen as one of the briefing papers and promoted the agency of the affected individual, which became one of the six core values of Decent Care and has acted as a unifying perspective of the individual's role in the process of health. Subsequent to the convening, the WHO assembled the papers as part of a book: *Restoring Hope: Decent Care in the Midst of HIV/AIDS* (Karpf et al. 2008).

Agency is in contrast to terms such as *patient-centered care* and *patient empowerment*, both of which begin with the assumption that healthcare providers give the patient certain roles and responsibilities that direct the process of developing or achieving health or affecting disease processes. Agency begins by recognizing an individual's innate right to determine if and how they will participate, and if they participate, how their care will be structured and provided. This also is where emic understandings of decent care begin to expand from the American/Western European emic view of the primacy of the individual and other cultures' emphasis on the relational nature of families, communities, and cultures. The individual, embedded in the complex web of social networks, family, and community as they define it, brings a deeper and perhaps more human perspective to the concepts of decent care.

The third outcome of the work was the convening on the values of decent care and the principles of palliative care. This took the basic decent care convening process and applied it to palliative care. This convening itself was a major outcome, with participants taking the concept of Decent Care and palliation and returning to their own context to develop plans for implementing regional, country, and local projects.

The concept of Decent Care and a process for applying it in a convening was developed, and it was diffused on a global basis through regional activities. The extension of the concept of Decent Care to regionally and locally based contexts is the true measure of the power inherent in a values-based approach to the delivery of healthcare. Decent Care created a process for the voices of local communities, families, and individuals to take center stage in global and local decisions on how healthcare should be provided and who should be driving the decision-making. It is through the interdependence of individuals, families, communities, and providers and their solidarity that Decent Care will assist in the appropriate delivery of health services around the global.

The Anthropological Difference

The most significant difference that the application of anthropology made in these projects was the focus on the need to develop an approach that provides space for the values of decent care to be translated repeatedly through cultures and bureaucracies and remain true to critical core central precepts. For this to happen, it was essential for a variety of perspectives, both cultural and positional, to be in conversation for each step of the design and development of Decent Care. This development sanctioned the space for the conversations to take place locally, regionally, and globally through the shared understanding of the importance of multiple perspectives. Rather than assuming that Decent Care and its core values are clear and understood constructs, the effort of the convenings was to find convergence among a variety of emic understandings.

It is likely that, without our engagement in the design of the convening processes, the crafting of the convenings, and the analysis and reporting of the convening outcomes, the specificity and nuance of the various understandings would simply have become a single model based in American/Western European English-language perspectives and applied to cultures across the globe. Instead, a conversation was constructed among cultures and across structural positions, in various languages, to identify relationships among a core set of values and how those values are reinterpreted in various cultural and linguistic contexts. Important developments from the Vevey and Tunis convenings and the CHRP planning process included alternatives to a Western European/ North American focus on the primacy of self and a shift from independence to interdependence and the critical role of community.

Without experienced anthropologists engaged in every activity, the process of concept development might have returned to a consensus process and frustrated or stopped the development. Without the concept of agency, breaking free of the current construction of health and healthcare would have been difficult or impossible. Anthropology was central to facilitating each of the processes across divides of culture, language, socioeconomic status, and gender and to finding points of convergence based in deeply understood values.

Epilogue

The Tunisia convening spurred further development and diffusion of Decent Care. The WHO, in collaboration with the US Agency for International Development (USAID) and Family Health International, conducted a series of regional consultations intended to encourage collaborations and stimulate support of Decent Care adoption. The LTG team functioned as observers and evaluators for a "Consultation on HIV Palliative Care and Decent Care Values" held in Vietnam, which hosted policymakers, practitioners, and activists from across Asia.

The Altarum Institute, a nonprofit research and consulting organization, designed a grant competition to further the adoption of Decent Care. Two sites were eventually chosen to receive funding, one in Kenya and one in Malaysia. We were gratified to participate in the development of the project, and we functioned as part of the steering committee, collaborated on the design of the data collection and analysis tools, and conducted an evaluation of the Hospice Malaysia project in Kuala Lumpur.

USAID had an ongoing interest in the development of Decent Care and has funded a global evaluation of the uptake and utilization of the concept. Our firm was chosen to conduct the evaluation, which resulted in a report and a briefing for USAID.[3]

Cathleen E. Crain and **Nathaniel Tashima** are the managing partners of LTG Associates, the oldest anthropologically based consulting group in North America, founded in 1982. Nathaniel holds a PhD from Northwestern University with a concentration in psychological anthropology. Cathleen holds an MA from McMaster University with a specialization in medical anthropology. For nearly four decades, they have been pathbreakers, influencing the discipline of anthropology by promoting, valuing, and modeling examples of innovative anthropologically based research, policy, and practice to address health disparities in populations and ethnic/cultural groups in numerous communities in the United States and across the globe.

Notes

1. Both "decent care" and "Decent Care" are found throughout the chapter. The lower case describes the fundamentals of the concept. The ongoing development and discussions of this then yielded a specific, constructed process that is Decent Care.
2. In addition to the two authors, LTG staff anthropologist Alberto Bouroncle, PhD, participated in aspects of the project.
3. In addition to the two authors, two other LTG anthropologists contributed to the USAID evaluation: Pamela Rao, PhD, and Carter Roeber, PhD.

References

International Labor Organization. 2021. "Decent Care." Quote from previous website text in 2009. Retrieved 22 January 2022 from https://www.ilo.org/global/topics/decent-work/lang--en/index.htm.

Karpf, Ted, et al. 2008. *Restoring Hope: Decent Care in the Midst of HIV/AIDS*. New York: Palgrave MacMillan, published on behalf of the World Health Organization Regional Office for Europe.

World Health Organization. 2010. "Consultation on HIV Palliative Care and Decent Care Values in the Context of Primary Health Care in Asia." 15–16 March 2010, Hanoi, Vietnam, p. 16.

~:~

CHAPTER 20

Persistent Undercounts of Race and Hispanic Minorities and Young Children in US Censuses

LAURIE SCHWEDE

Project Backgrounds

The US Census Bureau's decennial census of the US population is the largest peacetime mobilization of the country. To fulfill its mission of counting everyone living in the United States once, only once, and in the right place, the Census Bureau needed to reach out and count more than three hundred million persons in the 2000 and 2010 censuses. The Census Bureau invests years in planning, research, testing, and communications each decennial cycle. Yet the bureau's own extensive research documents the persistent differential undercounts of some race and Hispanic minority populations across decennial censuses. For example, 2000 Census coverage studies documented estimated net *undercounts* of non-Hispanic Blacks (1.84 percent), Hispanics (0.71 percent), and American Indians off reservation (0.62 percent) compared to estimated net *overcounts* for non-Hispanic Whites (-1.13 percent) and for the total US population (-0.49 percent).[1]

Children are also underrepresented. In the 2010 Census, the young child (0–4) age cohort had the highest net undercount rate of all age groups at 4.6 percent, with even higher estimated rates for young children who were of Hispanic origin (7.5 percent) or in the Census Bureau's racial category "Black alone or in combination" (6.3 percent).[2] Overall, an estimated one in twenty (one million) children, disproportionately minorities, were missed (O'Hare 2015). Although a known problem, it became a major Census Bureau concern when research showed a worsening young child undercount over the previous three decades, even as the adult count improved. The implication is that some areas with higher concentrations of undercounted children would not get their fair share of funding for critical education, health, and nutrition programs through most of these young children's school years.

How much is at stake in the census? Accurate counting across groups is critical for fairness and equity; census data are used to both allocate political power—apportioning seats in the House of Representatives and votes in the electoral college, as well as intrastate redistricting for the next ten years—and money. In 2019, the estimated allocation of federal funds from census data had grown to $1.5 trillion *per year.* That is real money.

The two projects described in this chapter demonstrate how an anthropologist employed in a federal agency can initiate research proposals and work internally to build consensus and obtain funding to conduct applied ethnographic evaluation research on complex research problems with social justice implications. The outcomes would benefit the Census Bureau and the public, especially undercounted race and Hispanic groups, as well as young children and their families. The research also demonstrates to the federal agency the value of employing and contracting with anthropologists to help address persistent agency issues. Both research skills and the ability to successfully navigate a complex culture (here a massive, labyrinthine bureaucracy) are applied in these cases.

Project Description 1: Comparative Ethnographic Studies of Enumeration Methods and Coverage across Race/Ethnic Groups

The first project was exploratory: the purpose was to deepen understanding of how and why undercounts occurred in the 2010 Census, what types of households and persons were affected, and whether these varied by race and Hispanic origin. The goal was to use our findings to generate recommendations to improve or replace existing methods and suggest new 2020 Census research and development proposals.

As a Census Bureau staff researcher, I had to first develop a detailed study plan, following the standardized evaluation study plan template, then send it for review and potential approval by supervisors, stakeholders in other Census Bureau divisions, and the evaluation administrators. I designed a study plan to include controlled-comparison ethnographic field observations of live 2010 Census interviews and a subsequent record check of rosters from observed census households.

The evaluation study plan I developed was based on approaches, methods, and holistic perspectives from anthropology. The basic approach that most anthropologists take for granted is going out and conducting fieldwork with one or more cultural groups in their local settings, directly observing and collecting data, and then analyzing. This approach was not typical in the Census Bureau until 2005 or so. Most of the decennial research until then, other than some small-scale ethnographic studies, was done by statisticians, demographers, and other headquarters researchers with large datasets; few of them ever went out to the field to do anything other than individual ad hoc observations for a few days. Around that time, in the middle of the 2010 Census research and development phase, survey research colleagues began planning some small-scale systematic and coordinated observations of interviews during census tests. I was fortunate to have been invited to participate in those early efforts, and I then used that experience as the basis for designing this evaluation.

The first methodological component was systematic ethnographic field observations of census interviewers conducting live, cold-call, standardized census interviews with respondents on their doorsteps over nine days. All ethnographers would use the same methods in nine sites, each targeted primarily, but not exclusively, to a particular race or Hispanic group—American Indian, Alaska Native, Native Hawaiian/Pacific Islander, Asian, Black, non-Hispanic White, Hispanic, Middle Eastern, and a quasi-control site—in three different data collections.

The first two proposed data collections were part of the actual 2010 Census in-person interviews in spring 2010. The first was conducted in remote areas without city-style addresses, i.e., remote Alaska and some Indian reservations, from January through April. The second data collection was the massive Nonresponse Followup operation for the forty-seven million households from which no complete census mail return was received, in the field from May to July.

Ethnographic observations of live interviews for the third data collection would occur during the Census Coverage Measurement Survey (or CCM, an abbreviation you will see frequently here) operation in August. The CCM was an independent Census Bureau survey of 187,000 housing units that collected in-depth household roster data that was later matched back to the actual 2010 Census rosters for the same households to estimate census coverage rates.

In each of these data collections, the ethnographers would quietly and unobtrusively observe, audiotape, and listen very carefully for potential coverage errors as the interviewer read the questions and respondents answered. At the end of the interview, if the ethnographers had detected any verbal or nonverbal cues that someone in the housing unit may have been left off the roster or counted in the wrong place, they were to conduct an immediate conversational debriefing with the respondent to elicit enough information to decide where the person(s) should be counted, according to the census residence rule. The ethnographers would prepare a verbatim transcript of the recorded interview for each household, analyze and summarize each transcript, decide where each person should be counted, and identify possible coverage errors and how and why they occurred, then write site reports to answer the research questions.

The proposed ethnographic design was innovative; I was proposing for the first time to embed ethnographers into the actual census field data collection operations with interviewers and respondents during live census interviews. This had not been allowed in earlier censuses. I was also proposing to send the same ethnographers to the same sites in both the census and the CCM operations, to try to hold observer, social, and environmental factors constant, if possible.

Internal stakeholders from two Census Bureau divisions raised concerns about my study plan. The first stakeholders, who plan and run the vast census field operations, were concerned that the presence of ethnographers observing and audiotaping live census interviews would make it harder for interviewers to get respondents to agree to participate. We checked, and responding experts told us refusal rates appeared to be low in the few relevant studies. We also agreed to respect privacy concerns by asking just once for respondent consent to tape and left the recorder off for those who refused or were reluctant.

Field colleagues were also concerned that interviewers—trained to read census questions verbatim—might change their behavior in subsequent interviews after hearing the ethnographers' ad hoc follow-up questions. My colleague Rodney Terry and I worked on compromises, including allowing interviewers to opt out of being accompanied, permitting them to continue choosing where and when to conduct interviews, having unobtrusive ethnographers, and limiting the ad hoc coverage debriefing to less than three minutes.

Mathematical statisticians who design and oversee the CCM survey had other concerns. In a meeting in the administrator's office with at least four of his high-level managers, they reminded us that the validity and reliability of the CCM program in accurately estimating census coverage rates depended on maintaining the absolute independence of the CCM from the prior census operations. Noting that sending the same ethnographers to the same sites in both the census and the CCM interviews would risk CCM contamination, they told us they would not approve my study plan.

I was aware that I was the only woman in the room and the administrator and managers outranked me. I needed to find a compromise. Fortunately, I had worked with this administrator before and knew he had supported a previous ethnographic evaluation, so I noted that their concern was valid and asked what compromises might be possible.

He suggested we either keep the same nine ethnographers for both operations but send them to different, very distant sites in the CCM (doubling the number of sites) or keep the same nine sites and send different ethnographers (doubling the number of ethnographers). Aiming to hold some of the wider sociodemographic, economic, and geographical factors as constant as possible, I agreed to the latter compromise. I did not take this decision lightly; the extra effort to recruit, write, and negotiate contracts with twice as many ethnographers, as well as to get security clearances for, train, and oversee them, would strain our resources. But on the basis of these compromises, I modified the study plan, and it was approved.

Implementation and Anthropologist's Role

Rodney and I sought eighteen expert ethnographers who had the requisite recent field research experience with one or more of our target race/ethnic groups and who could apply our modified participant observation methods with a holistic approach in the field. We networked by distributing flyers at annual anthropological meetings, talking to colleagues and fellow association members, and reaching out to other networks, especially those focused on specific race and Hispanic groups. We received 120 applications.

The final field interview sites included Blacks (Chicago); Alaska Natives (Kodiak Borough, Alaska); American Indians (Hopi and Zuni reservations); Asians (San Francisco Chinatown/Oakland); Hispanics (Dallas/Fort Worth); Middle Easterners (Wayne County, Michigan); Native Hawaiians and Pacific Islanders (Hawaii County, Hawaii); non-Hispanic Whites (Jackson County, Missouri); and a quasi-control generalized site (Broward County, Florida).

For each of the three data collection operations, we designed operations and training materials, trained the ethnographers, and sought concurrence for their observations from the local census offices in the nine field sites. The second evaluation component—the record check of actual census responses matched to ethnographer-observed household interviews—commenced after the ethnographers submitted their transcripts and summaries. Our team had grown to thirty, including ethnographers, staff, and interns, and the work was all-consuming.

We trained colleagues and interns to search in the vast, final, postprocessed census data files. The census record check involved finding, matching, and comparing the rosters of persons identified in the ethnographer-observed housing units on where to count each person from (1) the original verbatim census interview transcript, (2) the ethnographer's assessment, and (3) the postprocessed, unedited 2010 Census dataset. The phase 2 CCM persons had a fourth comparison with the final matched CCM/census postprocessing data records. Coders/matchers reviewed and coded data from all of these sources and then classified persons and households as consistent or inconsistent (census interviews) across those sources or, for CCM, as likely correct enumerations, possible omissions, and possible overcounts. Interns imported the spreadsheet data into SAS datasets for households and persons for the census or for CCM.

Rodney and I then analyzed the qualitative data from the site reports and wrote the overall evaluation report, incorporating the statistical results produced by Ryan King with the datasets created by Mandi Martinez, two of our team members.

One problem centered on developing two sets of standardized typologies (for the census and CCM interviews) for classifying inconsistencies and possible coverage errors across ethnographers and sites. As exceptions appeared to our initial, custom typologies, our understanding of coverage deepened, but the typologies had to be revised, cases reclassified, and data reanalyzed, sometimes yielding different outcomes.

A second difficulty was that in some sites, ethnographers had trouble reaching their targets of getting at least 50 percent of their observed interviews with their designated target race or Hispanic population in that site. Recall that we had agreed that ethnographers would let interviewers choose when and where to interview each day as the ethnographer tagged along. In such situations, ethnographers adapted by observing extra interviews, requested to go to wider or nearby areas, or ended with a relatively small proportion of target group interviews.

Outcomes

Our use of the mixed-methods controlled-comparison design enabled us to provide both qualitative and quantitative answers to our research questions (Schwede and Terry 2013; Schwede, Terry, and Childs 2014 on the CCM in phase 2; Terry et al. 2017 on the Nonresponse Followup in phase 1). We achieved a more in-depth understanding of how and why census miscounts occur, who is affected, and how these vary across race and Hispanic populations. Comparing the results from the census ethnographic observations, debriefings, and site reports, we identified five major cross-cutting sources of inconsistencies: (1) enumerator error and frequent question rewording; (2) difficulty gaining access to respondents; (3) language issues; (4) cultural differences; and (5) mobility and other factors.

The phase 1 record check showed that 13 percent of the 786 persons analyzed had count inconsistencies among the three data sources (inconsistencies may or may not be correct enumerations; the census form did not collect enough data to resolve them). Black and American Indian sites had higher proportions of inconsistencies.

Children ages zero to four had the highest proportion of inconsistencies per age group. We found no gender differences.

The phase 2 CCM ethnographers identified additional sources of possible coverage errors along with the five abovementioned issues, including (6) recall error and (7) respondent reactions to multiple cold-call interviewer visits. Other possible factors included tenuousness and cycling among places, distrust leading to deliberate concealment, and mismatches of respondents' concepts of who belonged in the household with the census concept of residence based on where one usually lives and was actually staying on Census Day. One ethnographer said that at one house, Middle Eastern residents were home but did not answer the door. The CCM, in a fluke of the calendar, happened to coincide with Ramadan, the Islamic fasting month. Recognizing Islamic decorations on the house, she assumed the residents were Muslims who were staying inside, fasting all day, and preparing then eating the evening meal, breaking the fast.

The CCM record check statistical analysis showed that 6 percent of the 953 persons analyzed had possible coverage errors at the ethnographer-observed housing units. Note that possible coverage errors could have been in the census or CCM, or both. The statistical analysis revealed respondent confusion and census processing errors as added factors.

"Complex households" (those including anyone other than, or in addition to, married partner, mother, father, biological or adopted child) were significantly more likely to have possible coverage errors than noncomplex households. (Keep the concept of "complex households" in mind, as it comes up quite a bit in discussions below of our findings.) Native Hawaiians/Pacific Islanders in the overall sample had significantly more possible coverage errors, and this is likely related to factors in the Native Hawaiian site, also statistically significant. The young child (age zero to four) cohort had the highest proportion (15 percent) of possible coverage errors, but there were just seven cases, not enough for testing statistical significance.

The most significant new finding for the Census Bureau was ethnographer documentation of frequent enumerator/interviewer error, specifically in frequent major rewording of questions that may have altered counts in households where this occurred. The anthropological approach of unobtrusively observing and recording behavior in the field and the Census Bureau's unprecedented agreement to allow systematic live observations in the 2010 Census were essential in documenting this. Some reasons for the question rewording, omission, or reordering included: to be more conversational; to get through an interview with a reluctant or resistant respondent, or one who does not speak English well, or who is hearing-impaired; to speed up an interview or, in some rare cases, to deliberately shorten questions to allow more interviews to be completed. The interviewer reward structure was based on the number of completed interviews per day: the more completed interviews, the more assignments, and thus the higher the paycheck for these temporary interviewers. Interviewers may not have realized how even simple wording changes could sometimes lead to incorrect counts and omissions, such as asking months after Census Day for the names of persons who live or stay there without reading the last clause of the question that stipulates listing only those who were there back on Census Day. That could result in coverage errors of including persons who had moved in since Census Day and not identifying those who had lived there on 1 April but had since moved out.

Our many findings led to specific recommendations to the Census Bureau in seven general areas: (1) reduce interviewer error and increase cultural awareness of minorities in training and monitoring interviewers; (2) review, revise, and test specific questions in the census questionnaire and related instruments; (3) translate materials into more languages and expand the capacity to interview in more languages; (4) improve access to hard-to-reach respondents; (5) conduct new research and consider amending the 2010 Census residence rule and situations document; (6) shorten the period between the census and the CCM operations; and (7) try to reduce the number of unannounced follow-up visits.

Our recommendations were accepted and entered into the overall permanent repository on census and CCM recommendations; these were distributed among the 2020 Census working groups forming at the time to incorporate into their discussions and planning. Rodney and I joined new, interdivisional working groups to design and plan research leading to the 2020 Census, focused on redesigning the Nonresponse Followup operation, measuring race and ethnicity, and reviewing and revising the census residence rule and situations, enabling us to share our findings and contribute to the improvement of 2020 Census planning.

Addendum: Final CCM results for the 2010 Census showed that differential undercounts appeared to have *increased* since 2000 for the three groups mentioned earlier: non-Hispanic American Indians off reservation (4.88 percent), non-Hispanic Blacks (2.07 percent), and Hispanics (1.54 percent), but non-Hispanic Whites were somewhat less *overcounted* at -0.84 percent (Mule 2012). Clearly more work needed to be done to prepare for the 2020 Census.

Project Description 2: Complex Households and the Undercount of Young Children in Decennial Censuses

As Rodney and I completed our comparative ethnographic report in 2013 and began presenting our qualitative and quantitative findings (Schwede et al. 2013), a new 2010 Census coverage problem came to light. For the first time, the age cohort with the highest undercount rate was that of young children, ages 0 to 4; that rate translates to about 1 million (1 in 20) young children missed in 2010. This became a major Census Bureau concern when historical research over 30 years showed a worsening young child undercount, from 1.4 percent in 1980 to 4.6 percent in 2010, even as the adult count improved to a slight *overcount* during the same period (Hogan et al. 2013). Young child undercounts have been identified in other countries as well; this has become a critical research issue in the fields of survey methods, demography, and statistics.

Also in 2013, Census Bureau mathematical statistician Deborah Griffin initiated a new Task Force on the Undercount of Young Children (UYC) to flesh out relevant problems and gaps, brainstorm, and propose new research. I shared with her our documentation of statistically significant associations between census inconsistencies and this young child age cohort, and between possible coverage errors and living in complex households (mentioned earlier). She read our report and then invited me to sift through the ethnographic case transcripts for qualitative and quantitative evidence on how and why young children may have been undercounted, and to present results to her task force. However, that observational study had not been designed to focus on children; there were just seven cases, but they were intriguing, piquing my curiosity. When the UYC research team formed in 2015 with Griffin as a member, I expressed interest and was invited to join.

As part of my independent research, I had already written a proposal for a new quantitative study to apply my new classification of complex household structure based on anthropological knowledge to all US households to document: (1) a wider range of household types and (2) how these vary by race and Hispanic origin.

My new UYC colleagues—mathematical statisticians Griffin and Scott Konicki, demographer Eric Jensen, and programmer Janet Wysocki—accepted my proposal and agreed to collaborate. We widened the scope to (1) expand the complex household typology to distinguish households with and without young children; (2) do custom recodes of 2000 and 2010 Census data to document distributions of complex and noncomplex household types with young children overall and within race and Hispanic groups; and then (3) link households across datasets to explore interrelationships of complex household types with young child omissions. We developed and tested hypotheses about changes between 2000 and 2010 in the proportions of young children living in complex households by race and Hispanic origin and the likelihood of being missed and then possibly being added back into the 2010 Census in a coverage operation.

This specific project should be viewed within the wider goals and objectives of the UYC research team: to deepen our understanding of the hows and whys of the growing young child undercount; to generate new hypotheses; to propose, conduct, and report on new research with extant datasets on relevant factors and correlates; and to recommend changes to reduce this undercount in the 2020 Census. The wider team of eight included demographers, mathematical statisticians, and me (the survey research anthropologist) and had a diversity of knowledge that led to stimulating discussions and new proposals. Team members worked jointly from 2015 to 2017 at Census Bureau headquarters in Suitland, Maryland, issuing fourteen reports by early 2019.[3]

Some background on how the Census Bureau's demographic subject matter experts classify the most basic household types is necessary to understand how the complex household typology was an innovation, how it contributed to the project design, and how it was linked to anthropology. The census household type variable is constructed from two questions on the census form: the relationship question that asks for each household person's relationship to Person 1 (aka "the householder," or "ego" in anthropological parlance) and the sex question. The 2010 Census relationship question had standalone checkboxes for close family relationships—categories mostly based on nuclear and stovepipe lineal family relationships, with newer categories for parents-in-law and siblings-in-law but not for distant relatives—and nonfamily relationships, such as unmarried partner or housemate/roommate.

The complex household typology concept I developed is innovative because it uses the same relationship categories as the standard census household types but groups some households differently. The groundwork for this was laid in my prior conceptualization of an independent complex household typology for my 2000 Census comparative ethnographic evaluation and book (Schwede, Blumberg, and Chan 2006). Complex households are defined as "households that include persons other than, or in addition to, nuclear family kin (i.e., parents and one or more of their own biological or adopted children). The typology distinguishes three types of *noncomplex* households (likely easier to enumerate): (1) married nuclear families with or without their own or adopted children and no one else; (2) single-parent families with their own or adopted children and no one else; and (3) single-person households. *Complex households* included all other types, e.g., blended, multigenerational, and family households with distant relatives or nonrelatives.[4]

To get approval for a new, exploratory research project to generate new statistics on the proportion of US complex households, I would need to convince senior decision-makers across divisional silos that there were likely to be enough complex households to justify the work time and costs. I would need to produce some statistical evidence in a research proposal on the prevalence of complex households to get approval to generate the first statistics. But I needed prevalence statistics to make a strong case. Catch-22.

Then, serendipitously, I found gold: secondary data in a demographer's appendix table showing census figures of the most common exact sets of intrahousehold relationships (e.g., husband + wife + biological child)—just the building blocks I needed! I inductively rearranged those exact household types and their frequencies into the first actual census-specific complex household typology, which could then allow me to document the proportions of US complex households; they had increased from 18 percent in 1990 to 21 percent in 2000. In our 2010 enumeration methods and coverage evaluation, my colleague Rodney Terry and I used this typology to show linkages among complex

Figure 20.1. Not all anthropology is exotic fieldwork. Undercount of Young Children (UYC) research team members Eric Jensen (*standing on left*) and Deborah Griffin (*seated on right*) exchange viewpoints on the maps showing the marked increase in the percentage of people living in complex households from 2000 to 2010, while Laurie Schwede (*standing on right*) and Karen Deaver (*sitting on left*) listen closely. Karen Deaver is the Census Bureau's chair of the 2020 Census Undercount of Young Children Task Force. *Not shown:* UYC team member Scott Konicki and programmer Janet Wysocki. © Amandamations Photography. Used with permission.

households, race/ethnicity, and census miscounts. This original typology did not, however, break out households with young children.

Interestingly, this team research is an outgrowth of my history of qualitative and quantitative work on complex households and coverage; past dissertation fieldwork on kinship and residence in an Indonesian matrilineal, matrilocal, Islamic society; and development of my complex household typology.

Implementation and Anthropologist's Role

As mentioned, I joined the UYC research team and proposed this research project. Three team members, including me, expanded the major categories of the complex household typology to differentiate households with and without young children. One colleague created a custom 2010 Census dataset that classified 117 million households into the expanded complex typology, enabling us to disaggregate complex household types by Hispanic and race groups for the first time. She and another team member confirmed that our recoding was reliable and accurate, and then used the same recodes to create a 2000 Census dataset of 105 million households. With comparable 2000 and 2010 data, we could identify and document trends in changing household complexity for race and Hispanic groups.

The team generated statistics, and we all participated in the excitement of interpreting our first-ever findings on multiple complex household types by race and ethnicity across a decade. A team member worked extensively with the new dataset and suggested new groupings. He also analyzed the complex household cases by race and Hispanic origin, providing many statistics and correlates.

Another team member matched and linked households and young children in our new 2010 Census dataset to those in another coverage dataset. This dataset is from the separate 2010 Census Coverage Followup telephone operation that starts after the end of census and is designed to follow up in cases in which respondents may not have been sure about whether someone in their household should have been listed on the census form. If the interview indicated one or more persons should have been included but had not been, those persons were added into the households for the final 2010 Census counts. She analyzed linkages among household complexity, race, and Hispanic origin for young children who may have been missed and were added to the census counts.

A fourth member matched and linked households and young children to the separate Census Coverage Measurement dataset designed to estimate census coverage rates. He analyzed possible child omissions in complex households overall and by race and Hispanic origin.

In summary, the team explored various data, analyzing linkages among household complexity, race, and Hispanic origin for young children who may have been missed. We drafted and revised our report through multiple versions until we agreed it was ready for stakeholder and administrative review.

Two major limitations of this research design could not be fixed with census datasets. First, the standard census relationship question and categories ask for relationships of all coresidents to Person 1 (the "householder") but no other interrelationships. This can lead to masking of important interrelationships among other residents that could affect classification of household types. The second major problem is with responses that do not have standalone checkbox categories for more distant relationships (e.g., uncle, niece, cousin, great-grandchild) that fall into the generic "other relative" category and cannot later be disaggregated. These types of intrahousehold relationships are relatively rare for non-Hispanic White families but more common among Blacks, Hispanics, Asians, American Indians/Alaska Natives, and Native Hawaiians/Pacific Islanders. The restricted response categories very much limit our ability to document the full range of household types across race and Hispanic groups.

Most other challenges, related to obtaining sufficient initial interest, buy-in, or approval from higher-ups, had already been dealt with. The Census Bureau is a hierarchical federal agency with more than three thousand headquarters workers in more than ten directorship "silos." The research and production silos need each other, but there is tension; sometimes researchers' recommendations are not viewed as important or practical by those on very tight schedules to finish required products. Researchers with new ideas and proposals must request and obtain approval, often through several levels of their own chain of managers and also through the other production directorate's chain. It helps to have a willing partner in the other directorate to convince their managers to approve, but that does not always work. Due to the high bar for getting these approvals, proposals must be well developed and supported by statistics showing why it is in the agency's interest to allow the requester to devote scarce time and funds so the researcher can do new research. This is why it took years to get buy-in for this project. Anthropologists in other federal agencies and even private companies likely face similar constraints.

Outcomes

Using 2000 and 2010 census datasets, our analysis of the interactions of the expanded complex households typology for households with and without young children by race and Hispanic origin was successful. We confirmed our hypotheses and recommended targeting certain at-risk households in the 2020 Census that may help reduce the persistent undercount of young children. Some of the major outcomes are discussed in turn.

First, our data revealed the trend of complex households (with or without young children) increasing from 18 percent in 1990 to 21 percent in 2000 and to 23 percent by 2010. Complex households with young children (about which we had a hunch but no preexisting data) increased from 34 percent in 2000 to 39 percent in 2010, showing that young child households are considerably more likely than all households in general to be complex, possibly putting them at risk of higher undercounts.

Second, very wide differences were found in both 2000 and 2010 censuses in complex households with young children in the proportions denoted by race and Hispanic origin. In 2000, the proportion of complex households with young children overall was 34 percent; these ranged from 25 percent for non-Hispanic White households to a high of 50 percent for Hispanics, non-Hispanic American Indians/Alaska Natives, and non-Hispanic Native Hawaiians/Pacific Islanders. Wide *within-group* increases in complex households with young children from 2000 to 2010 were found for non-Hispanic Whites (25 to 31 percent), Blacks (47 to 50 percent), Hispanics (50 to 54 percent), and

American Indians/Alaska Natives and Native Hawaiians/Pacific Islanders (50 to 58 percent).

Next, wide differences were noted in the proportions overall and by race and Hispanic origin of young children in complex households that were originally missed on census forms but added to the final census counts by the Coverage Followup operation. For example, the rate of original misses that were added back in were more than two times higher for young children who were Native Hawaiian/Pacific Islander than for non-Hispanic White children; numbers for Hispanic and children of other races fell somewhere in between.

Fourth, young children in complex households did have a greater likelihood of being initially missed and then added in during the Coverage Followup operation in the 2010 Census (7 per 1,000) than those in noncomplex households (3 per 1,000). Non-Hispanic White young children in noncomplex households had an undercount risk of 1.2 per 1,000, while Native Hawaiians/Pacific Islanders in complex households had many times the risk at 14.9 per 1,000. Hispanic young children in noncomplex households had a risk of 4 per 1,000.

The findings that Hispanic young children had the highest 2010 Census net undercount rate and that those in complex households are at higher undercount risk are concerning. Hispanic households in 2010 were already at higher undercount risk when undocumented Mexican and Central American immigrants were not a high-profile issue. From 2016 onward, immigration became a national hot-button issue, with political, economic, cultural, and other ramifications.

Finally, we documented the surprising major findings that just three types of young child complex households account for more than half of all 2010 Census Coverage Followup operation adding-in of young children to the 2010 Census: those with nonrelatives (26 percent), multigeneration households (21 percent), and family households with other (distant) relatives (15 percent). Moreover, these same three types accounted for at least half of young child "adds" *within* each of the race/Hispanic groups, from 50 percent for non-Hispanic White young children to 83 percent for non-Hispanic Native Hawaiian/Pacific Islander children. These high proportions show the need for special advertising, outreach, and enumeration in relevant, high-concentration areas in the 2020 Census. Targeting these areas would be a cost-effective way of possibly reducing the young child undercount, improving 2020 Census accuracy and completeness, and increasing the fairness of decisions and outcomes resulting from it over the next decade.

Our project showed that complex households with young children were strongly linked to the young child undercount and that a coverage improvement operation in 2020 like that in 2010 has the potential to identify and add substantial numbers of otherwise missed young children.

This project was innovative in five ways: (1) the interdisciplinary teamwork demonstrated by brainstorming and collaboration; (2) the conceptual development and expansion of the complex household typology to identify households with high young child undercount risk; (3) the methodological linking of 2010 census data with two other national coverage datasets to identify factors that may contribute to the young child undercount; (4) the rare generation of statistics on American Indians/Alaska Natives, Asians, and Native Hawaiians/Pacific Islanders that revealed marked differences from the overall pattern; and (5) identification of the 1990–2010 trend in increasing complex households with and without young children, by race/ethnicity and overall. We confirmed all hypotheses.

The final project report was posted as an official decennial 2020 planning document in the "Investigating the 2010 Undercount of Young Children" report series after a rigorous internal review (US Census Bureau 2018). Team findings that children in complex households and those in Hispanic and racial minority households were among those at highest coverage risk were documented in the executive summary of the wider Undercount of Young Children summary report (US Census Bureau 2019).

Our team produced important new findings and impacts, and Census Bureau management embraced our findings. They changed the 2020 Census questionnaire undercount probe wording on all census household questionnaires to add grandchildren or unrelated children, and they incorporated information on including young children into interviewer training, along with an exercise to include grandchildren. They worked on integrating complex household information, images, and messaging into the national communications materials and partnership programs targeted to different race/ethnic markets and created a young children website page with reports and other materials.[5]

In 2018, the Census Bureau authorized a new task force to address the 2020 child undercount issue. The following year, task force chair Karen Deaver identified complex households as the first on a list of correlates of households at high risk of young child undercounts in a formal presentation to the National Advisory Committee on Racial, Ethnic and Other Populations. In a personal communication, she said the complex household concept is the basic foundation upon which internal changes have been made for the 2020 Census regarding counting young children.

The Anthropological Difference

These two evaluations used a unique amalgam of methods from traditional anthropology and Census Bureau observational and statistical coverage studies. In the first project, the duration of using the anthropological method of participant observation was shorter than typical but still much longer than the usual one to three days for typical census observations. The ability to do intensive observations of verbal and nonverbal behavior while remaining unobtrusive and determining which follow-up questions to ask are hallmark behaviors of anthropologists.

The anthropological, holistic view and ethnographic observation methods were also critical in evaluating interviewer and respondent interactions. Anthropologists know and document cultural, linguistic, personality, and attitude/mood factors that can and do shape the interview context and sometimes influence outcomes, as can wider sociocultural, geographic, economic, and other factors not always considered by statisticians and demographers.

Another anthropological difference in the first project is that we purposely designed the evaluation to include sites targeted to each of the major race and Hispanic groups recognized by the federal statistical system and then selected contract ethnographers with recent field experience in one or more race or Hispanic communities, matching them to our corresponding race or Hispanic sites. Most Census Bureau quantitative survey reports only disaggregate results by Black and White race and Hispanic ethnicity, because very few surveys are large enough to produce valid and reliable statistics for small populations, such as Asians, American Indians/Alaska Natives, and Native Hawaiians/Pacific Islanders. Our goal was to identify and highlight similarities and differences across race/ethnic groups to aid in reducing future differential undercounts.

In the second, mostly statistical project, too, I politely persisted in urging my team colleagues (mathematical statisticians, demographer, and a programmer) to disaggregate young child undercounts and household structure for all of the standardized race and Hispanic groups. Doing so revealed our first evidence of very wide differences in the incidence and 2000–2010 growth of complex households by race and Hispanic origin. It was already known that census undercounts were higher for minorities and, separately, for complex households. Our new findings linked these factors to differential young child undercounts, suggesting ways to target areas for advertising, special outreach, enumeration, and evaluation.

Another anthropological difference is conceptual; because anthropologists are attuned to kinship and residence patterns in our field sites, we are open to a much wider range of household types and of multiple relationships between two persons, whereas Census Bureau demographers edit out additional relationships and record just one relationship for each person pair. For example, a person in a unilineal society (e.g., some American Indians) with cross-cousin marriage preference could be both a spouse and a cross-cousin to Person 1, but there is no specific cross-cousin checkbox, so the second relationship could only be marked in the "other relative" category and cannot be disaggregated later. And even then, the latter would be edited out to leave just the spouse category.

I also noticed an anthropological difference in conceptualizing some complex households. I tended to view multigenerational households and those with distant relatives as potentially stable, fully integrated unitary households, while my teammates—statisticians and demographers—tended to view them as sets of related, core nuclear or one-parent families with subfamilies that may split off.

Clearly, applying anthropological conceptions, perspectives, and methods in modified, unobtrusive participant observation in the field, attending to differences among all federally recognized race and Hispanic groups, and employing a holistic perspective on potential factors in the interviews, sociocultural settings, and wider sites were critically important to the success of these complex evaluations. In addition, the ethnographic reports we created answered the research questions and provided a wealth of extremely rich data and recommendations we incorporated into our final project report to inform 2020 Census research.

Epilogue

The results of our research, the first to show that household complexity is linked to the young child undercount, continued at the end of 2020 to influence initiatives to improve the 2020 Census. In early 2020, the Census Bureau sent postcards to fourteen million households in hard-to-count census tracts with messages about counting young children. They found that the percentage of young children in complex households was a key variable in predicting where young children and other hard-to-count groups might be missed in the census. Two main dimensions linked with the higher-risk tracts: (1) complex households and economic vulnerability, and (2) language barriers and large, foreign-born populations. A second initiative by the Population Reference Bureau developed tools to target communities where young children are at risk of 2020 undercounting. Communities with large shares of "female householders, no spouse present" households were a key variable for predicting possible young child coverage issues (O'Hare et al. 2020).

Ongoing complex household research was directly applied to targeted outreach in the 2020 Census, one of our original project goals. Separately, two 2020 Census-related reports listed our three complex household types at the top of charts of factors in young child undercounts (US Government Accountability Office 2018; Fernandez, Shattuck, and Noon 2018).

As for the 2020 Census itself, just a few days after massive field operations began in March 2020, it was shut down with the rest of the country in response to the coronavirus pandemic. After a four-month hiatus and major revamping to minimize COVID-19 infections, the operation resumed with a new end date of 31 October, only to have President Donald Trump suddenly announce a few weeks later that census fieldwork would stop in late September, cutting enumeration time in a very difficult year by roughly 25 percent. As a result of multiple lawsuits settled just days before that deadline, the count resumed, but it was again abruptly cut short on 15 October by the Supreme Court. Friends who worked in 2020 Census field operations told me that they and other staff felt whipsawed by these sudden, significant scheduling changes.

Moreover, in July 2020, just five months before the legal deadline for submitting the final 2020 Census apportionment counts, President Trump issued a sudden memorandum to change the apportionment policy to exclude "… illegal aliens from the apportionment base, to the extent feasible and to the maximum extent of the President's discretion under the law." The stated justification for this precedent-setting change was that large, undocumented populations inflate the total state populations, resulting in those states getting more House seats in apportionment than they otherwise would be allocated. To allow the president "to the extent possible" to carry out that policy, Commerce Secretary Wilbur Ross was to provide information on the "number of citizens, noncitizens, and illegal aliens in the country" obtained from matching 2020 Census person-level data to administrative records from other federal agencies, collected under an earlier July 2019 executive order.[6] In addition to enabling the exclusion of undocumented immigrants, the 2020 memorandum instructed Secretary Ross to submit the traditional apportionment file based on the official Census Residence Criteria and Residence Situations document that had, from 2010 onward, been carefully, systematically, and iteratively reviewed, tested, publicly reviewed, and then finalized in February 2018. In effect, there would be two different 2020 Census apportionment and possible federal funding files that would lead to very different apportionment outcomes: one including counts of unlawful immigrants, the other excluding them. President Trump asserted that he had the authority to decide which would be applied.

The renewed focus during live 2020 Census operations on lawful/unlawful status to exclude undocumented persons for apportionment could have rekindled fears in immigrant communities of deportation. That could have led some immigrants to choose to leave some coresidents, including young children, off their census forms, or avoid the census altogether, potentially increasing persistent undercounts even more.

If President Trump were ultimately to implement the new policy, the result would be a complete break from all past censuses, in which apportionment was based on total population, regardless of lawful status. This could result in some states with high proportions of undocumented immigrants losing seats in the House of Representatives, such as California, Texas, and Florida, to states with lower proportions, such as Alabama, Ohio, and Minnesota. Multiple lawsuits were filed within days and culminated in a Supreme Court hearing.

Meanwhile, this policy change required major changes to Census Bureau processing and reporting. The scheduled duration for such activities to produce quality statistics had been halved because the final reporting deadline was fixed by law and the Senate declined to follow the House in extending that deadline, even though the data collection had been delayed for four months by the pandemic.[7]

By the time of the Supreme Court hearing on 30 November, the government's lawyer had to admit a couple of things. First, it was not clear if the Census Bureau could, in a timely manner, reliably match the outside administrative records on legal status to person-level census data on more than a few segments of all persons in undocumented status. Nor could they feasibly exclude all of the estimated 10.5 million persons in unlawful status. And since the bureau indicated that the data might not be ready until late January 2021 or later (after Inauguration Day), the full court decided the case was premature; the appellants did not have standing and the case was not ripe for resolution. The Supreme Court vacated the decisions in the lower court cases that ruled the memorandum unlawful and/or unconstitutional. They said appellants could refile later if the president implemented the new policy and injury was clear.

In a dissenting opinion joined by Justices Sonia Sotomayor and Elena Kagan, Justice Stephen Breyer asserted appellant standing and case ripeness. He argued that "the plain meaning of the governing statutes, decades of historical practice, and uniform interpretations from all three branches of government demonstrate that aliens without lawful status cannot be excluded from the census solely on account of that status. The Government's effort to remove them from the apportionment base is unlawful, and I believe this Court should say so."[8]

Deep conflict and uncertainty about the apportionment outcome continued until just days before the end of President Trump's term. The Census Bureau issued a 30 December 2020 news release stating that the schedule was fluid and they "plan[ned] to deliver a complete and accurate state population count for apportionment in early 2021, as close to the statutory deadline as possible." In a final drive to deliver the data the president required before his term ended on 20 January 2021, Census Bureau Director Steven Dillingham pushed staff to produce tabulations by 15 January. Career staff whistleblowers resisted and informed the Commerce Department inspector general that the director was pressuring them to rush out data on noncitizens that would be "statistically indefensible," and that could be "misinterpreted, misused, or otherwise tarnish the Bureau's reputation" (Wang 2021). The inspector general sent questions to the director that he answered. On 12 January 2021, the director halted the effort to produce tabulations of citizenship or immigration status and announced his sudden retirement at the end of President Trump's term eight days later. He had risked damaging the Census Bureau's reputation for nonpolitical, objective, data-driven statistics. Incoming President Biden issued an Executive Order rescinding the call for citizenship and immigration status data while affirming that 2020 Census apportionment would be based on the total population, as had been done in every past census.

With these sudden, proposed massive changes to the core concept of usual residence, the census operations and reporting that had been very carefully planned and tested over the last ten years, as well as the lawsuits, are affecting the 2020 Census in ways that have yet to be known. They will likely reduce the accuracy and completeness of the 2020 Census, elevating persistent differential census undercounts, especially for traditionally undercounted populations, such as race and Hispanic groups and young children.

In early 2021, we are at a rare cultural inflection point due to the confluence of the pandemic shutdown, the concomitant massive spike in unemployment, a nationwide rethinking of racial discrimination after George Floyd's death in Minnesota at the hands (or literally, the knee) of police, the 6 January 2021 insurrection at the US Capitol, and the massive changes to the 2020 Census, the citizenship question and apportionment conflicts. The results will affect US House apportionment and annual funding allocations for the next ten years in as yet unknown ways.

Going back to our research, two factors suggest a trend of increasing complex households from 2010 to 2020. First, in 2010, non-Hispanic Whites of one race were 64 percent of the population, but with higher minority growth rates, they declined to 60 percent in the latest 2019 estimates. They have lower rates of complex households, so their decline may raise the overall proportion of complex households. Second, research has shown that household structure can fluctuate with economic conditions. Over the slow recovery since the 2007–9 recession, the proportion of complex households may have declined as more people could afford to live in noncomplex households, but with the 2020 unemployment shock, more people may be doubling up to share resources.

Two other factors countervail. First, public health experts recommend that younger persons stay away from elders and vulnerable persons at higher risk of serious COVID-19 effects. This could potentially result in breakups of some households with multiple generations, distant relatives, or nonrelatives that are more prevalent among minorities. These are the three complex household types we found to have the highest young child undercount risk in 2010. Second, disproportionate deaths of the elderly and of minorities have already resulted in significant differential declines in life expectancy and may at some point lead to a decline in complex households. My guess is that although US deaths from the pandemic exceeded 350,000 at the end of 2020, this may not be immediately noticeable in the overall US 2020 Census statistics when they are released; it might be discernible in statistics for hard-hit local areas.

The core research question that has not yet been adequately addressed is why the zero-to-four age cohort is most likely to be undercounted and why that undercount has been increasing. An article using results from a 2019 Count All Kids online survey found that only 82 percent of low-income parents would list their young child in their census household, with a lower proportion for children with more tenuous household ties (Griffin and O'Hare 2020). The authors conclude that misconceptions and confusion about listing young children on census forms exist and could lead to young child omissions. While Census Bureau researchers were planning a qualitative research program to identify at-risk households and to explore why young children are undercounted, more research is needed.

Anthropologists and sociologists are uniquely qualified to propose and conduct qualitative research to explore why this occurs and how to mitigate it. I share these reflections and invite you to engage with this knotty issue; I have retired, but am avidly following developments in this area.[9]

Laurie Schwede earned her University of Colorado MA (1976) and Cornell University PhD (1991) in anthropology after completing fieldwork among the matrilineal, Islamic Minangkabau in West Sumatra, Indonesia. As a US Census Bureau researcher, she designed and tested questionnaires, participated in interdisciplinary research and development teams, conducted on- and off-reservation research with American Indians and Alaska Natives, and proposed and managed 2000 and 2010 US census ethnographic evaluations on household structure, race/ethnicity, and census coverage. Among other publications, she coauthored *Complex Ethnic Households in America*. As an American Federation of Government Employees member on the Census Labor-Management Council and the Commerce Labor-Management Forum, she negotiated and collaboratively developed telework and phased retirement policies. She consulted on an Office of Personnel Management Federal Employee Viewpoint Survey experiment. Retired, Laurie presented a roundtable 2020 Census after-action review, served on the 2021 Praxis Award Committee, co-authored the "Best Practices" document on the National Association for the Practice of Anthropology website and in *The Applied Anthropologist*, and serves on the Washington Association of Professional Anthropologists board.

Notes

Editors' note: This chapter combines two separate projects, each of which received a Praxis Award in different years. Although both projects merit a standalone chapter, the anthropological endeavors for both were similar enough that the lessons are presented through a single, somewhat elongated chapter. The introductory "Project Backgrounds" and concluding "Anthropological Difference" and "Epilogue" sections combine details of both projects. *Author's note:* I would like to acknowledge several team members who made these efforts possible. Core research team members named with me in the Praxis Award submission for the first project whom I thank here include Rodney Terry, Mandi Martinez, and Ryan King. Ethnographers include Robin Albee, Rae Blumberg, Alexis Bunten, Ephrosine Daniggelis, Rachel Donkersloot, Ted Fortier, Angelina Foster, Victor Garcia, Eleanor Hubbard, Robin Jarrett, Karen Lacy, Sylvester Lahren, Dawn Lee Tu, Heather McMillen-Wolfe, Alison Newby, and Ruth Sando. Team members named with me in the Praxis Award submission for the second project whom I thank include Eric Jensen, Deborah Griffin, Scott Konicki, and Janet Wysocki.

1. The estimated 2000 Census rates for non-Hispanic Blacks, non-Hispanic Whites, and the overall population were statistically significantly different from zero; the rates for the other groups were not. Table 7 on page 15 of the following report shows estimated census net coverage rates by race and Hispanic origin in the 1990, 2000, and 2010 censuses (Mule 2012).

2. The Census Bureau tabulates official race data in two ways: to reflect persons of one race (e.g., "Black alone") or for both those who mark that race alone and those who show they are multiracial by marking more than one race (e.g., "Black alone or in combination"). To break down race by percentages, use the "race alone" category. "Black" is the term used in datasets, but the checkboxes on the census form itself show both Black and African American.

3. The Undercount of Young Children research team reports are available at https://www.census.gov/programs-surveys/decennial-census/decade/2020/planning-management/plan/undercount-of-young-children.html.

4. For more on the complex households typology, see US Census Bureau 2018, appendix.

5. US Census Bureau website: 2020 Census: Counting Young Children (Census Bureau webpage devoted to young child undercount, with news releases, fact sheets/memoranda, infographic, all research reports, task force report, and more. At https://www.census.gov/newsroom/press-kits/2019/2020-count-children.html.

6. That 2019 executive order was issued as part of a fallback strategy just a few weeks after the 28 June 2019 Supreme Court decision disallowing the addition of the citizenship question to the 2020 Census form. Collecting outside administrative records on citizenship and immigration status and matching them to the same persons in the 2020 Census would theoretically make it possible to subtract from the total population the numbers of citizens and legal noncitizens to derive counts of unlawful immigrants.

7. For more on the Commerce Department's unusually high level of engaging in Census 2020 technical matters under the Census Bureau's responsibility, see Wines 2022.

8. Donald J. Trump, President of the United States, et al., appellants v New York, et al. Breyer, J. dissenting. Docket No. 20-366. 592 US _____ (2020), December 18, p. 1.

⁻9. The 2020 Census undercount rates were released as we go to press (March 2022). Sadly, the young child net undercount rate increased from 2010 to 2020 (4.6 to 5.3 percent), and also increased for Hispanics (1.54 to 4.99 percent) and others. More research is clearly needed.

References

Fernandez, L., R. Shattuck, and J. Noon. 2018. "The Use of Administrative Records and the American Community Survey to Study the Characteristics of Undercounted Young Children in the 2020 Census." https://www.census.gov/library/working-papers/2018/adrm/carra-wp-2018-05.html.

Griffin, D., and W. O'Hare. 2020. "Are Census Omissions of Young Children Due to Respondent Misconceptions about the Census?" *International Journal of Social Science Studies*, 8(6), November. http://redfame.com/journal/index.php/ijsss/article/view/4994/5223.

Hogan, H., P. Cantwell, J. Devine, V. T. Mule, and V. Velkoff. 2013. "Quality and the 2020 Census." *Population Research and Policy Review* 32: 637–62.

Mule, T. 2012. "2010 Census Coverage Measurement Estimation Report: Summary of Estimates of Coverage for Persons in the United States," Memorandum for David C Whitford, Chief, Decennial Statistical Studies Division, DSSD 2010 Census Coverage Measurement Memorandum Series #2010-G-01, issued 22 May 2012. https://www2.census.gov/programs-surveys/decennial/2010/technical-documentation/methodology/g-series/g01.pdf.

O'Hare, W. 2015. "The Undercount of Young Children in the US Decennial Census." Springer Briefs in Population Studies.

O'Hare, W., L. Jacobsen, M. Mather, and A. Van Orman. 2020. "Predicting Tract-Level Net Undercount Risk for Young Children." https://www.prb.org/wp-content/uploads/2020/12/us-census-undercount-of-children-1.pdf For the mapping, see https://www.prb.org/new-strategies-to-reduce-undercount-of-young-children-in-2020-census/.

Schwede, L., R. L. Blumberg, and A. Chan. 2006. *Complex Ethnic Households in America.* Lanham, MD: Roman & Littlefield.

Schwede, L., R. Terry, and J. H. Childs. 2014. "Ethnographic Evaluations on Coverage of Hard-to-Count Minorities in US Decennial Censuses." In *Hard-to-Survey Populations*, edited by R. Tourangeau, B. Edwards, T. Johnson, K. Wolter, and N. Bates, pp. 293–315. Cambridge: Cambridge University Press.

Schwede, L., and R. Terry. 2013. "Comparative Ethnographic Studies of Enumeration Methods and Coverage across Race/Ethnic Groups." 2010 Census Program for Evaluations and Experiments Evaluation. 2010 Census Planning Memoranda Series, no. 255, 29 March. https://www.census.gov/content/dam/Census/library/publications/2013/dec/2010_cpex_255.pdf

Schwede, L., R. Terry, R. King, and M. Martinez. 2013. "Comparative Ethnographic Evaluations of Enumeration Methods across Race/Ethic Groups in the 2010 Census Nonresponse Followup and Update Enumerate Operations." *Joint Statistical Association Proceedings*, Survey Research Methods section, pp. 4479–4493. http://www.asasrms.org/Proceedings/y2013/files/400283_500781.pdf

Terry, R., L. Schwede, R. King, M. Martinez, and J.H. Childs. 2017. "Exploring Inconsistent Counts of Racial/Ethnic Minorities in a 2010 Census Ethnographic Evaluation." *Bulletin of Sociological Methodology/Bulletin de Methodologie Sociologique* 135(1).

US Census Bureau. 2019. "Investigating the 2010 Undercount of Young Children-Summary of Recent Research." https://www2.census.gov/programs-surveys/decennial/2020/program-management/final-analysis-reports/2020-report-2010-undercount-children-summary-recent-research.pdf.

US Census Bureau. 2018. "Investigating the 2010 Undercount of Young Children—Analysis of Complex Households," 4 December. https://www2.census.gov/programs-surveys/decennial/2020/program-management/final-analysis-reports/2020-report-2010-undercount-children-complex_households.pdf.

US Government Accountability Office. 2018. "2020 Census: Actions Needed to Address Challenges to Enumerating the Hard-to-Count Population." GAO-18-599. https://www.gao.gov/assets/700/693450.pdf.

Wang, H. L. 2021. "Census Bureau Stops Work on Trump's Request for Unauthorized Immigrant Count." NPR, 13 January. https://www.npr.org/2021/01/13/956352495/census-bureau-stops-work-on-trumps-request-for-unauthorized-immigrant-count.

Wines, M. 2022. "2020 Census Memo Cites 'Unprecedented' Meddling by Trump Administration." *New York Times*, January 15, 2022. https://www.nytimes.com/2022/01/15/us/2020-census-trump.html.

CHAPTER 21

~:~

Using the Concept
of Social Well-Being

*Developing and Implementing a Framework
for UNICEF Planning and Evaluating Efforts
to Achieve Rights and Development Goals
for Children and Families*

MARK EDBERG

Project Background

The United Nations Children's Fund (UNICEF) is an agency whose primary purposes include advocacy for the protection of children's rights (as detailed in the UN Convention on the Rights of the Child), helping to meet basic needs and expand opportunity for children, assisting in times of crisis, protecting highly vulnerable children, promoting gender equity and the elimination of discrimination, and generally promoting the achievement of social and economic development aims as set out originally in the UN Millennium Development Goals, now in the follow-up phase of Sustainable Development Goals, as these pertain to children. UNICEF works through agreements with country governments, typically set out in five-year plans.

In addition to the task of promoting and advocating rights and development as described, UNICEF also monitors progress both in countries where it works and throughout the globe. One of the key resources for monitoring is the Multiple Indicator Cluster Surveys (MICS), and UNICEF's synthesis of these data, along with US Agency for International Development (USAID)–funded Demographic and Health Surveys (DHS) as well as other global social/health data, including data collected by specific projects or initiatives. In monitoring with a focus on rights (or the lack thereof) and specific development goals (that are or are not met), there is often a "negative orientation" to the monitoring process, that is, a focus on data that are related to a problem, with resultant programs that are reactive and potentially even narrow in focus.

From an anthropological perspective, however, many of these specific problems are integrated in a larger sociocultural whole. For example, an issue of commercial sexual exploitation of minors (a rights concern) may be embedded in a multilevel context: a young, urban, female sex worker in Thailand originally migrates from a rural area because of the lack of work (due to a rural-urban economic configuration) to support her parents (her cultural responsibility) and ends up involved in sex work because of gender-limited options and minor status, which then puts her at risk for HIV/AIDS. Trying to understand that larger whole, and how dynamics within the larger context underlie barriers to rights and development, may lead to more effective and "upstream" points of intervention for UNICEF, where a given intervention can address more than one specific problem because it is focused on causal chains that connect multiple problems.

This broader focus is highly anthropological in orientation and also parallels the social determinants perspective now promulgated by the World Health Organization (WHO) (WHO 2011a and 2011b), the social-ecological orientation characteristic of recent public health approaches,[1] and the idea of syndemics[2] from critical medical anthropology (look for writings by Merrill Singer 2009, 1996, 1994; Singer and Clair 2003). Importantly, it implies a different, or at least additional, lens that UNICEF can consider for monitoring progress—a lens that identifies and monitors change at various levels within the broader causal chain, not just the final outcome. There is a more positive and less reactive character to such an approach because it aims to create change and build assets that may head off the problem in the first place.

At the same time, to take this kind of social-ecological approach to monitoring progress is challenging precisely because the data needed are no longer just problem focused in a narrow sense. Looking at progress through a social-ecological lens means developing a theoretical map or framework composed of multiple domains, potentially at several levels (e.g., proximal, underlying), collecting data in those domains, and linking specific programs, policies, or other interventions to their hypothesized domain outcomes, and then linking those outcomes to the ultimate impact on development goals and rights.

In other words, it is an ideal challenge for the theory, holistic connections, and tools that can be applied through anthropology.

Project Description

In the two linked projects I will describe here, I worked with UNICEF as a public health anthropologist in the Latin America–Caribbean (LAC) region to develop and help implement two variations of a social-ecological framework representing domains necessary for social well-being, which I framed as the precursor to the achievement of rights and development goals of key interest to UNICEF.

This work includes an Adolescent Well-Being Framework developed initially in 2008 (and continuing), tailored to the LAC region, and a 2011 Situation Analysis of Children and Women in Belize, which was based on a social-ecological framework outlining multiple levels of contributing factors and which served as the basis for continued work on behalf of UNICEF in that country. Both frameworks were intended to promote approaches to progress in achieving rights/development goals that address the connections between different domains (e.g., health, education, socioeconomic opportunity, capacity, protective systems, cultural/social identity, civic participation, and others) that together constitute social well-being across the life cycle.

The frameworks were informed by an anthropological perspective, current research (including ethnographic and qualitative research that I had previously conducted regarding homeless/runaway youth, injection drug users, and other populations at high risk for HIV/AIDS, substance abuse, and violence), the application of information from other social sciences, and country-specific data. Most importantly, both frameworks were developed as practical tools that incorporated the use of specific kinds of data to assess progress at the local, national, and potentially regional levels. Because the focus was on social well-being, most of the data to be used with these frameworks emphasized assessment of the positive assets necessary for social well-being, as opposed to just negative data, such as the prevalence of HIV/AIDS, violence, school dropout, gender inequity, or child exploitation, that are symptomatic of a lack of social well-being. For this reason, the frameworks can be used for planning and goal setting as well as evaluation.

Implementation and Anthropologist's Role

The project description below covers several sequential components, from the development of the Adolescent Well-Being Framework to the Situation Analysis of Children and Women in Belize to continuing work in Belize.

The Adolescent Well-Being Framework

Historically, UNICEF has focused on maternal and child programs as well as monitoring data. However, in recognizing that sufficient attention had not been paid to adolescent children, UNICEF established an Adolescent Development and Participation Unit at UNICEF headquarters in New York at the end of 2001 to provide program support and technical guidance in the area of adolescent health and development. As different regions began to increase their adolescent focus, basic questions arose as to how to monitor progress.

The Logic for a "Well-Being" Framework

The United Nations Convention on the Rights of the Child (CRC) establishes an extensive legal framework of rights that outlines legal and other conditions considered necessary for a fully protected existence during childhood, including adolescence. The CRC rights encompass safety, freedom from discrimination, exploitation, violence and trafficking, freedom of expression, thought and assembly, education, health and healthcare access, best interests of the child, and many others that pertain to positive conditions for development. At the same time, the indicators typically available to assess the state of affairs for adolescents aged ten to nineteen (or other related age brackets) often focused on the kinds of negative outcomes mentioned earlier. Conclusions about well-being among this age group were then based on the *reduction* or *absence* of negative consequences, in a sense presuming that adolescence amounts to "bad things waiting to happen."

However, from a social well-being perspective, the reduction or absence of negative outcomes is often a consequence of the positive assets, characteristics, and rights present in the social environment surrounding adolescents, as well as within them as individuals. Put simply, a negative consequence such as drug use or involvement in drug trafficking is likely to follow from such factors as the lack of educational and employment opportunities, the lack of available, positive social roles, poverty, discrimination, and lack of cultural respect for ethnic or religious minority groups, and many others. Thus, the logic of measuring well-being is based on tracking the presence of positive aspects of adolescents and their social ecology, which should serve as a guide to the social forces available to prevent negative consequences and to help adolescents thrive and become productive, contributing individuals. A key assumption underlying this approach is that adolescence is in fact "good things waiting to happen."

With this in mind, I worked through several steps with UNICEF in the LAC region to develop a proposed framework for identifying adolescent well-being indicators, and subsequently to develop a preliminary set of indicators, as well as training and implementation materials. The first step was an extensive background paper, titled "Development of UNICEF Latin America/Caribbean (LAC) Well-Being Indicators" (Edberg 2008), which sought to outline a comprehensive, social-ecological justification for defining adolescent well-being and to propose a preliminary set of domains for measurement that represented expected outcomes/impacts under that definition: the applied component. The justification came from my previous experience in assessing social ecologies of health risk and ethnographic research with high-risk youth,[3] qualitative research used for developing evaluation frameworks (see Edberg, Cory, and Cohen 2011), from social/behavioral theory related to adolescent development and risk, programmatic approaches to well-being drawn from the LAC region, and a range of legal and rights-based conventions pertaining to children and youth. The age range for adolescent well-being indicators was identified as ten to nineteen years, with an acknowledgment that the age of adolescence varies socially and culturally and that in a developmental sense, the adolescent age range is closely linked to younger age brackets as well as the nineteen-to-twenty-four age category following adolescence.

An effective strategy for developing a set of indicators to measure progress in adolescent well-being was to use a logic model structure that would (1) organize factors contributing to well-being into "actionable domains"; (2) identify the outcomes/impacts to be expected by domain in order for progress to occur; (3) define indicators for each of these outcomes/impacts; (4) identify any existing data sources for the indicators; and (5) set out the practical methods and means for collecting the data. Monitoring progress would be accomplished based on the collection and reporting of a selection of indicators within each domain, such that the entire set of domains represents adolescent/youth well-being from a positive viewpoint.

The second step, after finalization of my LAC background paper, was to accompany UNICEF LAC regional representatives to expert group meetings at UNICEF headquarters in 2009, where multiple UNICEF regions were meeting to identify a basis for developing an adolescent module for the upcoming fourth round Multiple Indicator Cluster Survey (or "MICS4 survey"). This was to be the first time that the survey included a module specific to adolescents. Each region came with ideas and rationales for defining the elements of such a module, but the LAC well-being framework ended up serving as one basis for the discussion and for the eventual module, which was in fact included in the MICS4 survey, administered globally.

Adolescent/Youth Well-Being Domains

The starting point for determining adolescent well-being domains had to be a consensus definition of adolescent age parameters and the characteristics of well-being. The definition is rather involved but generally frames adolescence as occurring between the ages of ten and nineteen, with unique developmental characteristics and needs, and with younger and older ages sharing many similar characteristics.

As part of the document prepared for the 2009 expert group meeting, I developed a set of indicators, a matrix of possible data sources, and a sample module formatted as if in a survey. Within each domain there are expected outcomes/impacts, viewed as short-term outcomes versus longer-term impacts, and as the *results* of some activity.[4] For purposes of planning, monitoring, and evaluation, progress toward adolescent well-being was framed as the aggregate result of progress in each of several domains, such as health status, subjective well-being, educational opportunity and performance, protection from abuse and exploitation, socioeconomic opportunity, equity of identity, access to supportive services, and opportunities for participation.

The third step, one that continued for some time following framework development, was the refinement and application of the theoretical framework and tool. First, the framework was utilized in a small evaluation exercise conducted in the Caribbean. I then presented the framework at several international UNICEF meetings. The framework was also integrated into the CARICOM (Caribbean Community) Youth Development Action Plan for 2012–17. UNICEF-Belize then signed an agreement with George Washington University to set up a "Center of Knowledge" relationship, which I directed. One task under this center was to develop an Adolescent Well-Being Framework training and application package, and to begin working with nongovernmental organizations (NGOs) in Belize to test its use. In the two years following that agreement, I was engaged in these (and other related) application tasks.

The Social Well-Being Framework and Belize Situation Analysis

In 2010, the primary contact person with whom I worked at the UNICEF LAC headquarters in Panama was appointed UNICEF country officer to Belize. She was determined to keep moving forward on the development and use of a social-ecological, well-being framework—particularly since UNICEF was seeking to realign itself toward more "upstream" strategic planning as well as evaluation work. Pursuant to this aim, she appointed me as the team leader of a small group of consultants who were to conduct a situation analysis of children and women in Belize.

Belize is a small but unique country, full of natural beauty, historical significance, and a vibrant and diverse cultural mix. It occupies an important political and cultural space between Central America and the Caribbean and is composed of at least four key cultural groups: the Afro-Caribbean (Kriol), Latino, Garifuna, and Maya. Belize also faces a number of challenges. On the one hand it had, at the time of this project, the highest HIV/AIDS prevalence rate in Central America along with serious problems of drug trafficking and violence; on the other, it had an emerging tourist industry and strong environmental protection stance. While it was technically a lower-middle income country (by World Bank rating), the postcolonial political and culture-group hierarchy is linked to significant inequities between population groups and regions. In the Maya region, for example, poverty levels at the time exceeded 60 percent.

Typically, a situation analysis for UNICEF is organized around the rights and development goals UNICEF monitors. For this situation analysis, however, I proposed the development of a social-ecological framework as the basis for organizing the document and its recommendations—again, meaning that the document was not just a narrative around current rights/development data but an explanatory and contextual narrative that sought to link current data to a causal, multidomain matrix. One challenge in following this path, however, was that once these broad, linked domains were set out, data would have to be identified (or in some cases, collected) for each domain. Such data are not always easy to find. A second challenge was to gain the buy-in of collaborating government agencies and NGOs, who were more accustomed to the traditional situation analysis format.

This is important because the situation analysis was to serve as the guiding document for the elaboration of a country cooperation program between UNICEF and the government of Belize and contribute to the development of a new country assessment and a UN assistance framework. As such, it incorporated a substantial number of surveys, assessments, evaluations, and studies that had been conducted by the government of Belize, the National Commission on Families and Children, various NGOs, UNICEF and other UN agencies, as well as other development and local organizations. These were used to update and provide additional information on the status of women and children in Belize and the factors contributing to their current status. Moreover, impacts of the changing economic environment in Belize as a consequence of the global recession were documented in this situation analysis.

To gain buy-in, we conducted several meetings with NGOs and Belize government representatives to explain the utility of a social-ecological framework, seeking their respective input and eventually gaining approval. Working with two consultant team members, an extensive network of sources, both in Belize and regionally, were tapped for data. We also conducted some interviews and focus groups (with youth, and with radio, internet, and other communications representatives) to gain additional understanding about youth perceptions of their role and future in Belize and about the availability of communications channels and programming for youth (the latter related to the communication and informational environment for youth).

The social-ecological framework around which the situation analysis was organized included domains arrayed at four levels:

1) Proximal/Immediate Domains ("what people experience")
   + Health (health status, risks, knowledge)
   + Education (availability, access, equity)
   + Protective asset equity (the types and equitable distribution of protections available against exploitation, abuse, identity discrimination, etc.)
   + Socioeconomic opportunity

2) Domains Related to Underlying Capacity
   - Policy and legal structure (policies/laws that support the proximal domains)
   - Educational capacity (capacity to provide educational access, equity, etc.)
   - Social/health services (capacity to provide these services)
   - Justice system (the capacity of the system to ensure protection)
   - Data and communication capacities (infrastructure, access, content relevant for multiple cultures)
3) Underlying Factor Domains Affecting Capacity
   - Inequity and poverty (as these interrelate by group and region)
   - Economic and crisis vulnerability
4) Broad Underlying Domains
   - Cultural factors (the cultural landscape in relation to inequity and poverty)
   - Geography (physical, resources)
   - Governance issues (e.g., longstanding patterns of political culture)

Figure 21.1 displays these social well-being domains, mapped to the UN rights and goals that UNICEF has to monitor.

Belize Situation Analysis: Domains

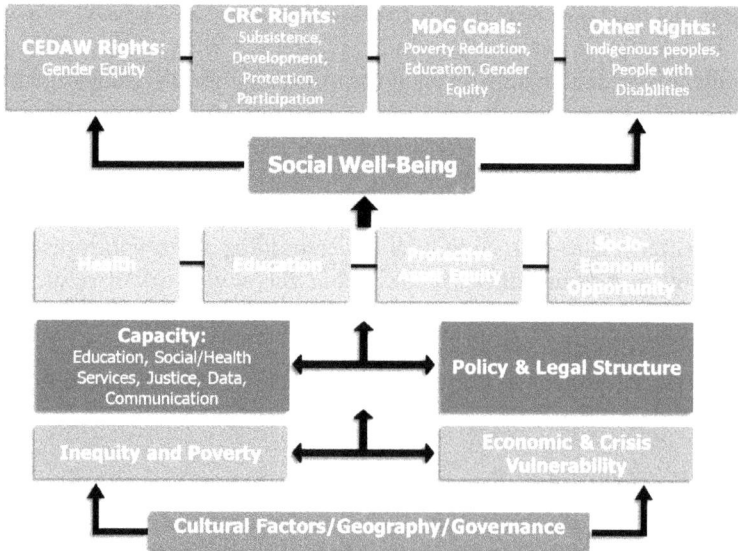

Figure 21.1. The social well-being domains of the social-ecological framework and how they map to United Nations goals. © 2020 Mark Edberg

Outcomes

Taken together, the Adolescent Well-Being Framework and the Social Well-Being Framework for the Belize Situation Analysis were and continue to be an attempt to develop and implement the kind of holistic, integrated understanding that is at the root of an anthropological perspective. There is no question that the implementation of these frameworks presented and will present challenges, because it is by nature more demanding, in terms of both the information and linkages that need to be considered in formulating policies and programs and in evaluating them. The next task for both of these frameworks is to increase the practicality of their use. That work is ongoing.

The following key points are useful to keep in mind when summarizing how this social well-being effort drew from anthropology and led to practical results.

First, UNICEF faced a challenge for how to impact and measure progress for adolescents, as well as children and families, vis-à-vis the rights and development goals they must promote and monitor, and in a way that would support a more "upstream," strategic role for UNICEF. [There has been a continued evolution of this effort, beyond what was done for the original Adolescent Well-Being Framework discussed here.]

Second, I worked with UNICEF in the Latin America–Caribbean Region, in Belize, and at UNICEF headquarters to develop frameworks for planning and evaluation that were based on a concept broader than just rights and development goals—the concept of social well-being as an integrative approach underlying rights and development goals.

Third, both frameworks drew extensively from an anthropological perspective related to the integration of social phenomena and from direct ethnographic and qualitative work (as well as social research, applied program experience, and youth development theory).

Fourth, the Adolescent Well-Being Framework was presented in numerous UNICEF meetings, was tested and applied at several locations in the LAC region, was a key source for a regional youth development plan and played a role in the development of a first adolescent module for the UNICEF Multiple Indicator Cluster Survey.

And finally, the Belize Social Well-Being framework became the underlying framework for the 2011 Situation Analysis of Children and Women in Belize, which was the basis of a subsequent five-year plan of action between UNICEF and the government of Belize and also the basis for follow-up work in Belize through a Center of Knowledge relationship between UNICEF-Belize and George Washington University. Key findings from the Belize Situation Analysis include the following:

+ The distribution of ethnic groups by region, and concomitant disparities and bottlenecks in access to political power, infrastructure, services,
  schools, and other resources, was integrally tied to broader inequities.
+ Communication access (and therefore information access) was low overall,
  hampering movement toward achievement of development/rights goals.
+ The capacity to provide education, cross-cultural, health, protective, communication, disaster, and other services was low, and the educational infrastructure was not sufficient to build this capacity (if increased, the capacity
  would also increase income-producing opportunities).
+ The political and cultural history of Belize undergirded an identity question (what is a Belizean?) that affected decisions about language, education, and political access.
+ Limited economic opportunities were clearly tied to youth involvement
  in the drug trade, violence, and sex-for-money (HIV/AIDS and sexually
  transmitted infection risk).

There were many other findings, and a total of seventy specific recommendations were made covering all the domains. The situation analysis was released
with some fanfare (Edberg, Chambers, and Shaw 2011) at a meeting in the town
of San Ignacio, not far from the western border with Guatemala. In attendance
were heads of a number of ministries, the prime minister's wife, and a range of Belizean as well as regional NGOs focusing on human rights, development, gender,
and other issues. Each ministry head was presented with a copy of the situation
analysis, followed by brief speeches. The Belizean press (television, radio, print)
covered the event, and even I—a non-Belizean—was interviewed several times.

Most importantly, the situation analysis became the working document for
UNICEF and the Belize government and the basis for other tasks under a follow-up UNICEF Belize/George Washington University Center of Knowledge, including the development of awareness and training materials related to
a social-ecological perspective, intended for ministry staff (program planners,
policymakers), NGO practitioners, and the general public. The Belize situation
analysis was also added to the UNICEF headquarters website as an example of
an approach to conducting a situation analysis. Moreover, the Center of Knowledge became the foundation for a center I chartered at the university, now called
the Center for Social Well-Being and Development (https://cswd.gwu.edu/).

The Anthropological Difference

The anthropological difference in these linked projects has three components.
The first component is the grounded, qualitative research experience. The
impetus for thinking about adolescent risk and adolescent well-being as ho-

listic, embedded phenomena came largely from having worked previously on a series of qualitative and ethnographic projects in which I saw youth who were at risk for multiple problems, including HIV/AIDS, violence, and substance abuse, in context. Those contexts clearly shaped their vulnerability to these health issues. Youth in high violence, high poverty communities were put in the position of having to think about violence and other health risks in a different way, as part of the territory, as necessary for establishing protective or otherwise advantageous reputations. Paul Farmer, in his multiple works on structural violence, talks about the social position of marginalized groups as curtailing their choices. That was certainly true for the youth I saw. The choices they faced were different from the choices available to youth in high-resource communities and population groups. It affected not only what they did but how they thought about it. The same perspective and experience informed the social-ecological framework for the Belize situation analysis, as part of the data collection effort involved traveling to several parts of the country and collecting some primary data.

Second is the use of anthropological theory and the anthropological "lens." Anthropologists are not trained to think of human "behavior" as discrete and decontextualized action. So what I saw on the ground was supported by the theoretical background and methods gained from anthropology. Based on the grounded work mentioned above, and that anthropological lens, it made sense to use a broad, social-ecological framework to assess and address factors that could be contributing to outcomes for adolescents in general and for children and youth in Belize, and to think of those factors as integrated. That was a key reason for the term "social well-being" as opposed to "individual well-being." The sociocultural world around those children and adolescents had to be "well" in order for individual children and adolescents to do "well."

Finally, but certainly not least, is anthropology and perspective. An anthropological background helped me, when interacting with multiple stakeholders in the process, to pay attention to where these stakeholders were coming from and to understand their perspectives in order to be able to work collaboratively and communicate with them about using these frameworks. Stakeholders often view situations from the perspective of their agency or organization's involvement, from concerns about practical application (for example, about collecting data), from specific disciplinary backgrounds, or through the lens of particular constituencies for whom they are advocates.

Epilogue

Much has occurred since the work done with UNICEF on the Adolescent Well-Being Framework, the 2011 Situation Analysis, and formation of the two-year UNICEF Center of Knowledge. In 2012, as noted above, I converted the Center of Knowledge into a chartered center at George Washington University, now called the Center for Social Well-Being and Development (CSWD, at https://cswd.gwu.edu/), which has engaged in multiple projects since then, primarily with UNICEF. In 2014, the CSWD was awarded a long-term agreement with UNICEF headquarters, under which we have conducted multiple projects in South Africa, Indonesia, Ghana, and Jamaica, following the same social-ecological approach and producing a number of reports and a published article (Edberg et al. 2017). More recently, we conducted a second Situation Analysis for UNICEF Belize, using a slightly different framework but still in line with the social-ecological approach. We also completed a small pilot research effort (with the anthropology department at GWU) to obtain life-history interview data from recent Central American migrants to the United States in order to assess transnational factors influencing health outcomes (see Edberg et al. 2020).

Mark Edberg, PhD, MA, is a professor in the Prevention and Community Health Department in the Milken Institute School of Public Health at George Washington University, with secondary appointments in the Department of Anthropology and Elliott School of International Affairs. He is a cultural anthropologist with almost thirty years' experience in social and community research, interventions, evaluation, and strategic planning (domestic and global), focusing on health disparities and vulnerable populations. He directs two centers, the Avance Center for the Advancement of Immigrant/Refugee Health (previous funding from the National Institutes of Health and Centers for Disease Control and Prevention) and the global-oriented Center for Social Well-Being and Development (CSWD), the latter with a record of projects for UNICEF in multiple countries. He has also directed or been coinvestigator on projects for the Gates Foundation and multiple US agencies. He was co-chair of the 2014 National Minority Health Disparities Conference, a 2015 Salzburg Seminar fellow, a Fulbright Senior Specialist awardee, and he is a Society for Applied Anthropology (SfAA) fellow and was the SfAA program director for the 2021 annual meetings. He has authored/edited five books and numerous journal publications and reports.

Notes

1. The idea that there is a "social ecology" in which health social and other situations are embedded, such that they cannot be addressed effectively in isolation from that context.
2. Co-occurring and interacting health issues that result from shared social and structural conditions.

3. For example, an extensive ethnographic study I did of HIV/AIDS and substance abuse risk among runaway/homeless youth (funded by the National Institute on Drug Abuse; see Edberg 1994); an ethnographic study on the US-Mexico border concerning popular media images of the narcotrafficker persona and connection to youth risk (see Edberg 2004a and 2004b); a needs assessment study (SAMHSA) of youth at risk for HIV/AIDS, STIs, substance abuse, and hepatitis (Edberg et al. 2009); an ethnographic study of young women at risk for commercial sex exploitation/trafficking (Cohen, Edberg, and Giles 2010); and mixed-methods research (funded by the CDC), as well as other work, on youth violence prevention (see Edberg et al. 2010a and 2010b; Edberg and Bourgois 2013; Edberg 2012).

4. https://publichealth.gwu.edu/pdf/UNICEF-LAC%20Core%20Adolescent%20Well-Being%20Indicators.pdf

References

Cohen, M. I., M. Edberg, and S. Gies. 2010. *Final Report on the Evaluation of the SAGE Project's LIFESKILLS and GRACE Programs.* Prepared by Development Services Group, Inc. (Bethesda, MD) for the National Institute of Justice (Washington, DC), 30 June.

Edberg, M. 1994. "HIV/AIDS Risk Behavior among Runaways in the Washington, DC Metropolitan Area." In *Runaways and HIV/AIDS.* Report for National Institute on Drug Abuse (NIDA). Bethesda, MD: National Institutes of Health.

———. 2004a. *El Narcotraficante: Narcocorridos and the Construction of a Cultural Persona on the US-Mexico Border.* Austin, TX: University of Texas Press.

———. 2004b. "The Narcotrafficker in Representation and Practice: A Cultural Persona from the Mexican Border." *Ethos (Journal of the Society for Psychological Anthropology)* 32(2): 257–77.

———. 2008. "Development of UNICEF Latin America–Caribbean (LAC) Adolescent Well-Being Indicators: Background and Proposed Indicators." Project Report. Panama City: UNICEF LAC.

———. 2009. "Preliminary Set of UNICEF/LAC Core Adolescent Well-Being Indicators for the MICS4 (and Beyond), with Rationale and Sample Module." UNICEF. Accessible via https://publichealth.gwu.edu/pdf/UNICEF-LAC%20Core%20Adolescent%20Well-Being%20Indicators.pdf.

———. 2012. "Youth Violence: An Issue in Search of Anthropology." *Anthropology News*, American Anthropological Association, September.

Edberg, M., J. Benavides-Rawson, I. Rivera, H. Shaikh, R. Monge, and R. Grinker. 2020. "Transnational Determinants of Health for Central American Immigrants to the U.S.: Results of a Qualitative Study." *Global Public Health.* http://dx.doi.org/10.1080/17441692.2020.1779329.

Edberg, M., and P. Bourgois. 2013. "Street Markets, Adolescent Identity and Violence: A Generative Dynamic." In *Economics and Youth Violence: Crime, Disadvantage and Community*, edited by R. Rosenfeld, M. Edberg, X. Fang, and C. S. Florence. New York: New York University Press, pp. 181–206.

Edberg, M., C. Chambers, and D. Shaw. 2011. *Situation Analysis of Children and Women in Belize, 2011: An Ecological Overview.* Report, Government of Belize/UNICEF Belize.

Edberg, M., S. Cleary, E. Andrade, et al. 2010a. "SAFER Latinos: A Community Partnership to Address Contributing Factors for Latino Youth Violence." *Progress in Community Health Partnerships* 4(3): 221–33.

Edberg, M., S. Cleary, J. Klevens, E. Collins, R. Leiva, M. Bazurto, I. Rivera, A. Taylor, L. Montero, and M. Calderon. 2010b. "The SAFER Latinos Project: Addressing a Community Ecology Underlying Latino Youth Violence." *Journal of Primary Prevention* 31: 247–57.

Edberg, M., E. Collins, M. Harris, H. McLendon, and P. Santucci. 2009. "Patterns of HIV/AIDS, STI, Substance Abuse and Hepatitis Risk among Selected Samples of Latino and African-American Youth in Washington, DC." *Journal of Youth Studies* 12(6): 685–709.

Edberg, M., K. Corey, and M. Cohen. 2011. "Using a Qualitative Approach to Develop an Evaluation Data Set for Community-Based Health Promotion Programs Addressing Racial/Ethnic Health Disparities." *Health Promotion Practice*, 15 June, doi: 10.1177/1524839910362035 (online version).

Edberg, M., H. Shaikh, R. N. Rimal, R. Rassool, and M. Mthembu. 2017. "Development of a Communication Strategy to Reduce Violence against Children in South Africa: A Social-Ecological Approach." *African Journal of Information and Communication* 20: 49–76. https://doi.org/10.23962/10539/23576.

Singer, M. 1994. "AIDS and the Health Crisis of the US Urban Poor: The Perspective of Critical Medical Anthropology." *Social Science and Medicine* 39(7): 931–48.

———. 1996. "A Dose of Drugs, a Touch of Violence, a Case of AIDS: Conceptualizing the SAVA Syndemic." *Free Inquiry in Creative Sociology* 24(2): 99–110.

———. 2009. *Introduction to Syndemics: A Critical Systems Approach to Public and Community Health.* San Francisco, CA: Jossey-Bass.

Singer, M., and S. Clair. 2003. "Syndemics and Public Health: Reconceptualizing Disease in Bio-social Context." *Medical Anthropology Quarterly* 17(4): 423–41.

World Health Organization (WHO). 2011a. *Social Determinants Approaches to Public Health: From Concept to Practice.* Geneva: World Health Organization.

———. 2011b. "Rio Political Declaration on Social Determinants of Health." World Conference on the Social Determinants of Health, Rio de Janeiro, 19–21 October 2011. Geneva: World Health Organization.

~:~

Conclusion

TERRY M. REDDING AND CHARLES C. CHENEY

In the introduction to *Anthropological Praxis*, Wulff and Fiske (1987: 1) note that the authors' book provides detailed, hands-on guidance for successful practice and can serve to convince current and prospective practitioners of the utility and marketability of their anthropological knowledge. The chapters highlight the use of knowledge and not solely the production of knowledge. As you have seen, the chapters in this book follow firmly in those footsteps.

This volume highlights the twenty-one most recent projects recognized by the Praxis Award. However, in four decades now of its existence, there has been a total of twenty-seven first place awards and sixty-seven honorable mentions or special recognitions. Keep in mind as well the additional dozens of other worthy applicants over the years that, due to the award's very competitive nature, did not receive special recognition. That is quite a legacy for our discipline, our profession.

Sadly, it is the nature of practice that many of our works go unreported, underreported, or unrecognized in the trade. Our findings and reports are often proprietary and under the control of a funder, or they are very sensitive in terms of identifying vulnerable groups. We are often barred by contractual agreement from presenting our work through the professional journals that academic anthropologists use to keep anthropology and their findings accessible.

Noble efforts are made to disseminate practitioner efforts, such as the journals *Practicing Anthropology* and the *Annals of Anthropological Practice*, the content of which tends to have a more practical focus than their more academic peers. Even the so-called "fugitive literature," a trove of technical reports, briefs, proposals, and other materials that might forever remain buried away on musty shelves, are brought forth by such efforts as John van Willigen's Applied Anthropology Documentation Project at the University of Kentucky (which has since morphed into an oral history project).

Still, many practitioners do not have the requisite time, funding, or other support to invest in producing materials for the profession. A purpose of the award and this book, as noted in the foreword, is to provide some incentive for our colleagues to share their efforts. Now that you see them on these pages, you should have a better sense of some of the work going on out there.

That being said, a fair number of our profession work in administrative, managerial, artistic, and other positions that do not lend themselves to the neat packets of information needed when applying for Praxis or other awards, such as start and end dates, goals and objectives, and outcomes. Although not doing research and collecting data, they do their work with the anthropological lens, consider all sides, do not take things for granted, and ask the "what if" questions that anthropology arouses. So again, while this book represents great work, it does not encompass all the great work we do. And even though your work may never lend itself to Praxis or other award criteria, the lessons you find here will, we hope, serve as a meaningful guide.

In every Praxis Award cycle in which the editors have participated, it is fascinating to watch applications roll in from peers doing compelling work in varied circumstances around the globe. Perhaps some of these efforts have been presented at a session during a professional meeting. But even more often, it is usually the first time the work has been described to a larger audience beyond the immediate stakeholders.

You may have come away with favorites here. Different readers with differing or even similar interests or specializations will harbor their own preferred chapters and projects. This is as it should be in our wide-ranging profession. We hope that you have also come away with some sense of the personalities of the authors from these narratives, which sometimes included personal impressions and musings. In the end, the nonmissing link throughout is how we take our basic tools and methods to address problems of our common humanity. We apply our experiences, specializations, and even our personalities to come up with workable results and solutions.

Readers should take away a few of the following principles:

+ Successful work involves engaging people. It is simply what we do. It is of course necessary to involve all levels of stakeholders, determine their needs and interests, consider all sides, and do your best to manage non-aligned interests accordingly when interests diverge.
+ There are many ways to approach a problem or situation. In the end, success can be found by taking a multifaceted view of how to achieve desired results. A specific, dogmatic focus usually does not work in anthropology.
+ Things may not always be clear or easy but think through the major issues first. Have a good plan and adapt along the way as needed.
+ Focus on what works, and be practical, dedicated, and persistent.
+ Keep in mind the big picture and how it affects all stakeholders.

It is hoped that, like the editors, you will come away from these narratives with a fuller sense of the richness of our profession and the useful ways that anthropology is being applied in real actions that benefit the world and the humanity therein.

Terry M. Redding is currently a strategic communications specialist with a maternal and child health project funded by the US Agency for International Development (USAID). He received an MA in anthropology from the University of South Florida in 1998. In 1999, he contributed to and edited *Applied Anthropology and the Internet*, the first-ever fully online publication of the American Anthropological Association. He joined LTG Associates, Inc. in 2000 on a USAID-funded population project and was then involved in a variety of research and evaluation projects before working for several years as an independent editorial and evaluation consultant. He has served as president of the Washington Association of Professional Anthropologists, communications chair for the National Association for the Practice of Anthropology, and chair of the Praxis Award competitions of 2013, 2015, and 2017.

Charles C. Cheney completed a dissertation on cultural change among the Huave Indians of southern Mexico and received a PhD in anthropology from the University of California, Berkeley, in 1972. He then began what would become a career in applied medical anthropology by taking the job of "culture broker" between a South Texas pediatric hospital and the predominantly Latino people of the Texas-Mexico borderlands. After that, he served as director of sociocultural research in the departments of community medicine and psychiatry of Baylor College of Medicine and later was director of program development for the National Association of Community Health Centers. Further, as an independent consultant, he has conducted extensive needs assessment and evaluation research into the provision of healthcare services to US low-income minority and immigrant populations for community health centers, public health departments, and a range of federal health agencies. He has served as president of the Washington Association of Professional Anthropologists, member of the board of directors of the Society for Applied Anthropology, and chair of the Praxis Award competitions of 2009 and 2011.

References

Wulff, R. M., and S. J. Fiske. 1987. *Anthropological Praxis: Translating Knowledge into Action*. Boulder, CO: Westview Press.

~:~
Afterword

RIALL W. NOLAN

The Book I Wish I'd Had

This collection describes in detail how anthropology is used to solve problems. Its twenty-one chapters detail how anthropologists work with others to create what Robert Chambers (1997) terms "good change." The application of anthropology to everyday problems—often termed *practice* or *praxis*, in the case of the Praxis Award and elsewhere—is arguably the most interesting and dynamic aspect of anthropology today.

This is the book I wish I'd had fifty years ago. As a newly minted graduate student, I would have found the book not only to have been inspiring but also helpful in answering a question I got asked with some regularity: "You're studying anthropology. That's nice, but what are you going to be able to actually do with it?" If that has ever happened to you, you now have your response. Just hand them this volume and say, "Read this."

Practice and *application*, as I use them here, are synonymous terms. *Applied anthropology* is simply anthropology put to use, and someone who does this is a *practitioner*, whether that person is a university-based academic or an anthropologist with no academic connections. Although the working conditions and context differ significantly across these two groups, both are engaged in practice—putting anthropology to use. As this collection of examples demonstrates very well, practice takes many forms and is done in a range of contexts by different sorts of anthropologists. Represented here are anthropologists from across the spectrum. Their work is equally diverse, taking place in a variety of domains and across the globe.

Practice, in other words, is not one thing but many. Underneath the variety, however, are important similarities in process and approach. Anthropologists involved in practice work are engaged with real problems, which have real consequences for people. These anthropologists are not outsiders looking in; they are client centered, working inside the context of what they are doing. Practitioners pay specific attention to the "so what" of their work; they are concerned not just with finding things out but also with understanding what can be done with what one finds out. Their work often involves the crafting and implementation of solutions, with all of the risk and responsibility that this implies. Practitioners have, in other words, skin in the game.

Unlike academics, practitioners don't usually get—or seek—individual credit for what they do. Instead, they lead from the side and work through others. They're not "studying" the people they work with; they are collaborating and cocreating with them in a process that closely resembles what Donald Schön (1991) has termed *reflective conversations*. It is this collaborative aspect of practice that is perhaps the most significant. The chapters in this book illustrate very well John van Willigen's reminder (1986:215) that there are no anthropological problems in the world, only client problems, and instead of worrying about whether what you are doing is "real" anthropology, think about how you would use anthropology to help people solve these problems.

Practice and Application Today

Paraphrasing Ernest Hemingway, practice in anthropology grew in two ways: gradually, and then suddenly. From promising beginnings in the 1940s and 1950s, practice was slowed by both the growth of the academy and the backlash against the Vietnam War. The academy became the public face of anthropology, and most "outside" work became ethically suspect.

Within the discipline, a prolonged period of what Rylko-Bauer and Singer (2006) have termed "diverted gaze"—where the work of practitioners was largely ignored—helped generate a vast area of ignorance among university-based anthropologists concerning how anthropology could be—or was being—used to solve societal problems. Instead, the discipline busied itself with theoretical discussion, and when it finally did begin to pay attention to the world outside the academy, it adopted the role of critic. Although much of this work has been both insightful and solid, it has rarely touched on the concerns of anthropologists working in these areas.

By the mid-1970s, however, practice had undergone a revival. Anthropology graduates began to enter and explore a variety of extramural domains, with each succeeding cohort of graduates willing—and increasingly able—to explore new territory. Eventually, nonacademic anthropologist practitioners came to outnumber their university-based colleagues. Today, practice has come fully into its own, with extensive networks of academic and nonacademic anthropologists working in virtually every area of human endeavor, increasingly visible to the public, and increasingly influential.

In recent years, the early controversies that swirled around nonacademic work seem to have largely subsided. Initial fears that practice was unethical, theory-free, and—worst of all—"not really anthropology at all" have lessened. The much-debated "fracture" between the academy and practice appears to have healed in the minds of most people, and although there continues to be a range of substantive and important differences between the conditions under which academics and practitioners perform their work, there is much more mutual recognition of the worth and value of both.

To take but one example, consider the application of anthropology to our understanding of contemporary large organizations. In the late 1960s, Laura Nader (1969) encouraged anthropologists to "study up." In 1987, Mary Douglas, drawing on Durkheim and Weber, published an influential set of essays on "how institutions think." In the 1990s, anthropologists were making their initial forays into corporations and other influential organizations, and a decade or so later, highly original work by practitioners like Brigitte Jordan (2012) and Melissa Cefkin (2009) had started to appear. The interplay between academic and nonacademic anthropology, and between theory and practice, is very evident here.

As the chapters in this book demonstrate, practice is strong, anthropologists are increasingly visible to the public, and they are having an impact in many ways. It could be argued that practice is the cutting edge of the discipline, the place where new ideas and approaches take shape, and where new opportunities—and challenges—first appear.

Improving Anthropological Training

As rich and meaningful as it is, the insights and lessons of practice have yet to find their way into many of our academic training programs.

Anthropology's core strength is skill in finding things out, and also in situating those findings within a context that both illuminates and enhances them, rendering understanding vivid and three-dimensional. We are good at training our students to do this. We are less good, however, at helping them understand what can actually be done with what they know.

In our academic training programs, practice is often mysterious. Introductory textbooks, by and large, pay little attention to application and practice. If applied anthropology is mentioned at all, it is usually in one of the final chapters and generally focused on something involving research by full-time academics. Nonacademic practitioners are seldom highlighted or even discussed.

As our students progress, they are taught the history and development of the discipline, but here again the development of practice as an alternative to an academic career may be given little mention. Much of what practitioners are up to is either unknown within the academy or ignored. Many of our undergraduates, in fact, can complete their major without ever meeting a nonacademic practitioner of the discipline they have studied. And although a great deal of attention is rightly paid to ethics in anthropological training, the issues discussed are centered primarily around research and publication and do not generally arise from situations of application.

Theory is usually given a prominent place in anthropological training and, often, methods. But for the most part, discussion is lacking on how either theories or methods can be used to get things done. The emphasis, rather, falls mainly on developing skill in analysis and writing, as well as in the production of dissertations, articles, books, and reviews of the work of others.

This lack of connection between anthropological training and extramural application has actual consequences. In a very real sense, practice work is fieldwork, and ideally it should serve the same useful functions as fieldwork has in the past—as a source of data, insight, and experience, helping to build theory, train students, define and test methodologies, and illuminate key questions. The diverse experiences of practitioners, such as those described in this book, are all too often not used in training, nor are they even recognized. It is hardly surprising, therefore, that so much of what anthropology students learn seems to have so little connection to what anthropologists working out in the world do.

Upon graduation, today's anthropology students face new challenges, beginning with the scarcity of academic jobs for which many of them were trained. Academic hiring began to taper off in the 1970s following postwar university expansion, but today, not only are those academic jobs fewer in number but tenure is also declining, and part-time teaching posts are on the rise. At the same time, although opportunities outside the university are growing for the kinds of things that anthropologists can do, there is increased competition for these jobs. Many of our students, sadly, have never been encouraged to think about anything other than a university career.

For these reasons, it is important to think about how academic preparation can best equip younger anthropologists for what lies ahead. Recent decades have seen increasing attention to broad, significant issues, now often termed "global grand challenges." Climate change is one of these, of course, but there are many others—health, poverty, inequality, and regional insecurity, just to name a few. Until relatively recently, anthropology was slow to engage with many of these. Indeed, for a considerable time, engagement was seen by many as a violation of the supposed objectivity that was to be brought to social research. Policy, in that view, is properly made by others, not us; plans, programs, and projects are things done by others. Anthropologists, to the extent that they are engaged with these activities at all, tend to play the role of sideline critic.

Bringing the experience of practice into our training programs will not only require us to connect practice to theory and methods but also compel us to train our students to apply knowledge gained, which will involve acquainting them with areas such as policymaking, program and project design, and the management of implementation.

Going Beyond Where We Are

Thanks to the growth and development of practice, we are slowly adding a professional dimension to our discipline. We are building skill and experience in using what we know and developing increasingly wide networks of like-minded individuals, both inside and outside the academy, who share an interest in application. We have begun, through forums like WAPA, EPIC, and others, to have professional conversations that take place alongside our traditional academic exchanges.

One of the most important things occurring now is the documentation of application work through a growing literature of practice—accounts written by anthropologists working in the field about what it is actually like to solve problems. The present volume is an excellent example of this, wherein one finds rich material relating to both theory and method, together with a wealth of ethnographic detail about what happened and why. Such accounts are vital to our developing an understanding of how best to use what we know and how to train others to do the same.

These accounts of anthropological practice are every bit as valuable for us as were the early ethnographies brought back by our disciplinary ancestors from faraway places. Just as those accounts made possible the development of our discipline, so too today's literature of practice constitutes an important body of "ground truth" about how our discipline works out in the world.

Professions feed disciplines, and disciplines feed professions, in synergistic fashion. Disciplines generate knowledge, and professions apply that knowledge. The lessons of application are then fed back into the discipline, enhancing both theory and methodology. This need for synergy is obvious; as Kant reminded us, theory without practice is empty; practice without theory is blind.

Continuing to engage with society's most pressing problems will involve us in a long-term project extending far beyond the lifetime of any individual now reading this. Documenting our efforts—our attempts, our successes, failures, and lessons learned—through a literature of practice is the best way to ensure that our work has sustainable impact.

Years ago, Fredrik Barth (1967) reminded us that institutionalization, not mere innovation, was the defining characteristic of social change. Finding new and better ways to apply anthropology is only a start. The future of our discipline will be determined in large part by how effectively anthropology's contributions come to be embedded in society at large. Although the world can always benefit from having more anthropologists, our job, at base, is to infuse anthropological thinking into the work of the world so that, eventually, such work is not only more successful but appears as simply sound and sensible procedure.

Riall W. Nolan is professor emeritus of anthropology at Purdue University and an affiliated lecturer at the Centre of Development Studies at the University of Cambridge. He received his PhD from the University of Sussex and spent the first third of his career as a development practitioner in Africa, Asia, and the Middle East. Subsequently, he directed international programs at several large US universities, including Pittsburgh, Cincinnati, and Purdue. His academic career has focused on research, teaching, and writing about anthropological practice, and preparing anthropology graduates for nonacademic careers. He is the author of eight academic books, including *Development Anthropology* (Westview Press, 2001) and *Using Anthropology in the World* (Routledge, 2017). He has also published nearly forty articles, including "Anthropology and Development" in the Oxford Research Encyclopedia of Anthropology (Oxford University Press, 2019).

References

Barth, F. 1967. "On the Study of Social Change." *American Anthropologist* 69(6): 661–69.

Cefkin, M., ed. 2009. *Ethnography and the Corporate Encounter: Reflections of Research in and of Corporations.* New York: Berghahn Books.

Chambers, R. 1997. "Responsible Well-Being: A Personal Agenda for Development." *World Development* 25(11): 1743–54.

Douglas, M. 1987. *How Institutions Think.* London: Routledge and Kegan Paul.

Jordan, B. 2012. *Advancing Ethnography in Corporate Environments: Challenges and Emerging Opportunities.* Walnut Creek, CA: Left Coast Press.

Nader, L. 1969. "Up the Anthropologist: Perspectives Gained from 'Studying Up.'" In *Reinventing Anthropology,* edited by D. Hymes, 284–311. New York: Random House.

Rylko-Bauer, B., and M. Singer. 2006. "Reclaiming Applied Anthropology: Its Past, Present, and Future." *American Anthropologist* 108(1): 178–90.

Schön, D. A. 1991. *The Reflective Practitioner: How Professionals Think in Action.* Farnham: Ashgate Publishing.

Van Willigen, J. 1986. *Applied Anthropology: An Introduction.* South Hadley, MA: Bergin & Garvey.

~: INDEX :~

www.ingramcontent.com/pod-product-compliance
Lightning Source LLC
Chambersburg PA
CBHW070610030426
42337CB00020B/3743